Quotes

⤜✥⤛

Soft, Strong and Not Too Long

Published in 2012 by Prion

an imprint of the Carlton Publishing Group

20 Mortimer Street

London W1T 3JW

Copyright © 2011 Carlton Books Limited

ISBN 978-1-85375-876-8

10 9 8 7 6 5 4 3 2 1

Printed and bound in Great Britain by
CPI Group (UK) Ltd, Croydon CR0 4YY

Quotes

Soft, Strong and Not Too Long

PRION

Are you sitting comfortably?

In our busy lives there are few opportunities to escape the daily pandemonium and make time for ourselves. That's why your bathroom break is so important, and you shouldn't be in a hurry to flush it away. Instead, why not use it to do something truly life-affirming like contemplating the wit and wisdom of the world's greatest thinkers, comedians, politicians, pundits and self-appointed experts?

Of course you don't have time to waste when you're caught short, so we haven't bogged this book down with categories or chapters, just oodles of wonderful quotes. Dive into a page and – who knows? – maybe your trip to the little room will be inspirational.

Auntie Lou

There are only two ways to live your life. One is as though nothing is a miracle. The other is as though everything is a miracle.

– Albert Einstein

There are just two types of coaches – those who have just been fired and those that are going to be fired.

– Bum Phillips

Suburban Chicago is virgin territory for whorehouses.

– Al Capone

It was the Wrong Kind of Snow.

– Terry Worrall explaining disruption on British Rail, 1991

It's not whether you win or lose – it's how you lay the blame.

– Fran Lebowitz

A gifted person ought to learn English (barring spelling and pronouncing) in thirty hours, French in thirty days, and German in thirty years.

– Mark Twain

Men who tell you they read the Ann Summers' catalogue for the articles are lying.

– Rita Rudner

My father, Denis, was fond of saying, 'Better to keep your mouth closed and be thought a fool than to open it and remove all doubt.'

– Carol Thatcher

I absolutely love Christmas... I've spent about £250, 000 in total celebrating Christmas every day for the past twelve years. I've also got through 36 ovens and 42 video recorders by watching the Queen's speech every day as well as Christmas films.

– Andy Park, a.k.a. 'Mr Christmas'

One of our Christmas rituals was always 'boiling the sixpences'. This was to sterilize them for incorporation in the pudding, which, in turn, was boiled. To this day, my sister still recycles the same old, now obsolete sixpences, some bearing the profile of King George VI, and spat out or choked on by at least two generations of the Humphries family... EU purists may prefer to interlard their festive dessert with recently excised credit cards...

  – **Barry Humphries**

I like the name 'Winterval' instead of 'Christmas' because it sounds as if it lasts for three months and involves ice-skating in a tiny silver fox-fur dress while off your face on schnapps.

  – **Caitlin Moran**

It's a shame to call somebody a 'diva' simply because they work harder than everybody else.

  – **Jennifer Lopez**

Chambers Dictionary defines the word 'Taghairm' as 'divination in the Scottish Highlands, especially inspiration sought by lying in a bullock's hide behind a waterfall'.

  – **Brian Greer**

I have a bumper sticker that says, 'Don't honk if you can't read this.' Everywhere I drive, I leave confused people in my wake.

  – **Craig Tanis**

The three great holiday gift lies are: 'Easy to assemble', 'Unbreakable', and 'One size fits all'.

  – **Pat Williams**

Things you won't hear a father say: 'Go ahead, take my car – and here's 50 bucks for gas'; 'Here, you take the remote'; 'Can you turn up that music? It really calms my nerves'; 'Waiter! More ice cream for the little one!'

  – **David Letterman**

My daughter brought home one of her 'Goth' friends – black nail polish, black lipstick, black eyeliner, black hair, Liquid paper-white face. I'm sorry, didn't we use to call that 'Hallowe'en'?

– Jeff Foxworthy

Whenever my mother sees me she says, 'Jenny, Jenny, why aren't you wearing a petticoat?' 'Mother, it's because I've got jeans on.'

– Jenny Eclair

Love wears a bumper sticker that says 'My other car is a hearse'.

– Julie Burchill, journalist

I never take notice of letters marked 'Urgent'. It merely means urgent to the writer.

– Napoleon Bonaparte

When you are 92 and you say, 'When I was 74,' it's almost like saying, 'When I was young'.

– Ernest Waring

I once replied to a street evangelist, 'You mean that Jesus is coming and you're dressed like that?'

– Scott Caparro

My dad said to me, on Christmas: 'You were the ugliest child the hospital had ever seen. When we took you home they gave us two blankets – one to put over your head.'

– Barbara Ellen, journalist

When I was young, I was told: 'You'll see, when you're 50.' I'm 50 and I haven't seen a thing.

– Erik Satie

When mom got mad she'd threaten, 'Wait 'til your father gets home.' 'Mom,' I'd say, 'it's been eight years.'

– Brett Butler

A good snow machine will cost $2,000 and last four to five years. With dogs, you've got regenerative powers. Snow machines don't have pups.

– Lou Schultz, trainer of Alaskan Huskies

As long as a woman can look 10 years younger than her own daughter, she is perfectly satisfied.

– Oscar Wilde

I keep fit. Every morning, I do 100 laps of an Olympic-sized swimming pool – in a small motor launch.

– Peter Cook

Two weeks ago we celebrated my uncle's 103rd birthday. 103 – isn't that something? Unfortunately he wasn't present. How could he be? He died when he was 29.

– Victor Borge

Mother nature is wonderful. She gives us 12 years to develop a love for our children before turning them into teenagers.

– Eugene Bertin

The sole Dutch Guiana entrant in the 1956 Olympics was runner Wim Esajas. He slept all morning to relax for the event and arrived at the stadium at 2p.m. only to learn that the race had been run in the morning. He returned home where he was beheaded.

– Peter Sherwood

My dream would be to build a 2,000-foot statue of Homer Simpson with a revolving head and a restaurant inside it. A monument to fatherhood.

– Matt Groening

If I had known when I was 21 that I should be as happy as I am now, at 70, I should have been sincerely shocked. They promised me wormwood and funeral raven.

– Christopher Isherwood

My eldest son is about to become 21, and all I can say is that he makes me feel incredibly old. He is an incredible help and assistance to me as I become increasingly decrepit.

– Prince Charles on Prince William

In Los Angeles, by the time you're 35, you're older than most of the buildings.

– Delia Ephron

I was recently stopped for driving at 39 mph in a 40 mph limit. 'Nobody does that at 2 am unless he's been drinking, sir,' said the policeman. After a negative breathalyser test, the officer asked why I had been travelling below the speed limit on a clear road. 'Because there was a police car behind me,' I said.

– Alan Calverd

When one is 20, yes, but at 47, Venus may rise from the sea, and I for one should hardly put on my spectacles to have a look.

– William Thackeray

You know you're getting old when a 4-letter word for something pleasurable two people can do in bed is R-E-A-D.

– Denis Norden

A loving wife is better than making 50 at cricket or even 99; beyond that I will not go.

– James Barrie

I visited a new dentist for my 6-monthly check-up. Having given me the all clear, he glanced at my notes, then remarked: 'Those should see you out.'

– Angela Walder, 72

I was watching Peter Pan with my 6-year-old daughter and she says,'Daddy, how does Captain Hook wipe his bottom?' I just said, 'Smee does it.'

– Bob Saget

I had a huge party for my 70th birthday with 800 guests. With so many familiar faces there, it was like driving through the rear-view mirror.

– Peter Ustinov

Funeral services were held this week for 82-year-old chewing gum magnate Philip K. Wrigley. In keeping with his last request, Wrigley's remains will be stuck to the bottom of a luncheonette counter.

– Jane Curtin

The trouble with reaching the age of 92 is that regrets for a misspent life are bound to creep in, and whenever you see me with a furrowed brow you can be sure that what is on my mind is the thought that if only I had taken up golf earlier and devoted my whole time to it instead of fooling about writing stories and things, I might have got my handicap down to under 18.

– P.G. Wodehouse

'On Christmas Eve,' I thought, as a child, 'even the furniture looks different!' The chests and cupboards, tables and chairs of my nursery shed on me, possibly, no more than the good nature which was in them always: I simply was more open to it that night.

– Elizabeth Bowen

A Russian and a Polish labourer repairing a derelict house chanced upon a hoard of gold. The Russian said eagerly 'We will share it like brothers'. 'No,' replied the Pole, 'fifty-fifty'.

– Peter Ustinov

To my father a school was not a seat of learning but a noisy detention compound to which children were sent for long periods of the year in order to be removed from under their parents' feet.

– R.F. Delderfield

When I was around nine, I cut a flat tree out of green wrapping paper and pinned it to my bedroom wall, next to my poster of Marc Bolan, and my wet bed chart. I covered all three in glitter.

– Tracey Emin

An archbishop is a Christian ecclesiastic of a rank superior to that attained by Christ.

– H.L. Mencken

I went into a pawnshop to buy a chess set, but they didn't have a full one.

– George Carlin

A lawyer is a person who writes a 10,000-word document and calls it a 'brief'.

– Franz Kafka

How to throw a children's party: dig a pit, throw in the kids and ice cream, add chocolate sauce; an hour later take out and send home.

– Tony Kornheiser

Can I take a punch? Now that's a question that is never likely to be answered.

– Muhammad Ali

The greatest service a parent can render a child is to throw school reports unread into the waste-paper basket. Any success I have achieved has been due to my father's unflinching and inexplicable confidence.

– Robert Morley

They say the first thing to go when you're old is your legs or your eyesight. It isn't true. The first thing to go is parallel parking.

– Kurt Vonnegut

A hole-in-one is an occurrence in which a ball is hit directly from the tee into the hole on a single shot by a golfer playing alone.

– Roy McKie

All Englishmen talk as if they've got a bushel of plums stuck in their throats, and then after swallowing them get constipated from the pits.

– W.C. Fields

My luggage trolley at Singapore airport had a notice saying: 'Not to be Removed from Crewe Station.'

– **Clive James**

Next time you're at the park, take a look at the new parents. At first they may appear to be basking in their new-found parental bliss. But look closer. See that facial twitch? – That's no twitch, my friend. That man's a hostage and he's trying to blink you a message.

– **Ray Romano**

At the reunion at a Washington party a few weeks ago there were three ex-Presidents, Carter, Ford and Nixon: See no Evil, Hear no Evil and Evil.

– **Bob Dole**

I'm ashamed to be your father. You're a disgrace to the family name of Wagstaff, if such a thing is possible.

– **Groucho Marx**

I'd much rather be a woman than a man. Women can cry, they can wear cute clothes – and they're the first to be rescued off sinking ships.

– **Gilda Radner**

We love television because television brings us a world in which television does not exist.

– **Barbara Ehrenreich**

Given a choice between Raquel Welch and a hundred at Lord's, I'd take the hundred every time.

– **Geoffrey Boycott**

You know those Christmas cards that play a tune when you open them? Well, I don't know if you've ever taken one apart but there's a little button attached to a wire. I once knew a TV producer who, as a dare, wrapped one of these up in smoked salmon and swallowed it. For half an hour after, if you went up to his stomach I swear you could hear 'Good King Wenceslas'.

– **Phillip Schofield**

I feel a bit guilty making such a good living out of something that I enjoy so much. Paid to dress up, pretend to be somebody, have all my friends around me, being part of a big gang, shouting and misbehaving.

— **Dawn French**

Only a friend can become an enemy. A relative is one from the start.

— **Harry Hirschfield**

Introduced to his child, he recoiled with a startled 'Oi!' The only thing that prevented a father's love from faltering was the fact that there was in his possession a photograph of himself at the same early age, in which he, too, looked like a homicidal fried egg.

— **P. G. Wodehouse**

If you think Christmas is commercialized, take a peek at Bethlehem. 'The Ninth Station Boutique' and 'The Manger Pizzeria' say it all.

— **Maureen Lipman**

If I'd been clever, I'd have been a sociologist or something, but I wasn't, so I became an actress.

— **Kristin Scott Thomas**

I like to conduct ballet music at a very fast tempo. That makes the buggers hop.

— **Thomas Beecham**

She is so cross-eyed, she can watch a tennis match without ever moving her head.

— **Phyllis Diller**

On my first day in New York a guy asked me if I knew where Central Park was. When I told him I didn't he said, 'Do you mind if I mug you here?'

— **Paul Merton**

Jim Morrison is dead now and that's a high price to pay for immortality.

— **Gloria Estefan**

Danny La Rue denies that he is a wealthy man, but I happen to know for a fact that he has a little bit tucked away.

– Jimmy Tarbuck

Custard is a detestable substance produced by a malevolent conspiracy of the hen, the cow and the cook.

– Ambrose Bierce

If Scotland ever discover that football is a team game, the rest of us will have to watch out.

– John Adams

When you can't do anything else to a boy, you can make him wash his face.

– Ed Howe

Humour keeps the elderly rolling along, singing a song. When you laugh, it's an involuntary explosion of the lungs. The lungs need to replenish themselves with oxygen. So you laugh, you breathe, the blood runs, and everything is circulating. If you don't laugh, you'll die.

– Mel Brooks

He has a future and I have a past, so we should be all right.

– Jennie Churchill, 64, marrying Montagu Porch, 41

Listen, if it's got four wheels or a dick you're gonna have trouble with it guaranteed.

– Annie Proulx, novelist

I do this great roast turkey with a difference – I chop sage, thyme and garlic, put it under the skin and massage it for 20 minutes, just like a human back. It's beautifully moist and tastes unbelievable.

– Carole Caplin

Retirement homes are great. It's like being a baby, only you're old enough to appreciate it.

– Homer Simpson, The Simpsons

Don't carry a grudge. While you're carrying a grudge, the other guy's out dancing.

   – Buddy Hackett

A lot of guys think the larger a woman's breasts are, the less intelligent she is. I think the larger a woman's breasts are the less intelligent men become.

   – Anita Wise

Who among us has not gazed at a painting of Jackson Pollock's and thought 'What a piece of crap'?

   – Rob Long

I seem to have been only like a boy playing on the sea shore, and diverting myself in now and then finding a smoother pebble or a prettier shell than ordinary, whilst the great ocean of truth lay all undiscovered before me.

   – Isaac Newton

An old wine-bibber having been smashed in a railway collision, some wine was poured on his lips to revive him. 'Pauillac 1873', he murmured, and died.

   – Ambrose Bierce

I thought that heavy water might have a practical use in something like neon signs.

   – Harold Urey

Bless my eyes, Here he lies, In a sad pickle, Kill'd by an icicle.

   – Epitaph, St Michael and All Angels' Church, Bampton, Devon

Dad taught me how to climb up a tree. But not how to climb down.

   – Mark Finch

The one luxury I would take to a desert island is a television set that does not work.

   – Robert Mark

As a boy, I was expelled from a Catholic College for casting doubt on the Bible by asking how Noah was able, in the Palestine desert, to take a penguin on board the Ark.

– Nikolaus Chrastry

Father told me if I ever met a lady in a dress like yours, I must look her straight in the eye.

– Prince Charles

If you can imagine a man having a vasectomy without anaesthetic to the sound of frantic sitar playing, you will have some idea of what popular Turkish music is like.

– Bill Bryson

Republicans understand the importance of bondage between a mother and a child.

– Dan Quayle

Put a pigeon in a partridge in a wild duck in a pheasant in a capon in a goose in a turkey – and that'll feed 50.

– Clarissa Dickson Wright

Never be alone in a lift with a man who has religious tracts on his desk.

– Pam Brown

Being a father is harder than being a rock 'n' roll singer on the road because any second your kid will run through the door with a 16-inch nail sticking through his head, going, – 'Daddy, daddy, I just got hit by a 4x2.'

– Ozzy Osbourne

Many a young man starts life with a natural gift for exaggeration which, if nurtured in congenial and sympathetic surroundings, or by imitation of the best models, might grow into something really great and wonderful. But as a rule, he comes to nothing. He either falls into careless habits of accuracy or takes to frequenting the society of the aged and the well informed, and in a short time he develops a morbid and unhealthy faculty of truth telling.

– Oscar Wilde

Throwing a football is comparable to painting a canvas or playing the piano. The difference is that Beethoven didn't play the 'Moonlight' Sonata, and Van Gogh didn't paint the Potato Eaters, with Mean Joe Green charging at them from the blind side.

– Oakland Raiders legend Jim Plunkett

I believe it is possible to obtain a divorce in the United States on the grounds of incompatibility. If that is true, I am surprised there are any marriages left in the United States.

– G.K. Chesterton

An Anglican clergyman is invisible six days a week and incomprehensible on the seventh.

– Dean Inge

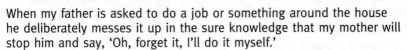

When my father is asked to do a job or something around the house he deliberately messes it up in the sure knowledge that my mother will stop him and say, 'Oh, forget it, I'll do it myself.'

– Bob Hayden

A tired chairman is a bad chairman. A dead one is usually worse.

– Nicholas Goodison

She has been kissed as often as a police-court bible, and by much the same class of people.

– Robertson Davies

The world we live in is in a funny state. Someone goes out and shoots John Lennon, but lets Des O'Connor live.

– Roy Brown

Children begin by loving their parents. After a time they judge them. Rarely, if ever, do they forgive them.

– Oscar Wilde

When a fellow says, 'Well, to make a long story short,' it's too late.

– Don Herold

One should never make one's debut with a scandal; one should reserve that to give interest in one's old age.
– **Oscar Wilde**

My father told me I should make a point of trying every experience once – except incest and folk dancing.
– **Leo Fallon**

My wife told me the baby had a runny nose. I asked if it was green or clean. We then had a 20-minute discussion about the boy's bodily fluids. It's like he's a tiny Bill Clinton.
– **Jimmy Cox**

My dad told me, 'Never sleep with a girl if you're going to be embarrassed to be seen on the street with her the next day.' I think that was more for the girl's benefit than mine. He didn't want me jumping on some girl and then leaving her in the lurch.
– **Ronald Reagan Jr**

This moment of meeting seemed to be a birth time for both of us: her first and my second life.
– **Laurie Lee**

If Everybody Else's Mother turned up at a PTA meeting and identified herself, she would be lynched.
– **Erma Bombeck**

When I told my dad I wanted a nose ring, he said, 'Have you considered lightning?'
– **Bob Hayden**

Every year, one of my children wants a game for Christmas. It is always one for which the demand exceeds the supply by about 355,000. Every kid in town has it on his list... The game is touted on television, beginning in June, with the approach that if it is not under your tree on Christmas Day you are an unfit parent and your child will grow up to rob convenience stores wearing pantyhose over his face.
– **Erma Bombeck**

Female streakers should not be allowed on a cricket pitch because you're allowed only one bouncer per over.

– **Bill Frindall**

In Hollywood it's not enough to have a hit. Your best friend should also have a failure.

– **Peter Bogdanovich**

Only a vegan nun who has taken a vow of silence lives without hurting anyone.

– **Tim Rayment**

My favourite photograph of us together is a picture of me aged about 9 or 10 helping the Queen Mother up the steps of Windsor Castle. I remember the moment because she said to me: 'Keep doing that for people and you will go a long way in life.'

– **Prince William**

The only function of a student at a lecture is to be present when a great mind communes with itself.

– **Denis Donoghue**

In the language of football, 'resign' is a code word meaning 'he was given the choice of quitting, being fired, or having the fans blow up his house.'

– **Gene Klein**

If it turns out that there is a God, I don't think that he's evil. But the worst you can say about him is that he's an underachiever.

– **Woody Allen**

Were I a philosopher, I should write a philosophy of toys, showing that nothing else in life needs to be taken seriously, and that Christmas Day in the company of children is one of the few occasions on which men become entirely alive.

– **Robert Lynd**

The infants' nativity play, in front of a packed house, is called 'Rock Around the Flock' and has a brisk run through the familiar story, together with ten songs, some more familiar than others. I'd never heard 'If We're Happy and We Know It' sung by angels at Christmas before.

– Stephen Bates

I'm at a point where I want a man in my life – but not in my house! Just come in, attach a VCR, and get out.

– Joy Behar

I saw this really annoying TV commercial. A woman takes a laxative and then goes hiking. What idiot would take a laxative and then hike up a mountain? What is more stupid is people hiking behind her.

– Jay Leno

Remember, your sales resistance is lower with a salesman who calls after the kids have gone to school. When you realise he isn't one of the kids that missed the bus, you're so happy you'll buy anything.

– Phyllis Diller

The murals in restaurants are about on a par with the food in art galleries.

– Peter De Vries

My dad, Tony Richardson, used to repeat a line of Samuel Beckett's so often that I had it pinned on my wall at home: 'Keep on failing. Only this time fail better.'

– Joely Richardson

After I stopped riding, I put on a lot of weight. When I lost it again, I asked my father, 'Do you love me more now I've lost weight?' He said, 'Yes.' It was so much the wrong answer.

– Clare Balding

'Sorry, Dad,' I said, 'I only got a third class degree. The lowest grade on the course. I've really let you down.' 'You haven't let me down, son,' my dad said. 'I never thought you'd pass.'

– Johnny Vegas

Winning a Golden Rose of Montreux is a non-event because for as long as I can remember British Television has always won all of them. Even Hale and Pace got one, through in what category I can't begin to imagine. It must be so dispiriting being an Andorran comedy writer.

– **A.A. Gill**

Australia was discovered by Captain James Cook who stepped off his ship, sniffed the air and declared, 'Yes. This would make a fantastic prison.'

– **Jeremy Clarkson**

A pre-teen is sort of like having a tornado before a hurricane hits.

– **W. Bruce Cameron**

Is there any sound more terrifying on a Sunday afternoon than a child asking, 'Daddy, can we play Monopoly?'

– **Jeremy Clarkson**

Winter in Madison Square was tamed like a polar bear led on a leash by a beautiful lady.

– **Willa Cather**

Tommy Smith could start a riot in a graveyard.

– **Bill Shankly**

West Wickham fire station is situated in a road which is blocked at both ends.

– **Frank Ruler**

I try to take one day at a time, but sometimes several days attack me all at once.

– **Jenny Eclair**

You can always tell what kind of a person a man really thinks you are by the earrings he gives you.

– **Audrey Hepburn**

I am a terrible realist about becoming a father. If it's a nice baby, obviously I will be over the moon, but I'm not going to be over the moon until I know what it's like.

– Louis de Bernières

Why is it that we rejoice at a birth and grieve at a funeral? Is it because we are not the person involved?

– Mark Twain

The worst thing that can happen to a man is to have his wife come home and he has lost the child. 'How did everything go?' 'Just great, we're playing hide and seek and she's winning.'

– Sinbad

I cannot see the sense of becoming a Commander of the British Empire. They might as well make me a Commander of Milton Keynes – at least that exists.

– Spike Milligan

A dad is the one who, after a roast dinner on Sunday, falls asleep in his comfy armchair with the newspaper over his face, while mum does the washing up.

– Jamie, aged 10

The girls on the top floor had a television set that gave you quite a good picture if you hit it with a clenched fist at the right angle.

– Clive James

Christmas is wishing there really was such a thing as an old-fashioned Christmas.

– Charles M. Schulz

Things For Guys to Consider Before Buying a Hairpiece: Will it appreciate in value? Is it possible a hairpiece will make me look too good? Will I be able to handle all the women? Have I explored all my comb-over options?

– David Letterman

Operator, we seem to have drifted into a position of somewhat redundant intimacy.

– **Alan Bennett**

It is better to go there with a lover because otherwise frustrations may set in.

– **Ilka Chase on Venice**

Next to listening to the minutes of a previous meeting, there is nothing as dull as a highbrow concert.

– **Kin Hubbard**

My father said to me, 'Never do a job that can be replaced by machines.' So I thought being an actor was a job that can't be replaced by machines. But it looks as though we might be getting nearer to that stage.

– **Michael Caine**

If you want to know how old a woman is, ask her sister-in-law.

– **Ed Howe**

When I go to the beach wearing a bikini, even the tide won't come in.

– **Phyllis Diller**

I can set up John Prescott with a trainer and I will guarantee he will become British champion within five fights.

– **Frank Malone**

All Shakespeare did was to string together a lot of old well-known quotations.

– **H.L. Mencken**

I would say we moved around quite a bit. Every time the rent came due, my father carried the furniture on his back to some new place. For 30 years, I thought we were in the furniture business.

– **Jackie Mason**

If the devil were to offer me a resurgence of what is commonly called virility, I'd decline. 'Just keep my liver and lungs in good working order,' I'd reply, 'so I can go on drinking and smoking.'

– **Luis Buñuel**

Middle age is when a man chases a girl only if she's going downhill.

– **George Burns**

I am careful when I break with a woman, not to break with her husband. In this way, I have made my best friends.

– **Guy De Maupassant**

Hollywood's a place where they'll pay you a thousand dollars for a kiss, and fifty cents for your soul. I know, because I turned down the first offer often enough and held out for the fifty cents.

– **Marilyn Monroe**

A very little wit is valued in a woman, as we are pleased with a few words spoken plain by a parrot.

– **Jonathan Swift**

I was the worst gift buyer as a child. When I was 13 my sister gave me an LP and a birdhouse, and in return I gave her one of those big-value, one-litre bottles of shampoo. I think it was 20p.

– **Ricky Gervais**

I'm not really wrinkled. I just took a nap on a chenille bedspread.

– **Phyllis Diller**

The best thing you can do with a horse that hangs left is to put a bit of lead in his right ear to act as a counterbalance with a shotgun.

– **Lester Piggott**

If logic tells you that life is a meaningless accident, don't give up on life. Give up on logic.

– **Shira Milgrom**

If one day you're going to be able to look back on something and laugh about it, you might as well laugh about it now.

– **Marie Osmond**

I hope there's a tinge of disgrace about me. Hopefully, there's one good scandal left in me yet.

– **Diana Rigg**

I was quite a good teenager for about two years till I got in with bigger boys. I thought I was a punk. I wasn't. I was 15, I hated doing any work, and I hated my parents because they were middle class and not on the dole.

– **Harry Enfield**

The worst thing anyone has ever said about me is that I'm 50. Which I am. Oh that bitch. I was so hurt.

– **Joan Rivers**

Cheops built the Great Pyramid of Gizeh about 3050 BC – then he felt better.

– **Will Cuppy**

Before I married I had six theories about bringing up children, but no children; now I have six children and no theories.

– **John Wilmot**

People say to me, 'Don't go on about fish today, please, Jack'. And I say, 'Just tell me one thing – can you breathe under water?' And of course, I have them there.

– **John Cleese**

Americans are a broad-minded people. They will accept the fact that a person can be an alcoholic, a dope fiend, a wife beater and even a newspaperman, but if a man doesn't drive, there's something wrong with him.

– **Art Buchwald**

Some people get terribly po-faced when talking about couples who disappear into the office filing cabinet together. But speaking as someone who has seen more than a couple of pencil sharpeners under cover of darkness, I can testify that it's fun, provided you preserve some modicum of discretion. Those amateurs who ignore this caveat are often left with faces redder than Rudolph's nose. How about the couple I heard of who retired to a City boardroom for a festive fumble, but forgot that the security cameras were keeping watch?

– Virginia Blackburn

I don't hold that Christmas is 'all about togetherness – it's all about watching telly and having impressively resonant wind.

– Caitlin Moran

One of the things Father specially detested about guests was the suddenness with which they arrived.

– Clarence Day

In the House of Commons, Peter Snape accused Transport Secretary Nicholas Ridley of being 'a hypocrite' and 'an old Etonian twerp.' He was immediately asked by the speaker to withdraw the word 'hypocrite'.

– Graham Jones

A private railroad car is not an acquired taste. One takes to it immediately.

– Eleanor Robson Belmont

Have you ever noticed how the best acting at the Academy Awards ceremony is done by losers congratulating the winners?

– George Roberts

Some of those Gerber baby desserts are actually pretty good. Gerber Apple and Blackberry Crumble Dessert tastes so good I served it at a dinner party.

– Pete Austen

I could have been sexually abused, but after I was born – my parents were hardly interested in having sex with each other.

– P.J. O'Rourke

According to research... British homes will be adding to Santa's fat belly this year by leaving him 18 million mince pies, 9 million glasses of sherry and at least a million chocolate biscuits, giving him two million times as many calories as he needs and five million times the recommended number of units of alcohol.

– William Hartston

Burt Reynolds sings like Dean Martin with adenoids and dances like a drunk killing cockroaches.

– John Barbour

Americans adore me and will go on adoring me until I say something nice about them.

– George Bernard Shaw

The only obvious advantage to being an adult is that you can eat your dessert without having eaten your vegetables.

– Lisa Alther

The value of marriage is not that adults produce children but that children produce adults.

– Peter de Vries

At New York University I majored in advanced fondling. I minored in foreplay.

– Woody Allen

I was telling my son about the advantages of being over 50. 'As you get older,' I explained, 'you get wiser.' He just looked at me and said, 'In that case you must be a genius.'

– Angus Walker

Scientists say that women who have children after 40 are more likely to live to be 100, but they don't know why. I think the reason is, they're waiting for the day when their kids move out the house.

– Lorrie Moss

If your hat blows off never run after it: others will be delighted to do it; why spoil their fun.

– **Mark Twain**

Experience is a comb life gives you after you lose your hair.

– **Judith Stern**

Doctors say it's okay to have sex after a heart attack, provided you close the ambulance door.

– **Phyllis Diller**

I knew it was okay to die after the Wimbledon final, but not during it. It would have put Goran off.

– **Srdjan Ivanisevic**

The snow was thick, and in the afternoon the sky cleared, and the landscape looked as if it had gone to heaven.

– **Sylvia Townsend Warner**

A person's maturity consists in having found again the seriousness one had as a child at play.

– **Friedrich Wilhelm Nietzsche**

If I had my life to live again, I'd make the same mistakes, only sooner.

– **Tallulah Bankhead**

People keep asking me if I'll marry again. It's as if after you've had one car crash you want another.

– **Stephanie Beecham**

Thomas Wolfe wrote, 'You can't go home again.' You can, but you'll get treated like an 8-year-old.

– **Daryl Hogue**

I'm 101 years old and at my age, honey, I can say what I want! .

– **Bessie Delany**

A lawyer is one who protects us against robbery by taking away the temptation.
- **H.L. Mencken**

I didn't have the balls to vote against my father, Ronald Reagan, but I couldn't vote for him.
- **Patti Davis**

I used to call anyone over the age of 35, R. F. C – Ready For Chrysanthemums.
- **Brigitte Bardot**

I don't eat health foods. At my age I need all the preservative I can get. Age does not diminish the extreme.
- **George Burns**

So people think I'm lying about my age all the time? It's the records that are wrong. I've never told anyone how old I am. The minute they ask me I say 'That's none of your business.' So that means I've never once lied about my age. Now that's true!
- **Calista Flockhart (born 11/11/64)**

The Christmas card perfectly sums up our age – impersonal, garish, emotionally threadbare and egotistical. An age when what things look like is more important than what they actually mean.
- **Janet Street-Porter**

Love. Everyone says that looks don't matter, age doesn't matter, money doesn't matter. But I never met a girl yet who has fallen in love with an old ugly man who's broke.
- **Rodney Dangerfield**

When it's Fall in New York, the air smells as if someone's been frying goats in it, and if you are keen to breathe, the best plan is to open a window and stick your head into a building.
- **Douglas Adams**

I'm 59 and people call me middle aged. How many 118-year-old men do you know?

    – Barry Cryer

Youth is something very new: twenty years ago no one mentioned it.

    – Coco Chanel (in 1971)

I have everything I had 20 years ago, only now it's 6 inches lower.

    – Gypsy Rose Lee

My best Christmas was a few years ago, when there was a power cut from Christmas Eve morning until Boxing Day afternoon. We had no lights, no heating and ate smoked salmon sandwiches round the fire. It was such fun with all the candles. My nephews adored it.

    – Christine Hamilton

I had Christmas in LA ten years ago; the sun was shining and it wasn't fun. I need cold, snow, grim London and repeats of The Two Ronnies and Bruce Forsyth.

    – Paul McKenna

Nursing homes. Ugh. I hate those places. All the old people want to touch my hair.

    – Claire Fisher, Six Feet Under

A homely face and no figure have aided many a woman heavenward.

    – Minna Antrim

How full of creative genius is the air in which these are generated! I should hardly admire them more if real stars fell and lodged on my coat.

    – Henry David Thoreau

Reality may not be the best of all possible worlds but it's still the only place where you can get a decent steak.

    – Woody Allen

I can't cook. I use a smoke alarm as a timer.

– Carol Siskind

If I didn't have a problem with alcohol, I would drink all the time.

– Havelock Ellis

Since Christmas is a big feast for all corporate brands, we might as well reposition it as that. Enjoy Christmas for what it really is: swap all the religion for what really matters – material possessions. With that in mind, pick any of the following stars and worship them. Merry Christmas (from: PlayStation, Apple, Coca-Cola, Gucci, Barbie, Microsoft, Calvin Klein, Fisher-Price, Mattel, Nokia, Disney, H&M, McDonald's, Nike, Mercedes, Panasonic, Ericsson, Motorola, Sony, Hewlett-Packard, Ford, Gillette, MGM, Compaq, Honda, Budweiser, Pepsi, Oracle, Samsung, Holiday Inn, Penguin group, Morgan Stanley, Dell, Toyota, Nintendo, Kodak, Gap, HSBC, Kellogg's, BMW, Canon, Heinz, Volkswagen, Ikea, Champion, Harley-Davidson, Louis Vuitton, MTV, L'Oreal, Xerox, KFC, Orange, Accenture, Avon, Philips, Nestlé, Warner Bros, Chanel, Kraft, Selfridges, Yahoo!, Hoover, Bacardi, Adidas, Rolex, Omega, Tiffany, Duracell, IBM, Hermès, Jack Daniels, Levi's, Hertz, Hennessy, Shell, Smirnoff, Prada, Moët & Chandon, Nissan, Heineken, Nivea, Electrolux, Starbucks, Polo Ralph Lauren, FedEx, Visa, Topshop, Guinness, Boots, British Airways, Paul Smith, Cartier, Audi, Diesel, Bally, Burton, Lacoste, Harrods, Boss, Fila, Seiko, Hallmark, Kronenbourg, Lancome, Minolta, Puma, Red Bull, SAAB, Volvo, Siemens, Whirlpool...)

– 'Mother' Advertising Agency, rebranding Christmas

A father is a plaster that cures all the ills of his children.

– Sean Cooper

The snow hid all the grass, and all signs of vegetation... We played at cards, sat up late. The moon shone upon the water below Silver-How, and above it hung, combining with Silver-How on one side, a bowl-shaped moon, the curve downwards; the white fields, glittering roof of Thomas Ashburner's house, the dark yew tree, the white fields gay and beautiful. William lay with his curtains open that he might see it.

– Dorothy Wordsworth

The trouble with trouble is that it all starts out as fun.

– Naomi Judd

Christmas is a time when people of all religions come together to worship Jesus Christ.

– Bart Simpson, The Simpsons

The Christmas tree inspires a love/hate relationship. All that time spent selecting and decorating, and a week after, you see it by the side of the road, like a mob hit. A car slows down, a door opens and a tree rolls out. People snap out of Christmas spirit like it was a drunken stupor. 'There's a tree inside the house! Throw it anywhere!'

– Jerry Seinfeld

My best Christmas is a composite of all those I spent between the ages of four and ten at my grandfather's house in Hampshire – opulent, traditional, magical, with Father Christmas and little velvet dresses and tinsel from the tree in your hair. Then my parents split up and I went to a boarding school and it was never the same.

– Rose Tremain

The voice was marvellously clear and we all went into the wings to see the cause of the improvement. There was Frank Benson, hanging upside down in a tree as Caliban, and for the first time on the whole tour the false teeth fitted him properly.

– Robert Morley

My eleven-year-old daughter mopes around the house all day waiting for her breasts to grow.

– Bill Cosby

Between the possibility of being hanged in all innocence, and the certainty of a public and merited disgrace, no gentleman of spirit could long hesitate.

– Robert Louis Stevenson

An Englishman named Robert Browning wrote: 'Grow old along with me, the best is yet to be.' Clearly this man was a minor poet. Or else he wrote those lines when he was 12.

– Joan Rivers

I can't cheat on my score – all you have to do is to look back down the fairway and count the wounded.

– Bob Hope

Some people get so rich they lose all respect for humanity. That's how rich I want to be.

– Rita Rudner

... I have something which makes it all bearable, the presents, the in-laws, other people's children, your own children, the games, the noise, the mess, the ridiculous meals. It consists of one part French cooking brandy, one part Irish whiskey and four parts fresh milk. The hard part is remembering to have put milk instead of water into one of your ice trays the previous night. Drink the mixture immediately on rising, while the others are having breakfast or throwing up behind the snowman.

– Kingsley Amis

If women ruled the world and we all got massages, there would be no war.

– Carrie Snow

There are to us no ties at all in being a father. A son is distinctly an acquired taste.

– Heywood Broun

The smell of wee-wee is still there all right, but these days the fresh and healthy smell of oranges has long gone. It's all crisps now, and giant cardboard cartons of Coke, bars of melting chocolate and great packets of cheap sweets. A colleague with the terrifying task of taking three young children round pantos... found he had to cope with impressive bouts of projectile vomiting... as well as the usual umpteen trips to the loo.

– Charles Spencer

Some day we will look back on all this and plough into the back of a parked car.

– Scott Adams

A child, like your stomach, doesn't need all that you can afford to give it.

– Franklin A. Clark

The ant sets an example to us all, but it is not a good one.
  – **Max Beerbohm**

An Englishman, even if he is quite alone, forms an orderly queue of one.
  – **George Mikes**

Why should I have a kid? I already have girlfriends who call me 'Daddy'.
  – **Bill Maher**

The Scots invented golf – which could also explain why they invented Scotch.
  – **James Dent**

Diane Keaton believes in God. But she also believes that the radio works because there are tiny people inside it.
  – **Woody Allen**

Dame Kiri Te Kanawa is a viable alternative to valium.
  – **Ira Siff**

My wins are merely beginner's luck, gentlemen, although I have devoted some time to the game.
  – **W.C. Fields**

Before you buy a tree, you should always have Dad pick it up and bang it hard on the ground a couple of times.
  – **Dave Barry**

I've tried to lose weight but I've always had this problem with my feet. I can't keep them out of the fish and chip shop.
  – **Roy Brown**

The two sides of industry have traditionally always regarded each other in Britain with the greatest possible loathing, mistrust and contempt. They are both absolutely right.
  – **Auberon Waugh**

Whether it is summer or winter, I always like to have the morning well aired before I get up.

— **Beau Brummell**

I never sleep through a performance. I always make sure I am awake for the intermission.

— **Max Benchley**

Whenever I pick up someone hitchhiking I always like to wait for a few minutes before I say anything to them. Then I say, 'Put your seatbelt on – I wanna try something. I saw it in a cartoon but I'm pretty sure I can do it.'

— **Steven Wright**

I have no fear of death and am optimistic, if not convinced, that there will be some kind of after-life, which I look forward to as an interesting change from Hay-on-Wye.

— **Peggy Causton**

Secretariat [the race horse] is everything I am not. He's young, he's beautiful, he has lots of hair, he's fast, he's durable, he has a large bank account, and his entire sex life is ahead of him.

— **Si Burick**

The thing that impresses me most about America is the way the parents obey their children.

— **Duke of Windsor**

Depressingly, Drop Dead Fred became popular in America, but then so did serial killing.

— **Christopher Tookey**

Professor Toad used to play Bach on an odd sort of pianola contrivance not because he was particularly enamoured of the fugues, but because the exercise of pedalling was good for constipation.

— **Beverly Nichols**

Due to the shape of the North American elk's oesophagus, even if it could speak, it could not pronounce the word 'lasagne'.

— **Cliff Clavin**

You cannot underestimate the intelligence of the American people.

— **H.L. Mencken**

Hollywood is the only place where an amicable divorce means each one gets fifty per cent of the publicity.

— **Lauren Bacall**

The thing that takes up the least amount of time and causes the most trouble is sex.

— **John Barrymore**

You can judge your age by the amount of pain you feel when you come in contact with a new idea.

— **Pearl S. Buck**

Every aunt, if fed enough liquor, becomes amusing. If not, pour yourself more liquor.

— **Grace Bradberry**

Eamon D'Arcy has a golf swing like an octopus falling out of a tree.

— **David Feherty**

In the city a funeral is just an interruption in the traffic; in the country it is a form of popular entertainment.

— **George Ade**

Most human problems can be solved by an appropriate charge of high explosive.

— **Blaster Bates**

I see the Church of England as an elderly lady, who mutters away to herself in a corner, ignored most of the time.

– George Carey

Our ability to delude ourselves may be an important survival tool.

– Jane Wagner

I have a fear that there is an afterlife but no one will know where it's being held.

– Woody Allen

The roughest thing I ever said to an umpire was, "Are you sure?"

– Rod Laver

It is part of prudence to thank an author for his book before reading, so as to avoid the necessity of lying about it afterwards.

– George Santayana

There is no question that there is an unseen world. The problem is, how far is it from midtown and how late is it open?

– Woody Allen

The worst misfortune that can happen to an ordinary man is to have an extraordinary father.

– Austin O'Malley

My theory is that if you buy an ice cream cone and make it hit your mouth, you can play tennis. If you stick it on your forehead, your chances are less.

– Vic Braden

Every time an Oscar is given out, an agent gets his wings.

– Kathy Bates

There are just two golden rules for an orchestra – start together and finish together. The public doesn't give a damn what goes on in between.

– Thomas Beecham

I'd just opened a card from Carol and Sam. I have no idea who they are either, but Carol, Sammy, you have the ugliest children on God's earth. The thing on the left is a real monster, and they're getting pride of place just above the coal scuttle.

– A.A. Gill

There are only a few original jokes and most of them are in Congress.

– Will Rogers

Old age means a crown of thorns, and the trick is to wear it jauntily.

– Christopher Morley

I walked home again with great pleasure, and there dined by my wife's bed-side with great content, having a mess of brave plum-porridge and a roasted pullet for dinner, and I sent for a mince pie abroad, my wife not being well to make any herself yet.

– Samuel Pepys, Diary, 25 December, 1662

We're obsessed with age. Numbers are always and pointlessly attached to every name that's published in a newspaper: 'Joe Creamer, 43, and his daughter, Tiffany-Ann, 9, were merrily chasing a bunny, 2, when Tiffany-Ann tripped on the root of a tree, 106.'

– Joan Rivers

You walk into an estate agent's office and all the roulette tables become desks.

– Dylan Moran

How could Tristan and Isolde, or Romeo and Juliet, have survived if there had been a child? All the poetry would have been lost in irritation at feeding time.

– Peter Ustinov

Two elderly women are in a restaurant and one of 'em says, 'Boy, the food in this place is really terrible.' The other one says, 'Yeah, I know, and such small portions.' Well, that's essentially how I feel about life. Full of loneliness and misery and suffering... and it's all over much too soon.

– **Woody Allen**

Most people who are as attractive, witty and intelligent as I am are usually conceited.

– **Joan Rivers**

If you leave aside Three Mile Island and Chernobyl, the safety record of nuclear power is really very good.

– **Paul O'Neill**

The only difference between a female lawyer and a pit bull terrier is the lipstick.

– **Patrick Murray**

I loved giving breakfast to the girls, and I loved it after Abigail became old enough to understand that, remarkable as I was, I did not deserve total credit for making such good corn flakes.

– **Calvin Trillin**

An elderly lady came into the chemist and asked for a bottle of euthanasia. I didn't say anything. I just handed her a bottle of echinacea.

– **Lydia Berryman**

I will honour Christmas in my heart, and try to keep it all the year.

– **Charles Dickens**

I've been a dad for some years, and I still don't have any answers. Only big, mind-bending questions like, 'What is that mysterious, semi-buoyant brown crud your children leave in your glass whenever they take a sip of your iced tea?'

– **Michael Burkett**

A horse is dangerous at both ends and uncomfortable in the middle.

– Ian Fleming

Gin is a dangerous drink. It's clear and innocuous looking. You also have to be 45, female and sitting on the stairs.

– Dylan Moran

This book is dedicated to my brilliant and beautiful wife without whom I would be nothing. She always comforts and consoles, never complains or interferes, asks nothing and endures all. She also writes my dedications.

– Albert Malvino

One day the don't-knows will get in and then where will we be?

– Spike Milligan

Even though all fathers are physically exhausted and mentally denuded, they like to talk. Encourage Dad to talk. Probably no one has for years.

– Elizabeth Hawes, fashion designer

Let the child's first lesson be obedience, and the second will be what thou wilt.

– Benjamin Franklin

I've been smoking for thirty years now and there's nothing wrong with my lung.

– Freddie Starr

Your mom is full of Christmas cheer and enough tranquillizer to take down an elephant.

– Peter Griffin, Family Guy

One Christmas, my wife stuffed the turkey and I cooked it. I kept putting it back in the oven because there seemed to be blood everywhere, only to find out she'd used a red berry stuffing. So the bird got horribly overcooked – and we all got completely tanked waiting for it.

– Michael Praed

She saw the funny side of life and we laughed till we cried. Oh, how I shall miss those laughs and the wonderful wisdom born of so much experience and of an innate sensitivity to life.

– Prince Charles

The urge to gamble is so universal and its practice so pleasurable that I assume it must be evil.

– Heywood Brown

The English should give Ireland home rule and reserve the motion picture rights.

– Will Rogers

Another crisis! I've heard that Santa's drunk and he's holding a painting by a French 18th century pastoral artist and a piece of paper out of a cracker. Oh no! He's blotto in the grotto with a Watteau and a motto.

– I'm Sorry I Haven't a Clue radio show

The writings of Henry Brougham are long and vigorous, like the penis of a jackass.

– Sydney Smith

My wife and I have five children and the reason why we have five children is because we do not want six.

– Bill Cosby

Better an eternity in Hell with Little and Large, Max Bygraves and Dick Emery than a single Christmas with the Osmonds.

– Clive James

Christmas is not in tinsel and lights and outward show. The secret lies in an inner glow. It's lighting a fire inside the heart... It's a glorious dream in the soul of man.

– Wilford A. Peterson

Advice is like kissing: it costs nothing and it's a pleasant thing to do.

– George Bernard Shaw

When the force is with Devon Malcolm and he puts his contact lenses in the correct eyes, he can be devastating.

– **Mike Selvey**

I've never really learnt how to live, and I've discovered too late that life is for living.

– **John Reith**

Family are the main source of guilt and therefore must be got rid of, either by suffocation or alienation.

– **Jenny Éclair**

Women used to make great mince pies and fake orgasms. Now we can do orgasms but have to fake mince pies. Is this progress?

– **Allison Pearson**

Zsa-Zsa Gabor got married as a one-off and it was so successful she turned it into a series.

– **Bob Hope**

A friend told me to shoot first and ask questions later. I was going to ask him why, but I had to shoot him.

– **John Wayne**

Bad luck is meeting your date's father and realizing he's the pharmacist you bought condoms from that afternoon.

– **Lewis Grizzard**

Nothing soothes me more after a long and maddening course of piano recitals than to sit and have my teeth drilled.

– **George Bernard Shaw**

Even if I read about a disease and it says, "This disease is present only in seventy-year-old Asian men," I feel, Oh! I could be the first white woman to have this disease.

– **Fran Lebowitz**

The cleaners thought my art was rubbish and put it in the bin.

   – Damien Hirst

When I had my baby, I screamed and screamed. And that was just during the conception.

   – Joan Rivers

I went to Naples to see Vesuvius and would you believe it, the bloody fools had let it go out.

   – Spike Milligan

I'm on a new diet – Viagra and prune juice. I don't know if I'm coming or going.

   – Rodney Dangerfield

Never put anything on paper, my boy, and never trust a man with a small black moustache.

   – P.G. Wodehouse

Given a good play, a good team and a decent set, you could have a blue-arsed baboon as director and still get a good production.

   – Peter O'Toole

Get your haggis right here! Chopped heart and lungs, boiled in a wee sheep's stomach. And it tastes as good as it sounds.

   – Matt Groening

It was about Santa Claus and elves and stockings hung by the fireplace and good cheer and a big dinner and sugar cookies and gifts, gifts, and more gifts.

   – Binnie Kirshenbaum

One of the secrets of a long and fruitful life is to forgive everybody everything every night before you go to bed.

   – Bernard M. Baruch

There are four sexes: men, women, clergymen and journalists.

— **Somerset Maugham**

The average minister should be unfrocked immediately and prevented, by force if necessary, from communicating any ideas to persons under thirty-five.

— **W.C. Fields**

I decided to stop drinking with creeps and to drink only with friends. I've lost 30 pounds.

— **Ernest Hemingway**

I believe in the discipline of silence and could talk for hours about it.

— **George Bernard Shaw**

If you're given the choice between money and sex appeal, take the money. As you get older, the money will become your sex appeal.

— **Katharine Hepburn**

It is nice to make heroic decisions and to be prevented by 'circumstances beyond your control' from ever trying to execute them.

— **William James**

A woman went to a plastic surgeon and asked him to make her like Bo Derek. He gave her a lobotomy.

— **Joan Rivers**

My father liked to collect yellow neckties and Yiddish curses. He never met a book he didn't finish.

— **Calvin Trillin**

Edith Evans bought an incredibly expensive Renoir and, when a friend asked her why she had hung it so low on the wall, out of the light behind the curtain, she replied curtly, 'Because there was a hook.'

— **Stephen Fry**

I've always wanted to be a spy, and frankly I'm a little surprised that British intelligence has never approached me.

   – Liz Hurley

When you wake up in the morning and nothing hurts, you can be sure you are dead.

   – Herbert Achternbusch

When I wake up in the morning and nothing hurts, I know I must be dead.

   – George Burns

I must particularly warn you against laughing; and I could heartily wish that you may be often seen to smile, but never heard to laugh. Frequent and loud laughter is the characteristic of folly and ill manners: it is the manner in which the mob express their silly joy at silly things. To my mind there is nothing so illiberal, and so ill-bred, as audible laughter.

   – Lord Chesterfield

I thought I was an honest guy, and just doing what everyone else was doing – bending the rules.

   – Manny Goldstein

If you keep working you'll last longer and I just want to keep vertical. I'd hate to spend the rest of my life trying to outwit an 18-inch fish.

   – Harold S. Geneen

I drink to your charm, your beauty and your brains: which gives you a rough idea of how hard up I am for a drink.

   – Groucho Marx

Fall is my favourite season in Los Angeles, watching the birds change colour and fall from the trees.

   – David Letterman

They're all mine... Of course, I'd trade any of them for a dishwasher.

   – Roseanne Barr on her children

A lot of today's new parents are annoying, giving their kids time-outs for slaying their friends, strapping safety helmets on them every time they walk down a flight of stairs, and displaying those stupid 'Baby on Board' stickers in their cars. They just wanna protect their kids at every moment from every thing. Have they considered large safe-deposit boxes with air holes?

— **Bill Geist**

The Basques are said to understand one another, but I don't believe a word of it.

— **Nicolas Scalinger**

I was talking to my nan about Ant and Dec. She didn't know which one Dec was. I said, 'Do you know which one Ant is?' She said, 'Yes.'

— **Jimmy Carr**

Thanks to modern medical advances such as antibiotics, nasal spray and Diet Coke, it has become routine for people in the civilized world to pass the age of 40, sometimes more than once.

— **Dave Barry**

'Sex,' she says, 'is a subject like any other subject. Every bit as interesting as agriculture.'

— **Muriel Spark**

Anyone can become a writer. Merely consider any novel by Judith Krantz and you'll know it's true.

— **Harlan Ellison**

It is to be noted that when any part of this paper appears dull, there is a design in it.

— **Richard Steele**

Did you ever notice they never take any fat hostages? You never see a guy come out of Lebanon going 'I was held hostage for seven months and I lost 175 pounds. I feel good and I look good and I learned self-discipline. That's the important thing.'

— **Denis Leary**

My father never raised his hand to any one of his children – except in self-defence.

– Fred Allen

I would rather see a woman die, any day, than see her happy with someone else.

– Pablo Picasso

One word sums up the responsibility of any vice-president, and that word is 'to be prepared'.

– Dan Quayle

I wouldn't ever set out to hurt anybody deliberately unless it was, you know important – like a league game or something.

– Dick Butkus

Happiness in old age is, more than anything else, preserving the privileges of privacy.

– Harold Azine

I know God will not give me anything I can't handle. I just wish that He didn't trust me so much.

– Mother Teresa

Nine out of ten males will believe anything, especially if it confirms their virility.

– Andrea Martin

When I was younger I could remember anything, whether it happened or not, but I am getting old and now that I am 71, I shall soon remember only the latter.

– Mark Twain

I believe I am the only Irishman apart from the staff who has ever set foot in the National Gallery of Ireland.

– George Bernard Shaw

A person who publishes a book wilfully appears before the populace with his pants down.

– Edna St Vincent Millay

'Credit' and 'Aaaargggh' – those two words are usually coupled together in the Old Pink Dog Bar.

– Douglas Adams

I am glad all the old masters are dead and I only wish they had died sooner.

– Mark Twain

The happy people are failures because they are on such good terms with themselves they don't give a damn.

– Agatha Christie

A schoolgirl was asked, 'In what countries are elephants found?' She answered, 'Elephants are very large and intelligent animals and are seldom lost.'

– James Agate

Marriage is a ceremony in which rings are put on the finger of the lady and through the nose of the gentleman.

– Herbert Spencer

Men love their children, not because they are promising plants, but because they are theirs.

– Charles Montagu

In the United States of America there are no trappings, no pageants, and no gorgeous ceremonies. I saw only two processions: one was the Fire Brigade preceded by the Police, the other was the Police preceded by the Fire Brigade.

– Oscar Wilde

The Irish are excellent timekeepers because they are used to working with watches that are an hour fast and ten minutes slow.

    – Patrick Murray

Parents are not interested in justice, they are interested in peace and quiet.

    – Bill Cosby

French fries. I love them. Some people are chocolate and sweets people. I love French fries. That and caviar.

    – Cameron Diaz

For every New Man changing nappies, there are 99 Newish Men dreaming about changing wives for one with a little less bounce around the bikini line.

    – Julie Burchill

My kids hate me. Their three goldfishes are named 'We', 'Hate' and 'Dad.'

    – Herb Gold

Blurbs that appear on the back cover are written by friends of the author who haven't read the book but owe the poor guy a favour.

    – Art Buchwald

People who insist on telling their dreams are among the terrors of the breakfast table.

    – Max Beerbohm

The other lads on the rugby team are calling me 'Lurpak' – the best butter in the world.

    – Steve Hampson

There are two politicians drowning and you are allowed to save only one. What do you do? Read a newspaper or eat your lunch?

    – Mort Sahl

The Greasy Spoon served plates of fat. You could have sausages in your fat or fried eggs in your fat. You could have the sausages and the fried eggs together, but that meant you got double the amount of fat.

  – Clive James

Why fear Taliban terrorist reprisals? Women who are having cosmetic surgery are waging chemical and germ warfare on themselves at £250 a pop.

  – Kathy Lette

Anybody who thinks that the Liberal Democrats are a racist party is staring the facts in the face.

  – Paddy Ashdown

There are two theories about how to argue with a woman. Neither one works.

  – Walter Matthau

People who count their chickens before they are hatched act very wisely: because once hatched, chickens run about so absurdly that it is impossible to count them accurately.

  – Oscar Wilde

People who define themselves by their age are about as appealing to be with as feminists who drone on about women's rights, homosexuals who are obsessed with being gay, or environmentalists who mention recycling every time they drop by for green tea.

  – Marcelle D'Argy-Smith

I suppose you think that persons who are as old as me are always thinking about very grave things, but I know that I am meditating on the same old themes that we did when we were 10 years old, only we go more gravely about it.

  – Henry David Thoreau

There is no more sombre enemy of art than the pram in the hall.

  – Cyril Connolly

Does Grandpa love to babysit his grandchildren? Are you kidding? By day he is too busy taking hormone shots at the doctor's or chip shots on the golf course. At night he and Grandma are too busy doing the cha-cha.

– **Hal Boyle**

The questions new dads care most about are: Will I ever have sex again? How are we going to pay for all this stuff? Will I be like my father – and is that good or bad?

– **Bradley Richardson**

Those press-on towels are a real rip-off, aren't they? I used six of them and I couldn't even get my arms dry.

– **Jack Dee**

I detest life insurance agents; they always argue that I shall some day die, which is not so.

– **Stephen Leacock**

My dad used to purposefully provoke polemical arguments. He'd say things like – I mean, he never said actually this – but you'd be eating away and he'd go, 'Ah, y'know, that fella Hitler, he had a few good ideas.' The next minute, the place would erupt. He'd sit back and me and my two sisters would argue passionately that we didn't fucking believe it at all. That was the way we were. It was fairly explosive.

– **Bob Geldof**

A foreign correspondent is someone who flies around from hotel to hotel and thinks that the most interesting thing about any story is the fact that he has arrived to cover it.

– **Tom Stoppard**

Setting off to a costume party dressed as a ghost, I was given a lift by a car full of men in white sheets. When those Klansmen discovered I was a New York Jew, they wanted to lynch me on the spot, but I calmed them down with an eloquent discourse on brotherhood. Not only did they cut me down and let me go, but that night I sold them two thousand dollars' worth of Israel bonds.

– **Woody Allen**

If I had as many love affairs as the media have given me credit for, I would now be speaking to you from a jar in the Harvard Medical School.

   – Frank Sinatra

I have three daughters and I find as a result I played King Lear almost without rehearsal.

   – Peter Ustinov

Mexican food is delicious and perfectly safe as long as you are careful never to get any of it in your digestive system.

   – Dave Barry

Never have I enjoyed youth so thoroughly as I have in my old age.

   – George Santayana

Remembering something at first try is now as good as an orgasm as far as I'm concerned.

   – Gloria Steinem

I am as fond of beauty spas as I am of being flayed alive with barbed wire.

   – Kathy Lette

H.G. Wells throws information at the reader as if emptying his mind like a perpetual chamber pot from a window.

   – Henry James

If a circus is half as good as it smells, it's a great show.

   – Fred Allen

Rossini addressed his letters to his mother as 'mother of the famous composer'.

   – Robert Browning

My dad didn't like people as much as he liked his car. He even introduced it to people. 'It's my Bonneville,' he'd say, 'my family's over there.'
- **Louie Anderson**

There's this interior linesman who's as big as a gorilla and as strong as a gorilla. If he was as smart as a gorilla, he'd be fine.
- **Sam Bailey**

This is the man who, as far as inventions go, thinks Wonderbra and La Perla are up there with the wheel.
- **Jane Moore**

They say a man is as old as the woman he feels. In that case, I'm 85.
- **Groucho Marx**

My father taught me to regard him as a warning and not a model... and I now see that this anxiety on his part was admirable and lovable; and that he was really just what he so carefully strove not to be: that is, a model father.
- **George Bernard Shaw**

People always ask me, 'Were you funny as a child?' Well, no, I was an accountant.
- **Ellen DeGeneres**

It is a mistake to regard age as a downhill grade towards dissolution. The reverse is true. As one grows older, one climbs with surprising strides.
- **George Sand**

The attention span of a computer is as long only as its electrical cord.
- **Eugene Turnaucka**

A motto for New Jersey – Not as bad as you might have expected.
- **Calvin Trillin**

Diaries are full of indispensable information, such as the recommended tyre pressures for North Korea.

– Leslie Mallory

Operas have a plot that is roughly as complex as The Magic Roundabout, only louder obviously.

– Joe Joseph

Not believe in Santa Claus! You might as well not believe in fairies! You might as well get your papa to hire men to watch all the chimneys on Christmas Eve to catch Santa Claus, but even if they did not see Santa Claus coming down, what would that prove? Nobody sees Santa Claus, but that is no sign that there is no Santa Claus. The most real things in the world are those that neither children nor men can see.

– Francis P. Church

When a man says his word is as good as his bond, always take his bond.

– Hugo Vickers

A classic is a book everyone is assumed to have read and which they often assume they have read themselves.

– Alan Bennett

Whatever women do they must do twice as well as men to be thought half as good. Luckily this is not difficult.

– Charlotte Whitton,

Every actor yearns to have a voice as resonant and penetrating as those in the audience who whisper.

– Cullen Hightower

I have yet to hear a man ask for advice on how to combine marriage and a career.

– Gloria Steinem

Monogamy is OK in the office but at home I prefer white pine.

– Samuel Goldwyn

In politics, if you want anything said, ask a man; if you want anything done, ask a woman.

- **Margaret Thatcher**

On my 60th birthday my 4-year-old grandson asked me if I was now a 'superior citizen'.

- **Anon**

Walking in a churchyard I have often asked myself, 'Where are all the bad people buried?'

- **Charles Lamb**

You may be a pain in the ass, you may be bad, but child, you belong to me.

- **Ray Charles**

Diana Barrymore, my daughter, is a horse's ass; quite a pretty one, but still a horse's ass.

- **John Barrymore**

Going into the drawing room, [Mark] was astonished to see that during the night the brightly coloured glass balls hanging from the branches of the tree had been added to by long looping garlands of French letters. Luckily, with Jane's and my help we managed to remove them all in time for the Reverend and Mrs Worsley, who were popping in for their annual pre-Christmas lunch drink.

- **Annabel Goldsmith, describing the antics of her father, the 8th Marquis of Londonderry**

If I wanted to start an insane asylum, I would just admit applicants that thought they knew something about Russia.

- **Will Rogers**

I was asked to be a linesman at the Wimbledon tennis championship. I excused myself by expressing myself flattered by the offer, but begged them to renew it when my eyesight had deteriorated sufficiently to be able to make wrong decisions with absolute conviction.

- **Peter Ustinov**

It is time, at 56, to begin, at least, to know oneself – and I do know what I am not .

– John Constable

I've got a bit of a situation at home. My eldest daughter brought a boy home for the first time. And I think it's safe to say I reacted rather badly. She said, 'Hello, Dad, this is Billy.' I said, 'Billy? Billy is it?' and I went up to this... person and said, 'If you so much as fucking touch her I'll cut you.' This Billy started crying. Still, that's 7-year-olds for you.

– Phill Jupitus

In Hollywood the girl throwing the bouquet at a wedding is just as likely to be the next one to marry as the girl who catches it.

– Geraldine Page

To be positive is to be mistaken at the top of one's voice.

– Ambrose Bierce

It's extraordinary. My mother doesn't need glasses at all and here I am 52, 56 – well, whatever age I am – and I can't see a thing.

– Queen Elizabeth II

No matter how much time you save, at the end of your life, there's no extra time saved up. You'll be going, 'What do you mean there's no time? I had a microwave oven, Velcro sneakers, a clip-on tie. Where's the time?' But there isn't any. Because when you waste time in life, they subtract it. Like if you saw all the Rocky movies, they deduct that.

– Jerry Seinfeld

I thought nothing of firing a revolver at a man or of thrusting a glass in his face, but as an Englishman I would never use a knife.

– Arthur Harding

Kids love to play the dropping game at mealtimes, but you can beat that. You have only to fasten a rubber band on the cup handle and wrap it around the child's wrist. That way the kid digs the rubber band and has all the fun of dropping the cup too.

– Bill Cosby

Nature gives you the face you have at 20. Life shapes the face you have at 30. But at 50 you get the face you deserve.

    – Coco Chanel

In stark contrast to grown-up parties, partygoers at children's parties don't become embarrassingly drunk. It is the birthday-boy's or girl's father who becomes embarrassingly drunk.

    – Jeremy Hardy

Husbands are afraid to touch the child at first. The mother learns immediately that you can sling it over your shoulder and it will be just fine. My husband never changed a diaper; he was very proud of that. My child flew through the air; he'd say, 'She's wet' and toss her to me.

    – Joan Rivers

Physicians of the Utmost Fame, Were called at once, but when they came, They answered, as they took their fees, 'There is no cure for this disease.'

    – Hilaire Belloc

England had Thatcher. We had Reagan. But at least we have one thing we can hold over England's head. We tried to kill Reagan.

    – Denis Leary

The organ of Winchester Cathedral is audible at five miles, painful at three, and lethal at one.

    – Thomas Beecham

It's the friends you can call up at 4 a.m. that matter.

    – Marlene Dietrich

He claims to be a great sexual athlete, just because he always comes first.

    – Ellie Laine

Harold Acton's Humdrum reads like a painstaking attempt to satirize modern life by a Chinaman who has been reading Punch.

    – Cyril Connolly

My advice to all who want to attend a lecture on music is "Don't." "Go to a concert instead."

– Ralph Vaughan-Williams

When I'm in a wig I'm pretty attractive. I stare at myself in mirrors because I'm my type.

– Kevin McDonald

The first white man to sail near Australia was the world's most useless explorer, a Dutchman called Abel Tasman. In a three-year voyage he found Fiji, Tasmania and New Zealand, but in one of the most inept pieces of navigation ever, he completely missed the big bit in the middle.

– Jeremy Clarkson

Typical of Margaret. She produced twins and avoided the necessity of a second pregnancy.

– Denis Thatcher

Sometimes I would rather have someone take away years of my life than take away a moment.

– Pearl Bailey

A survey shows moms are better at baby talk than dads. Duh. For a dad, baby talk is, 'Here, you take him.'

– Jay Leno

Signs you're getting on a bit: your back hurts; you eat food past its sell-by date; your carpet is patterned; you go supermarket shopping in the evening to pick up marked-down bargains; you can spell; you hang your clothes on padded coat hangers; you save the hearing aid flyer that falls out of the colour supplement; you try to get electrical gadgets repaired when they go wrong; you save the free little packets of sugar from cafés; you have worn a knitted swimsuit; when you watch black and white films you spend the whole time pointing at the screen going, 'He's dead... She's dead...'; your car stereo is tuned to Radio 2.

– Colin Slater

People who say they sleep like a baby usually don't have one.

– **Leo J. Burke**

If you were to open up a baby's head – and I am not suggesting for a moment that you should – you would find nothing but this enormous drool gland.

– **Dave Barry**

I don't think the Israelis should give back the land they won from the Arabs. I think they should sell it back.

– **Woody Allen**

My mother is 96, and had a bad fall and a blackout a few days ago. The doctor who examined her in the A&E clearly thought she was a bit gaga, so asked her to count down from 20. 'Better than that,' she said, 'I'll do it in French,' and got down to 'douze' before the doctor, chastened, said, 'OK, OK.'

– **David Horchover**

The Queen Mother seemed incapable of a bad performance as a national grandmother – warm, smiling, human, understanding, she embodied everything the public could want of its grandmother..

– **John Pearson**

He had an eternity to play that ball, but he took too long over it.

– **Martin Tyler**

If you go long enough without a bath, even the fleas will let you alone.

– **Ernie Pyle**

Last Christmas, I gave my kid a BB gun. He gave me a sweatshirt with a bullseye on the back.

– **Rodney Dangerfield**

Men who have a thirty-six-televised-football-games-a-week habit should be declared legally dead and their estates probated.

– **Erma Bombeck**

There ain't no answer. There ain't gonna be any answer. There never has been an answer. That's the answer.

– **Gertrude Stein**

You have to be careful not to be upstaged by your nipples.

– **Susan Sarandon**

Think what a better world it would be if we all, the whole world, had cookies and milk about three o'clock every afternoon and then lay down on our blankets for a nap.

– **Barbara Jordan**

How absurd and delicious it is to be in love with somebody younger than yourself. Everybody should try it.

– **Barbara Pym**

A golf ball hitting a tree shall be deemed not to have hit the tree. Hitting a tree is just bad luck and has no place in a scientific game. The player should estimate the distance the ball would have travelled if it had not hit the tree and play the ball from there.

– **Arnie Kunz**

The plot of many old films can be summarized as follows: 'Separated at birth for a crime he did not commit.'

– **Des MacHale**

The ideal board of football directors should be made up of three men – two dead and one dying.

– **Tommy Docherty**

Life is too short but it would be absolutely awful if it were too long.

– **Peter Ustinov**

I realized I should try harder to be an actress because I'd never make it as a waitress.

– **Jane Krakowski**

When Prince Charles speaks, everybody pretends to be fascinated, even though he has never said anything interesting except in that intercepted telephone conversation wherein he expressed the desire to be a feminine hygiene product.

   – **Dave Barry**

A Christmas Day, to be perfect, should be clear and cold, with holly branches in berry, a blazing fire, a dinner with mince pies, and games and forfeits in the evening. You cannot have it in perfection if you are very fine and fashionable.

   – **Leigh Hunt**

I told my wife I want to be cremated. She's planning a barbecue.

   – **Rodney Dangerfield**

In a world without men, there would be no crime and a lot of fat happy women.

   – **Nicole Hollander**

I hate a woman who seems to be hermetically sealed in the lower regions.

   – **H. Allen Smith**

Knowledge of the world is only to be acquired in the world, and not in a closet.

   – **Lord Chesterfield**

'Merry Xmas Everybody' is, and always will be, the great British Christmas hit, because it's an unapologetic party song... The song instantly conjures images of Noddy Holder, frizzy hair exploding from either side of his head like a doodle in the phone book, his fringe obediently plastered to his forehead, or wedged under that ridiculous mirrored top hat. Father Christmas may not exist, but I believe in Noddy Holder.

   – **Andrew Collins**

Music hath charms to soothe a savage beast, but I'd try a revolver first.

   – **Josh Billings**

Par is anything I want it to be. For instance, the hole right here is a par 47, and yesterday I birdied the sucker.

– **Willie Nelson**

All the men in my family were bearded, and most of the women.

– **W.C. Fields**

In my day, women were still stud beasts, and feminine wit wasn't fashionable. It was a privilege reserved exclusively to the men.

– **Rachel Ferguson**

Sex is one of the most wholesome, beautiful and natural things that money can buy.

– **Steve Martin**

Having a child is surely the most beautifully irrational act that two people in love can commit.

– **Bill Cosby**

This guy says, 'I'm perfect for you, because I'm a cross between a macho and a sensitive man.' I said, 'Oh, a gay trucker?'

– **Judy Tenuta**

My dad said, 'You'll never be someone because you procrastinate.' I said, 'Just you wait.'

– **Ted Carnes**

Lots of men are jealous of me because I have this extraordinarily beautiful wife who does great Indian and Italian.

– **Michael Caine**

A man knows he is growing old because he begins to look like his father.

– **Gabriel García Márquez**

He's on the mend, sitting up in bed blowing the froth off his medicine.

– **Flann O'Brien**

Of course, the placenta is very useful because it is so very hideous that by comparison, the baby is quite attractive.

– **Jenny Eclair**

The English church-goer prefers a severe preacher because he thinks a few home truths will do his neighbours no harm.

– **George Bernard Shaw**

I didn't hire Scott as assistant coach because he's my son. I hired him because I'm married to his mother.

– **Frank Layden**

I call my son the boomerang kid because he keeps on moving back.

– **Ross Cooper**

Fathers send their sons to college either because they went to college, or because they didn't.

– **L.L. Hendren**

I always astonish strangers by my amiability, because no human being could be so disagreeable as they expect me to be.

– **George Bernard Shaw**

Everyone told me to pass on Speed because it was a 'bus movie'.

– **Sandra Bullock**

I really want to have a child because Christmas without one is rubbish.

– **Hugh Grant**

The holidays are welcome to me partly because they are such rallying points for the affections which get so much thrust aside in the business and preoccupations of daily life.

– **George E. Woodberry**

You don't know how difficult it has been being a closet heterosexual.

– **David Bowie**

Don't drink until your children are in bed. I tried this rule once – they got so sick of being tucked in at 4.30 in the afternoon.

  – Phyllis Diller

Darling, if I get excited during this bedroom scene, please forgive me. And if I don't get excited, please forgive me.

  – Tom Berenger

English vegetables taste as though they have been boiled in a strong soap.

  – W.C. Fields

English coffee tastes like water that has been squeezed out of a wet sleeve.

  – Fred Allen

A nuclear fallout shelter in Barnsley has been damaged by vandals.

  – Steve Race

Basil Blackwell said that he had certainly been depraved by the book, Last Exit to Brooklyn, but as he was in his 80s at the time the matter didn't seem to be of great practical significance.

  – John Mortimer

If God had intended us to drink beer, He would have given us stomachs.

  – David Daye

Now, son, you don't want to drink beer. That's for daddies and kids with fake IDs.

  – Homer Simpson

The toughest job in the world isn't being a President. It's being a parent.

  – Bill Clinton

A plumber who has Latin is a better plumber than one who does not.

  – Enoch Powell

I believe that mink are raised for being turned into fur coats and if we didn't wear fur coats, these little animals would never have been born. So is it better not to have been born or to have lived for a year or two and be turned into a fur coat?

– **Barbi Benton**

Only one arrest was made at the Belgium v. Ireland match in Brussels. It was an Irishman with a painted moustache who attempted to kiss a police horse.

– **Patrick Murray**

If the English could only learn to believe in fairies, there wouldn't ever have been any Irish problem.

– **W.B. Yeats**

I know from experience that I myself benefited from being whipped as a child so I want and command you to whip my son when he is bad and to make him understand why.

– **Henry IV, to his son's tutor**

A competitor of Irving Berlin's complained that Berlin has used up all the holidays: 'I'm Dreaming of a White Christmas', 'Easter Parade', and so on.

– **Groucho Marx**

Whatever they try and sell you, the best aphrodisiac for women is eating oysters because if you can swallow oysters, you can swallow anything.

– **Hattie Hayridge**

A man's gotta make at least one bet every day otherwise he could be walking around lucky and never know it.

– **Jimmy Jones**

Statistics show that attendance at work is better among married men with children and spikes even higher among fathers of newborns. Quite a coincidence, huh?

– **Thomas Hill**

The English rugby team – I've seen better centres in a box of Black Magic.

— **Max Boyce**

Sometimes I believe that some people are better at love than others, and sometimes I believe that everyone is faking it.

— **Nora Ephron**

People often ask me, 'What's the difference between couple-hood and babyhood?' In a word? Moisture. Everything in my life is now more moist. Between your spittle, your diapers, your spit-up and drool, you got your baby food, your wipes, your formula, your leaky bottles, sweaty baby backs, and numerous other untraceable sources, all creating an ever-present moistness in my life, which heretofore was mainly dry.

— **Paul Reiser**

I can discern no difference in behaviour between English Protestant and English atheist.

— **Cyril Connolly**

We gave our presents on Christmas morning between opening our stockings and church. Nancy once despised my present so much that she threw it straight on the fire. Strangely enough I did not mind a bit; I knew it was a hopeless present and admired her courage in demonstrating her displeasure.

— **Diana Mitford**

Adolescence is a time of rapid change. Between the ages of 12 and 17, for example, a parent can age as much as 20 years.

— **Anon**

After 40 a woman has to choose between losing her figure or her face. My advice is to keep your face, and stay sitting down.

— **Barbara Cartland**

Should a father be present at the birth of his child? It's all any reasonable child can expect if Dad is present at the conception.

— **Joe Orton**

For the first baby, we spent a big part of each day just gazing at her. For the second baby, we spent a big part of each day watching to be sure our elder child wasn't squeezing or hitting her. For the third baby, we spent a big part of each day hiding from the children.

– **Anon**

My father never escaped into heartiness: 'Hi, Bill! My son Biff has told me a lot about you,' and so on. No fellow human, however small, should be subjected to 'How do you like your school, Sonny?'

– **Wilfred Sheed**

What's Christmas but a time of paying bills without money, a time for finding yourself a year older and not an hour richer etc. Old Ebenezer was not wholly without reason. Though it is not for riches I long, but repose of the soul...

– **Robertson Davies**

The harpsichord is a performance on a bird-cage with a toasting fork.

– **Percy A. Scholes**

Just as I was about to give birth, Mick arrived at the hospital bearing diamond earrings and caviar. The wives and nurses were very excited to find him there with a pot of caviar, and asked for lemon slices and toast.

– **Jerry Hall, ex-Mrs Jagger**

I got my figure back after giving birth. Sad, I'd hoped to get somebody else's.

– **Caroline Quentin**

It's like getting ready for your own birth. Nothing prepares you. When those eyes meet your eyes – I was feeling things I never had feelings like before. But let us make no mistake as to why the baby is here: it is here to replace us. We'll see who's wearing the diapers when all this is over.

– **Jerry Seinfeld**

My performances tend to be a little bit off-centre, whatever that means.

– **Rachel Weisz**

I was invited to Hugh Hefner's 75th birthday party but I couldn't figure out what gift to buy him. What do you give the man who's had everyone? Then I thought of it: monogrammed Viagra!

– David Letterman

The best way to remember your wife's birthday is to forget it once.

– Joseph Cossman

It's time to stop denying the 'inner bitch' in ourselves. Stop apologising for her. Set her free.

– Elizabeth Hilts

Robins and reindeer, bunches of gilt bells, black cats, red-berried holly, Pickwickian coaches-and-four, candles, angels, fir trees... Each of us probably has in mind one ideal and absolute of the Christmas card, as received in childhood.

– Elizabeth Bowen

I'm not offended by all the dumb blonde jokes because I know I'm not dumb... and I also know that I'm not blonde.

– Dolly Parton, singer-songwriter

Funny how a wife can spot a blonde hair at twenty yards, yet miss the garage doors.

– Corey Ford

You can't help feeling that goalkeeper Peter Bonetti looks rather like a member of the public who just happens to have wandered on to the pitch.

– Nick Hancock

Lots of guys like to drive a BMW because it's the only car name they can spell.

– Jeremy Clarkson

I'm not to blame for an old body, but I would be to blame for an old soul. An old soul is a shameful thing.

- **Margaret Deland**

I don't try to be a sex bomb. I am one.

- **Kylie Minogue**

I could get into bed with James Bond, then take my false leg off and it would really be a gun.

- **Heather Mills**

There's a store in New York called Bonjour Croissant. It makes me want to go to Paris and open a store called Hello Toast.

- **Fran Lebowitz**

I see girls in their miniskirts, their boobs hanging out and stuff. In Melbourne, the girls who wear that shit, they get beaten up. By other girls!

- **Holly Valance**

If you are in difficulties with a book, try the element of surprise; attack it at an hour when it isn't expecting it.

- **H.G. Wells**

Spiro Agnew's library burned down and both books were destroyed – and one of them hadn't even been coloured in.

- **Mort Sahl**

Once you've put one of Henry James' books down, you simply cannot pick it up again.

- **Mark Twain**

Some men borrow books; some men steal books; and others beg presentation copies from the author.

- **James Roche**

I don't need stuff like pot or booze. My high is my wife and kids.

   – Bill Cosby

It would be rude to say that Boris Johnson looks as if he dresses at a charity shop because no charity shop would accept stuff in that condition.

   – Simon Hoggart

The difference between owning a book and borrowing a book is that when you own a book you can get food on it.

   – Susan Catherine

A good reducing exercise consists of placing both hands against the edge of the table and pushing back.

   – Robert Quillen

All these cereals they have: Cracklin' Oat Bran and Honkin Fibre Chunks. Cereal used to come with a free prize and now it comes with a roll of toilet paper in every box.

   – Denis Leary

If Everton were playing down at the bottom of my garden, I would draw the curtains.

   – Bill Shankly

I'm one of seven children. My dad bought an MG sports car once. Nice car, but where the bloody hell were we supposed to sit? We had to go to school like the White Helmets Motorcycle Display team, all balanced on each other's shoulders. My dad'd be at the front, 'Low bridge!'

   – Jeff Green

Signs you're on a Bad Cruise: the brochure boasts the ship was the subject of a 60 Minutes exposé; as you board, a personal injury lawyer hands you his business card; no matter what you order from the bar, it tastes of salt; every time you see the crew, they're wearing life-jackets; the vessel's name is the S.S. Scurvy.

   – David Letterman

My mother-in-law was very depressed so I bought her one of those do-it-yourself suicide guides. It told her to place a gun just below her left breast and pull the trigger. She kneecapped herself.

– **Les Dawson**

I saw a guy driving down Hollywood Boulevard with a tree on his front bumper and I said, 'Getting ready for Christmas?' He said, 'No, teaching the wife how to drive!'

– **Bob Hope**

Life expectancy would grow by leaps and bounds if green vegetables smelled as good as bacon.

– **Doug Larson**

You've got the brain of a four-year-old boy, and I bet he was glad to get rid of it.

– **Groucho Marx**

'He's tired'; 'She's teething'; 'He's a real boy'; 'She's a bit of a tomboy' are all euphemisms for 'Whatabrat!'

– **Tom Kaplan**

In my Rogues' Gallery of repulsive small boys I suppose he would come about third.

– **P.G. Wodehouse**

Every four weeks I go up a bra size... it's worth being pregnant just for the breasts.

– **Natasha Hamilton**

It was like the referee had a brand new yellow card and wanted to see if it worked.

– **Richard Rufus**

A coward dies a hundred deaths, a brave man only once. But then once is enough, isn't it?

– **Harry Stone**

A nutrient is a chemical added to breakfast cereal to allow it to be sold as a food.

— **Mike Barfield**

At 50, the madwoman in the attic breaks loose, stomps down the stairs, and sets fire to the house. She won't be imprisoned anymore.

— **Erica Jong**

Trevor Brooking stings like a butterfly.

— **Brian Clough**

Belgium is a country invented by the British to annoy the French.

— **Charles De Gaulle**

It never occurred to Stalin that the British electorate would remove Churchill from office in the very moment of victory. The result not only surprised but startled him, confirming his rooted belief that elections where the outcome was not guaranteed were too dangerous to be allowed.

— **Alan Bullock**

Her expression as she eyed my grubby brood implied that I had conceived them all in a drunken stupor with a series of nameless and unsuitable fathers.

— **Birna Helgadottir**

My father used to play with my brother and me in the yard. Mother would come out and say, 'You're tearing up the grass.' 'We're not raising grass,' Dad would reply, 'we're raising boys.'

— **Harmon Killebrew**

England's coach Jack Rowell, an immensely successful businessman, has the acerbic wit of Dorothy Parker and, according to most New Zealanders, a similar knowledge of rugby.

— **Mark Reason**

My father was very hairy. When my brother and I were little, he liked to amuse us by setting his chest hairs alight and then blowing them out.

– **Grace White**

When I die, I wish to be buried in the no smoking section of the cemetery.

– **David Story**

When I was introduced to a Texan businessman he looked aghast: 'Tarquin Olivier,' he said, 'now there's a name that smacks of overkill.'

– **Tarquin Olivier**

Though Love and all his pleasures are but toys, They shorten tedious nights.

– **Thomas Campion**

My father was an eminent button maker, but I had a soul above buttons. I panted for a liberal profession.

– **George Colman**

Cantonese will eat anything in the sky but airplanes, anything in the sea but submarines and anything with four legs but the table.

– **Amanda Bennett**

Men kick friendship around like a football, but it doesn't seem to crack. Women treat it like glass and it goes to pieces.

– **Anne Morrow**

I may not be making a living, but I'm making a difference.

– **Rachel Hickerson**

They caught the first female serial killer, but she didn't kill the men herself. She gained access to their apartments, hid their remote controls and they committed suicide.

– **Elayne Booster**

I sometimes got birthday cards from fans. But it's always the same message – they hope it's my last.

– **Al Norman**

Don't be over-impressed by time. Accept it, but don't kowtow to it. We should still be able to stick two fingers in the air as the diminishing amount of sand trickles through the hourglass.

– **George Melly**

I have been dead for two years, but I don't choose to have it known.

– **Lord Chesterfield**

You should never say anything to a woman that even remotely suggests you think she is pregnant unless you can see an actual baby emerging from her at that moment.

– **Joan Rivers**

My wife had half-a-dozen sex change operations, but couldn't find anything she liked.

– **Woody Allen**

There are no handles to a horse but the 1910 model has a string to each side of its face for turning its head when there is anything you want it to see.

– **Stephen Leacock**

During the war I consumed German wine but I excused myself that I was not drinking it but interning it.

– **Winston Churchill**

Immortality is a long shot, I admit. But somebody has to be first.

– **Bill Cosby**

I think a lot of Leonard Bernstein, but not as much as he does.

– **Oscar Levant**

I wouldn't say my father hated me, but at my christening, he tipped the vicar a fiver to hold me under.

– **Bob Monkhouse**

There are many mysteries in old age but the greatest, surely, is this: in those adverts for walk-in bathtubs, why doesn't all the water gush out when you get in?

– **Alan Coren**

I have bursts of being a lady, but it doesn't last long.

– **Shelley Winters**

George Gershwin died on 11 July 1937, but I don't have to believe it if I don't want to.

– **John O'Hara**

I wear the pants in our house but I also wash and iron them.

– **Denis Thatcher**

Of course a platonic relationship is possible, but only between a husband and wife.

– **Irving Kristof**

There was a point to this story, but it has temporarily escaped the chronicler's mind.

– **Douglas Adams**

Science has taught us to pasteurise cheese, but what about the H-bomb? Have you ever thought what would happen if one of those fell off a desk accidentally?

– **Woody Allen**

Age does not protect you from love. But love, to some extent, protects you from age.

– **Jeanne Moreau**

She had lost the art of conversation, but not, unfortunately, the power of speech.

   – George Bernard Shaw

I didn't want to look my age, but I didn't want to act the age I wanted to look either. I also wanted to grow old enough to understand that sentence.

   – Erma Bombeck

I do want to have Brooklyn christened, but I'm not sure which religion.

   – David Beckham

I don't mean to be a diva, but some days you wake up and you're Barbra Streisand.

   – Courtney Love

My parents stayed together for 40 years but that was out of spite.

   – Woody Allen

I have often wished to cultivate modesty, but I am too busy thinking about myself.

   – Edith Sitwell

President George W. Bush is being criticized by Christian groups because his holiday cards don't have the word 'Christmas' in them. In response the President said, 'You try spelling it.'

   – Conan O'Brien

When my father caught me imitating him by pretending to smoke a toy pipe he advised me very earnestly never to follow his example in any way; and his sincerity so impressed me that to this day I have never smoked, never shaved, and never used alcoholic stimulants.

   – George Bernard Shaw

In one year I travelled 450,000 miles by air. That's eighteen and a half times around the world, or once around Howard Cosell's head.

   – Jackie Stewart

The child who is being raised strictly by the book is probably a first edition.

   – Aldous Huxley

The American poet Lindsay began his career by codifying the ways in which a poet can get a free meal. Here was a seer, here was a man with a strong grasp of essentials.

   – Christopher Morley

After a sleepover, my daughter is returned by her friend's mother who tells me what a lovely child we're raising – so polite, so helpful – I want that child!

   – Jason Rose

American football consists of committee meetings separated by outbreaks of violence.

   – George Will

I have certainly seen more men destroyed by the desire to have a wife and child and to keep them in comfort than I have seen destroyed by drink or harlots.

   – William Butler Yeats

I have never seen Jaws 4 but by all accounts it is terrible. However, I *have* seen the house that I bought with the money I got for doing it, and it is terrific.

   – Michael Caine

Marriage is a sort of friendship recognized by the police.

   – Robert Louis Stevenson

In Canberra, even the mistakes are planned by the National Capital Development Commission.

   – Alan Fitzgerald

You can't fight City Hall but you can crap on the steps and run like mad.

   – Alexei Sayle

A couple in Maryland has 'raised' a Cabbage Patch doll as their only son for 19 years. Pat and Joe Posey treat the doll, christened Kevin, as a human. He goes everywhere with them, they talk to him and he 'replies' by Joe putting on his voice. Joe says the doll's favourite hobby is fishing, and father and son go on frequent trips to a pond near their home.

– **Ananova News**

Historians have now definitely established that Juan Cabrillo, the discoverer of California, was not looking for Kansas, thus setting a precedent that continues to this day.

– **Wayne Shannon**

Britain has invented a new missile. It's called the civil servant – it doesn't work and it can't be fired.

– **Walter Walker**

In the old days, it was not called the Holiday Season; the Christians called it 'Christmas' and went to church; the Jews called it 'Hanukka' and went to synagogue; the atheists went to parties and drank. People passing each other on the street would say 'Merry Christmas!' or 'Happy Hanukka!' or (to the atheists) 'Look out for the wall!'

– **Dave Barry**

I watched a small man with thick calluses on both hands work 15 and 16 hours a day. He taught me all I needed to know by the simple eloquence of his example.

– **Mario Cuomo**

Job endured everything – until his friends came to comfort him. Then he grew impatient.

– **Soren Kierkegaard**

You can take a man's wife, you can even take his wallet. But never on any account take a man's putter.

– **Archie Compston**

There are all kinds of presents one can get for Christmas. The best is love.

– **Helen Hayes**

Another awful thing about these Christmas parties can be coming face to face with a hackette or secretary that you featured with 20 years ago. Embarrassing for both parties but less so for the one with the worse memory. There are women who have etched in their eyes the unspoken question, 'Why didn't you telephone?'

– Jeffrey Bernard

You stay young as long as you can learn, acquire new habits and suffer contradiction.

– Marie von Ebner-Eschenbach

Islington is about as far as you can get from London without needing yellow-fever jabs.

– A.A. Gill

'Strong Woman', used by men, means 'she can take it'. And if she can take it, why not do it to her again?

– Julie Burchill

What's all this fuss about Plutonium? How can something named after a Disney character be dangerous? Anyway radiation cannot kill you because it contains absolutely no cholesterol.

– Johnny Carson

Don't buy shares in companies whose chairmen can play consistently below their handicap. Either they are playing too much golf or they cheat.

– Jeff Randall

What every woman knows and no man can ever grasp is that even if he brings home everything on the list, he will still not have got the right things.

– Allison Pearson

You can have long hair, or you can have grey hair. But you can't have both. So choose carefully.

– Justin Rosenholtz

My grandmother was utterly convinced I'd wind up as the Archbishop of Canterbury. And, to be honest, I've never entirely ruled it out.
– **Hugh Grant**

I'm a philosophy major. That means I can think deep thoughts about being unemployed.
– **Bruce Lee**

The only way my wife and I can afford to have kids is if she breast-fed them for 18 years.
– **Paul Alexander**

Why talk with the monkey when you can talk with the organ grinder?
– **Winston Churchill**

It is amazing what the human body can do when chased by a bigger human body.
– **Jack Thompson**

There are a lot of things money can't buy. None of them are on my Christmas list.
– **Joan Rivers**

You remind me of a poem I can't remember, and a song that may never have existed, and a place I'm not sure I've ever been to.
– **Grampa Simpson, The Simpsons**

If all of the salmon caught in Canada in one year were laid end to end across the Sahara Desert, the smell would be terrible.
– **Alan Fleming**

There is no good reason why good cannot triumph as often as evil. The triumph of anything is a matter of organization. If there are such things as angels, I hope they are organized along the lines of the Mafia.
– **Kurt Vonnegut**

There are few situations in life that cannot be resolved promptly, and to the satisfaction of all concerned, by either suicide, a bag of gold, or thrusting the despised antagonist over a precipice on a dark night.

– Ernest Bramah

A mind of the calibre of mine cannot derive its nutriment from cows.

– George Bernard Shaw

My gently lachrymose grandmother had an extraordinary capacity for reliving the events of the Bible as though they were headline news in the paper.

– Peter Ustinov

To simulate the birth experience, take one car jack, insert into rectum, pump to maximum height and replace with jack hammer. And that would be a good birth.

– Kathy Lette

To say that Agatha Christie's characters are cardboard cut-outs is an insult to cardboard cut-outs.

– Ruth Rendell

All women should know how to take care of children. Most of them will have a husband some day.

– Franklin P. Jones

Christmas is coming. In Beverly Hills the carollers are already going round singing, 'Oh come all ye facelifts...'

– Joan Rivers

I used to be taken to Christmas carols in Salisbury Cathedral. It always was cold in that shrine to austerity. The Anglican chants are drear: there is no joy in the ecclesiastical attempt at doo-wop... I would never dream of taking my children to such a place. We'll do what we always do. I will have obtained, during the autumn, several hallucinogenic heads of the mushroom amanita muscaria. I have dried them and powdered them. We make cocktails of them. We get out of our heads.

– Jonathan Meades

The day is coming when a single carrot, freshly observed, will set off a revolution.
- **Paul Cézanne**

Always be prepared for a mistletoe ambush. Carry a can of mace spray.
- **Christopher Douglas and Mick Newman, Mastering the Universe radio show**

Football is football; if that weren't the case, it wouldn't be the game it is.
- **Garth Crooks**

Needless to say, the film Farinelli: Il Castrato ended on a high note.
- **Tony Clayton-Lea**

I have studied many philosophers and many cats. The wisdom of cats is infinitely superior.
- **Hippolyte Taine**

I don't see myself certainly as a celebrity, as a star, because people are so familiar with me... Basically, people say 'Hey Oprah, come on over here and sit down.' Every day, at the end of the show, they say, 'Want to go to lunch, want to come to my house? I'm fixing so and so for dinner.'
- **Oprah Winfrey**

When I had to fill in a census paper, I gave my profession as genius and my infirmity as talent.
- **Oscar Wilde**

One hundred dollars invested at seven per cent interest for one hundred years will become $100,000, at which time it will be worth absolutely nothing.
- **Lazarus Long**

Of all the '-isms' of the twentieth century, tourism may yet turn out to have been the worst.
- **Aga Khan III**

Something happens when a man reaches a certain age, that the news becomes the most important thing in his life. All fathers think one day they're going to get a call from the State Department. 'Listen, we've completely lost track of the situation in the Middle East. You've been watching the news. What do you think we should do?'

– **Jerry Seinfeld**

On one occasion when the Reverend Laurence Chaderton had been preaching for over two hours, he is said to have shown signs of flagging. The congregation then cried out, with one voice: 'For God's sake, Sir, go on!'

– **Henry Button**

Richard Baerlein's father decided to calculate the chances of life after death. He requested his family to give him a pile of sandwiches and a Thermos flask of coffee and he then retired to his room for the weekend. He emerged on Monday morning announcing that the chances were 'little better than five to two against'.

– **Jeffrey Bernard**

Politicians are like nappies. They should be changed regularly and for the same reason.

– **Patrick Murray**

FOR SALE: Christmas Pudding Charms: sterling silver charms to bring good luck. Potential choking hazard: do not use with food.

– **Past Times catalogue**

I was thrown out of NYU for cheating – with the dean's wife.

– **Woody Allen**

It now costs more to amuse a child than it once cost to educate his father.

– **Vaughan Monroe**

Give a student from the University of Chicago a glass of water and he says: "This is a glass of water. But is it a glass of water? And if it is a glass of water, why is it a glass of water?" And eventually he dies of thirst.

– **Shelley Berman**

I don't know which came first, the chicken or the egg? Were the people satanic and the media just reported on that?

– **Lily Tomlin**

He that doth get a wench with child and marries her afterwards it is as if a man should shit in his hat and then clap it on his head.

– **Samuel Pepys**

By the age of 6, the average child will have completed the basic American education. From television, the child will have learned how to pick a lock, commit a fairly elaborate hold-up, prevent wetness all day long, get the laundry twice as white, and kill people with a variety of sophisticated armaments.

– **Anon**

The most extraordinary thing about having a child is that people think I'm a responsible human being.

– **Colin Farrell**

Daddy's favourite tools are numbered among a child's favourite toys. Every kid wants to get her hands on Dad's retracting tape measure and his hammer.

– **St Clair Adams Sullivan**

My dad claimed he had a tough childhood. He told me he had to walk 20 miles to school in 5 feet of snow, and he was only 4 feet tall.

– **Dana Eagle**

My own wife had a lot of children – eight if I remember rightly.

– **Frank Pakenham**

Finish your vegetables! There are thousands of children in Hollywood with eating disorders.

– **John Callaghan**

Liszt's so-called piano music is nothing but Chopin and brandy.

– **James Huneker**

I married your mother because I wanted children. Imagine my disappointment when you came along.

– **Groucho Marx**

Christmas is about a child, and for children: like parenthood, if you don't throw yourself into it body and soul you will have a wretched time.

– **Amanda Craig**

You have to go back to the Children's Crusade in AD 1212 to find as unfortunate and fatuous attempt at manipulated hysteria as the Women's Liberation Movement.

– **Helen Lawrenson**

Yes, I did take money from the children's piggy banks, but I always left an IOU.

– **W.C. Fields**

I refuse to think of them as chin hairs. I think of them as stray eyebrows.

– **Janette Barber**

My dad used to say, 'Keep your chin up, son.' He once broke his jaw walking into a lamppost.

– **Adam Sandler**

It's a marriage. If I had to choose between my wife and my putter, I'd miss her.

– **Gary Player**

Pardon my long preamble. It's like a chorus girl's tights – it touches everything and covers nothing.

– **Gertrude Lawrence**

The Queen has sent about 37,500 Christmas cards during her reign.

– **Eighty Things About Queen Elizabeth II, 2006**

The better sort of cannibals have been Christian for many years and will not eat human flesh uncooked during Lent, without special and costly dispensation from their bishop.

– **Evelyn Waugh**

Happy Christmases are all alike; every unhappy Christmas is unhappy in its own way.

– **Ann Patchett**

My first attempt at cooking was a Christmas cake, made in Domestic Science and carried home proudly. I'd iced it with smooth white icing and painted a picture of the three kings on top of it. But I'd omitted to put any glycerine in the icing and it set like concrete. Parental pride turned first to amusement and then to fury as my father, unable to cut the thing, called for a hammer and hammered his thumb and then proceeded to split my mother's favourite bone-handled knife by using it as a chisel.

– **Pru Leith**

Christmas is sights, especially the sights of Christmas reflected in the eyes of a child.

– **William Saroyan**

Every idiot who goes about with Merry Christmas on his lips should be boiled with his own pudding, and buried with a stake of holly through his heart.

– **Charles Dickens, A Christmas Carol**

Hey kids! I made your favourite cookies: Christmas trees for the girls and bloody spearheads for Bart.

– **Marge Simpson, The Simpsons**

As you get older, you may think Christmas has changed. It hasn't. It's you who has changed.

– **Harry Truman**

Schubert sweated beauty as naturally as a Christian sweats hate.

– **H.L. Mencken**

The Toronto Sun's summary of Perry Como's Christmas Special read as follows: 'The members of a Greek family are murdered systematically in a bizarre fashion.'

– **William Marsano**

Never worry about the size of your Christmas tree. In the eyes of children, they are all thirty feet tall.

– **Larry Wilde**

In our family we sometimes play the Christmas card game. All Christmas cards received are dealt out to players, who then take it in turns to nominate a category, such as the ugliest Christmas card, the one with the most cherubs, the snowiest, or whatever. Each player then offers his best for the category and all argue about who should win.

– **Charles Moore**

I bought my brother some gift-wrap for Christmas. I took it to the Gift Wrap department and told them to wrap it, but in a different print so he knows when to stop unwrapping.

– **Steven Wright**

Yes, Bob, we do know it's bloody Christmas. There won't be snow in Africa this Christmas? Kilimanjaro. Snowy peaks all year round.

– **Jimmy Carr**

The gifts aren't the important thing about Christmas. The important thing is having your family around resenting you.

– **Reno Goodale**

It had all the hallmarks of a CIA operation; the bomb killed everybody in the room except the intended target.

– **William F. Buckley**

When people run around and around in circles, we say they're crazy. When the planets do it we say they are orbiting.

– **Dave Barry**

The United States will never be a civilized country until we spend more money on books than we do on chewing gum.

– Elbert Hubbard

I contemplated buying a new cream that claimed to stop the 7 signs of ageing and wondered what they might be. Incontinence? Talking about the weather? Wearing slippers? Memory loss? Compulsive need to queue up at the post office? Memory loss? Inability to comprehend the lyrics of pop songs?

– Maria McErlane

There is no distinctly native American criminal class except Congress.

– Mark Twain

When I was a Sunday presenter on Classic FM I was not allowed to say goodbye to the listeners at the end of the programme in case they thought the station was closing down.

– Tom Conti

I see my body just as a classy chassis to carry my mind around in.

– Sylvester Stallone

What example of family bonding does Santa Claus set, deserting his wife and kids on Christmas Eve for an all-night house-crawl?

– Francis Wheen

If Senator Donovan can get a resurrection clause into his death penalty bill, I will be willing to give it a second look.

– Hugh Carey

Winter could drop down out of a clear sky, sharp as an icicle, and, without a sound, pierce your heart.

– Jessamyn West

Beware of all enterprises that require new clothes.

– Henry Thoreau

Football hooligans? Well, there are the 92 club chairmen for a start.
  – **Brian Clough**

The best pitch I ever heard about cocaine was back in the early eighties when a street dealer followed me down the sidewalk going 'I got some great blow, man. I got the stuff that killed Belushi'.
  – **Denis Leary**

The only way to get rid of cockroaches is to tell them you want a long-term relationship.
  – **Jasmine Birtles**

My young daughter disposed of my £2 coins in the dustbin because they had no chocolate inside.
  – **Chris Jeffrey**

There are three intolerable things in life: cold coffee, lukewarm champagne and overexcited women.
  – **Orson Wells**

Ocean racing is like standing under a cold shower tearing up £5 notes.
  – **Edward Heath**

The word 'Toxteth' it appears is a combination of 'toxic' and 'death'.
  – **Paul Hoggart**

For men, childbirth is that cruellest of combinations: stressful and boring.
  – **Marcus Berkmann, Fatherhood: The Truth**

The day the Catholic and Protestant churches combine, it's the end of all drinking. I'll have to go to Rome to sabotage the affair.
  – **Brendan Behan**

If ants are such busy workers, how come they find the time to go to all the picnics?
  – **Marie Dressler**

When my 4-year-old daughter asked where babies come from, I thought she was too young for a frank explanation, so I gave her the whole bit about 'Daddy planted a seed in Mummy's tummy.' Then one day just as I was trying to reverse the car into a tight parking space with a queue of traffic behind me she asked, 'Daddy, did you plant the seed with your hand or did you use a trowel?'

– **Nick Cavender**

Whenever I go to Homebase, I always come back with something I didn't need. Because it was a bargain. But I do like a bit of DIY. I put some shelves up. Did it properly. Nice and straight. Then some idiot goes and puts something on them.

– **Jack Dee**

With every passing hour our solar system comes forty-three thousand miles closer to a globular cluster, M13 in the constellation Hercules, and still there are some misfits who continue to insist that there is no such thing as progress.

– **Ransom Ferm**

A rare book is a book that comes back to you when lent to a friend.

– **Alan King**

If I knew that a man was coming to my house with the conscious design of doing me good, I should run for my life.

– **Henry Thoreau**

I'm back... and you knew I was coming. On my way here I passed a cinema with the sign 'The Mummy Returns'.

– **Margaret Thatcher**

The teenager seems to have replaced the Communist as the appropriate target for public controversy and foreboding.

– **Edgar Friedenberg**

Spanish wine is foul. Catpiss is champagne compared to this sulphurous urination of some aged horse.

– **D.H. Lawrence**

The only constant factor of American eating competitions is the basic rule of competition: 'Heave and you leave.'
  – **Frank McNally**

Even the most respectable woman has a complete set of clothes in her wardrobe ready for a possible abduction.
  – **Sacha Guitry**

Christmas in Britain these days is almost completely ruined by the office party. The streets become full of ordinary people who have suddenly lost the ability to walk in a straight line. And the atmosphere in every restaurant is firebombed by the table of 60 who order food not for its taste but its aerodynamic efficiency.
  – **Jeremy Clarkson**

My kids learn how to operate a computer but never learn how to use a clothes hanger.
  – **Andy Tate**

Experts agree that the best type of computer for your individual needs is one that comes on the market about 2 days after you actually purchase some other computer.
  – **Dave Barry**

Intelligence was a deformity which must be concealed; a public school taught one to conceal it as a good tailor hides a paunch or a hump.
  – **Cyril Connolly**

I'm lucky that people have a negative conception of me: I can only look nice after that.
  – **Sarah Ferguson, former Duchess of York**

Marilyn Monroe is good at playing abstract confusion in the same way that a midget is good at being short.
  – **Clive James**

The chopper has changed my life as conclusively as it did for Anne Boleyn.

– **Elizabeth Bowes-Lyon**

Ice hockey is a form of disorderly conduct in which a score is kept.

– **Doug Larson**

Edith Sitwell's interest in art was largely confined to portraits of herself.

– **John Fowles**

I'm going to take a moment to contemplate most of the Western religions. I'm looking for something soft on morality, generous with holidays, and with a very short initiation period.

– **David Addison**

It's tough to feel a sense of control when you've got to stop six times during the half-hour ride to Grandma's.

– **Hugh O'Neill**

The Victorians had too much sense to converse with children as though they were human beings.

– **Clarence Day**

My parents' marriage left me with two convictions: that human beings should not live together and that children should be taken from their parents at an early age.

– **Philip Larkin**

If a woman likes another woman, she's cordial. If she doesn't like her, she's very cordial.

– **Irvin S. Cobb**

A restaurant I used to frequent in Cork advertised: 'Eat here and you'll never eat anywhere else again.'

– **Niall Toibin**

The Hotel Carvery: as much gristle and cornflour as you can stuff down for a tenner.

– A.A. Gill

We're not sure about kids yet. They cost a lot of money, don't they? Maybe we can get one who's about 22 and a solicitor so he can bring a good wage in.

– Ricky Gervais

If Mr Vincent Price were to be co-starred with Miss Bette Davis in a story by Mr Edgar Allan Poe directed by Mr Roger Corman, it would not fully express the pent-up violence and depravity of a single day in the life of the average family.

– Quentin Crisp

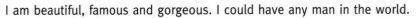

I am beautiful, famous and gorgeous. I could have any man in the world.

– Anna Kournikova

Growing up, my father told me I could be whoever I wanted. What a cruel hoax! I'm still his son.

– Ken Smith

New Year was the only thing we could afford that was really new.

– George Burns

Mathematics was always my bad subject. I couldn't convince my teachers that many of my answers were meant ironically.

– Calvin Trillin

I'm glad I'm not bisexual – I couldn't stand being rejected by men as well as women.

– Bernard Manning

Education is a wonderful thing. If you couldn't sign your name you'd have to pay cash.

– Rita Mae Brown

It's official – retired builder and local councillor Danny Meikle, 56, puts on Britain's biggest home-made festive lights extravaganza with his annual shrine to Yuletide. It has taken him six weeks to decorate his home in Coalburn, Lanarkshire, with one million Christmas lights, musical trees and Santa's grotto – resulting in a display so bright it's used by pilots as a turning point...

– Daily Express, 2003

Fifteen years ago, Britain was a great country in which to have a heart attack in the street.

– John Le Carré

One out of four people in this country is mentally unbalanced. Think of your three closest friends – and if they seem OK then you're the one!

– Ann Landers

There are very few shops in the country, but the ever resourceful farm folk have come up with a number of ingenious if disgusting ploys to circumvent this inconvenience. They won't just go out and buy a carton of milk like proper people, so what do they do? They squeeze it out of a cow! God only knows who first came up with that one, but it seems to work. Apparently cows are full of the stuff.

– Russell Bell

I was under the care of a couple of medical students who couldn't diagnose a decapitation.

– Jeffrey Bernard

Critics – unless the bastards have the courage to give you unqualified praise, I say ignore them.

– John Steinbeck

I think the whole world should be covered with snow; it would be so much cleaner.

– Norma Shearer, Idiot's Delight

The only good thing I know of Cranmer is that he burned well.

– Richard Froude

After my father was cast as the Cowardly Lion in The Wizard of Oz he was typecast as a lion.

– **Bert Lahr**

The most loathsome of all this year's crass Yuletide innovations is surely the 'ethical Christmas gift'. Instead of the DVD or handsome pair of socks you'd been hoping to receive, an ecologically crazed friend posts you a charity card informing you that 'the money I would have spent on your present has been used to buy six chickens for an African farmer' or 'a camel for a Bedouin tribesperson', and you're supposed to look pleased that he's given you precisely nothing, while he basks in a nauseating glow of self-satisfied eleemosynary.

– **Victor Lewis-Smith**

All this Christmas madness is driving me crazy. I hate the sound of sleigh bells (where in Britain can you see a sleigh in action?) and the fact that thousands of spruce trees are sacrificed to the cause. I abhor the enforced cheerfulness of strangers, and the lunatic jollity of 'Jingle Bells' blaring out of a thousand loudspeakers. I hate Nigella telling me that Christmas in the kitchen doesn't have to be a horror show...

– **Debra Craine**

Drugs have nothing to do with the creation of music. In fact, drugs are dumb and self-indulgent. Kind of like sucking your thumb.

– **Courtney Love**

I have a face that is a cross between two pounds of halibut and an explosion in an old clothes closet.

– **David Niven**

A good old age can be the crown of our life's experience, the masterwork of a lifetime.

– **Helen Nearing**

My television contribution went down like a cup of warm Dettol with a hair in it.

– **Hugh Leonard**

The only difference between me and General Custer is that I have to watch the films on Sunday.

– **Rick Venturi**

My grades were four F's and a D. My tutor suggested I was spending too much time on one subject.

– **Shelby Metcalf**

My mother was like a drill sergeant. Dad was the commanding general.

– **George W. Bush**

What's for dinner when Mom's away and Dad's 'cooking'? Well, there's pizza; chips and salsa; Cocoa Puff surprise; cold pizza; 'Kids Eat Free' night at the local steak house; back-of-the-fridge goulash (with lots of pepper); but best of all... whatever's cooking at Grandma's.

– **David Letterman**

If the children's name for me is Dad-Can-I, then my name for them is Yes-You-May.

– **Bill Cosby**

Most kids at school had accountants for dads. Mine was the archetypal rock 'n' roller, in the band Status Quo. I kept away from music for a long time but now my dad's my biggest fan. He said, 'I'm pleased you're not crap.'

– **Rick Parfitt Jr**

The roses and raptures of vice are damned uncomfortable as you will soon find out. You have to get into such ridiculous positions.

– **John Mortimer**

The secret of my long life? Swim, dance a little, go to Paris every August, and live within walking distance of two hospitals.

– **Dr Horatio Luro**

When Stalin says "dance", a wise man dances.

– **Nikita Khrushchev**

There were days last winter when I danced for sheer joy out in my frost-bound garden in spite of my years and children. But I did it behind a bush, having a due regard for the decencies.

   – Elizabeth von Arnim

'Middle of the road' music can be dangerous. While listening to one of those albums, I almost got hit by a truck.

   – Yakov Smirnoff

Ted Kennedy. Good senator, but a bad date. You know what I'm saying folks?

   – Denis Leary

The cell phone was invented purely for daughters to call their fathers at any time and you will go get her.

   – Brad Houston

There would have been serious trouble between David and Jonathan if either had persisted in dropping catches off the other's bowling.

   – P.G. Wodehouse

Like everyone who talks of ethics all day long, one could not trust Koestler half an hour with one's wife, one's best friend, one's manuscript or one's wine merchant.

   – Cyril Connolly

Father's Day is the same as Mother's Day but you don't spend as much.

   – Bill Cosby

I smoke ten to fifteen cigars a day – at my age I have to hold on to something.

   – George Burns

I smoke eight to ten cigars a day – I drink five martinis a day and surround myself with beautiful women. And what does my doctor say? Nothing. My doctor is dead.

   – George Burns

My grandmother started walking five miles a day when she was sixty. She's ninety-three today and we don't know where the hell she is.
 – Ellen DeGeneres

'Oh no,' said God on the fourth day, 'I've gone and made a spider which can kill a man just by looking at them. I need somewhere to put it.' So on the fifth day he created Australia.
 – Jeremy Clarkson

The trouble with being a hypochondriac these days is that antibiotics have cured all the good diseases.
 – Caskie Stinnet

I know I'm getting older because these days, before I leave in the morning, I have to ask myself, 'Did I remember to pluck my ears?'
 – Christopher Moore

When people run up to me these days, it's not to ask for my autograph, but to get a closer look at my wrinkles.
 – Elizabeth Taylor

I don't drink or take drugs these days. I am allergic to alcohol and narcotics. I break out in handcuffs.
 – Robert Downey Jr.

At 87, 'someday' and 'one of these days' are losing their grip on my vocabulary; if it's worth seeing or hearing or doing, I want to see and hear and do it now.
 – Anon

Great storytellers, even ones who have been dead for a hundred years, show up extant television writers as semi literate, unimaginative comatose cliché-mongers.
 – A.A. Gill

I don't think you ever manage to deal with politics. You just cope with it.
 – Zola Budd

Death in life; death without its privileges, death without its benefits. Who would want that? If you find you can't make 70 by any but an uncomfortable road, don't you go. When they take off the Pullman and retire you to the rancid smoker, put on your things, count your cheques, and get out at the first way station where there's a cemetery.

   – **Mark Twain**

There are worse things in life than death. Have you ever spent an evening with an insurance salesman?

   – **Woody Allen**

I work for a company that makes deceptively shallow dishes for Chinese restaurants.

   – **Woody Allen**

An election is coming. Universal peace is declared, and the foxes have a sincere interest in prolonging the lives of the poultry.

   – **George Eliot**

Always keep tubes of haemorrhoid ointment and Deep Heat rub well separated in your bathroom cabinet.

   – **P. Turner, Top Tip, Viz**

My Uncle Joe was a philosopher, very deep, very serious. Never eat chocolate after chicken he'd tell us, wagging his finger.

   – **Mel Brooks**

One can love a child, perhaps more deeply than one can love another adult, but it is rash to assume that the child feels any love in return.

   – **George Orwell**

When one is 18, one has very definite dislikes, but as one grows older, one becomes more tolerant, and finds that nearly everyone is, in some degree, nice.

   – **The Queen Mother**

Skiing? Why break my leg at 40 degrees below zero when I can fall downstairs at home?

– Corey Ford

A king, realizing his incompetence, can either delegate or abdicate his duties. A father can do neither. If only sons could see the paradox, they would understand the dilemma.

– Marlene Dietrich

Watching children grow up is a great delight. You see in them your own faults and your wife's virtues, and that can be a very stabilizing influence.

– Peter Ustinov

Meryl Streep will do whatever a part demands even if it demands speaking in a foreign accent whose origins only Streep and her dialogue coach know.

– Joe Joseph

Oswald Mosley was a cross between a demented Terry Thomas and Bill Clinton.

– David Aaronovitch

The Russian police have a Missing Persons Department; that's where they decide which persons are going to be missing.

– Yakov Smirnoff

Old age is like waiting in the departure lounge of life. Fortunately, we are in England and the train is bound to be late.

– Milton Shulman

Christmas, that time of year when people descend into the bunker of the family.

– Byron Rogers

Like most men, I am consumed with desire whenever a lesbian gets within 20 feet.

– Taki

'Vacation' is the word Americans use to describe going someplace different to have fun and get away from all their trials and tribulations. The English call it 'holiday'. In Russia it's known as 'defecting'.

– **Yakov Smirnoff**

Jill Tweedie once wrote me a letter describing her Christmas: 'All we did was shop, cook, wash up; shop, cook, wash up...' Every household member believes that he or she is the only person who ever renews the loo-paper or the bin-liner, deals with coffee-grounds in the cafetiere, or empties the dishwasher (all too eagerly filled).

– **Valerie Grove**

In 1932 President Herbert Hoover was so desperate to remain in the White House that he dressed up as Eleanor Roosevelt. When FDR discovered the hoax in 1936, the two men decided to stay together for the sake of the children.

– **Johnny Carson**

Two-thirds of the world's rainforest has been destroyed during the past ten years of my environmental campaigning. That shows how effective I've been.

– **Sting**

The genitals themselves have not undergone the development of the rest of the human form in the direction of beauty.

– **Sigmund Freud**

My wife is in league with the Devil. I don't know how much he pays her.

– **Emo Philips**

Taking care of a newborn baby means devoting yourself, body and soul, 24 hours a day, seven days a week, to the welfare of someone whose major response, in the way of positive reinforcement, is to throw up on you.

– **Dave Barry**

Charlemagne either died or was born or did something with the Holy Roman Empire in 800.

– **Robert Benchley**

So let me leave you with this Dickensian remedy for the morning after the night before. It's the inspiration of the great writer's great-grandson Cedric Dickens – the living embodiment of Pickwick himself. Make a well in the centre of a steaming hot bowl of porridge. Fill it with Drambuie, then pour single cream round the bowl. Sprinkle brown sugar all over the top. It's guaranteed to set you up for the new year.

– Godfrey Smith

They were a people so primitive they did not know how to get money except by working for it.

– Joseph Addison

It's funny that those things your kids did that got on your nerves seem so cute when your grandchildren do them.

– Raymond Holland

A 'Bay Area Bisexual' told me I didn't quite coincide with either of her desires.

– Woody Allen

Troubadours travelled from town to town. They didn't really sing too good, which is the main reason they kept going.

– Art Linkletter

Even now, 21 years after my father died, not a week goes by that I don't find myself thinking I should call him.

– Herb Gardner

We must make our boys understand the difference between making a baby and being a father.

– William Raspberry

Eighty's a landmark and people treat you differently than they do when you're 79. At 79, if you drop something it just lies there. At 80, people pick it up for you.

Helen Van Slyke

Love is a painful but not a dignified malady, I think, like piles.

– Cyril Connolly

There are people who are beautiful in dilapidation, like houses that were hideous when new.

– Logan Pearsall Smith

A picture is a representation in two dimensions of something wearisome in three.

– Ambrose Bierce

The first time my wife cooked me dinner I almost choked to death on a bone in her chocolate pudding.

– Woody Allen

Last week I bought a frozen Mexican dinner, but now I wish I had brought him into the house and let him warm up a little.

– George Carlin

In case of a nuclear attack, go directly to RKO. They haven't had a hit in years.

– David Niven

The length of a film should be directly related to the endurance of the human bladder.

– Alfred Hitchcock

My four-year-old daughter Amy and I were discussing the Nativity. She told me baby Jesus had to sleep in a manger in a stable. I asked why baby Jesus had to resort to a stable and she immediately replied: 'Oh, that's easy. There was no room left at the Holiday Inn.'

– Keith Young

I realize I'm succumbing to the occupational disease, the father-jitters or new-parenthood-shakes, expressed in: 'Hark, the child's screaming, she must be dying.' Or, 'She's so quiet, d'you think she's dead?'

– Laurie Lee

Every small boy wonders why his father didn't go into the ice cream business.

– Anon

... Christmas dinner – the single most disgusting meal ever invented, with the exception of American Thanksgiving... Nobody sane or loving could invent Christmas food from scratch.

– A A. Gill

It's not hard to create an ugly display. All you have to do is get carried away. I look like Christmas regurgitated all over my balcony. There are very few displays that look that good. And if they look that good, it's kinda boring. When I see Christmas lights, I want to laugh.

– Llori Stein

How to eat spinach like a child. Divide into piles. Rearrange again into piles. After five or six manoeuvres, sit back and say you are full.

– Delia Ephron

Conrad Hilton gave me a very generous divorce settlement – I wound up with 5000 Gideon Bibles.

– Zsa Zsa Gabor

Divorce comes from the old Latin word divorcerum meaning 'having your genitals torn out through your wallet'. And the judge said, "All the money and we'll shorten it to alimony."

– Robin Williams

The first thing a writer has to do is find another source of income.

– Ellen Gilchrist

People wish their enemies dead, but I do not; I say give them the gout, give them the stone!

– Mary Montagu

A married man with a family will do anything for money.

– Talleyrand

I wonder if George Gershwin had to do it all over again, would he fall in love with himself again?

    – Oscar Levant

To get back my youth, I would do anything in the world, except take exercise, get up early, or be respectable.

    – Oscar Wilde

I became a newspaperman. I hated to do it, but I couldn't find honest employment.

    – Mark Twain

The most important thing for poets to do is to write as little as possible.

    – T.S. Eliot

In my house I'm the boss. My wife is just the decision maker.

    – Woody Allen

I cannot stand whispering. Every time a doctor whispers in the hospital, next day there's a funeral.

    – Neil Simon

My father wanted me to become a doctor, but I wanted to do something more creative, so we compromised and I became a hypochondriac.

    – Wally Wang

It is difficult to produce a television documentary that is both incisive and probing when every twelve minutes one is interrupted by twelve dancing rabbits singing about toilet paper.

    – R. Serlking

It is customarily said that Christmas is done 'for the kids'. Considering how awful Christmas is and how little our society likes children, this must be true.

    – P.J. O'Rourke

A man who for an entire week does nothing but hit himself over the head has little reason to be proud.

– **Stanislaw Lem**

My grandmother is over 80 and still doesn't need glasses. Drinks right out of the bottle.

– **Henny Youngman**

I'm on a diet as my skin doesn't fit me any more.

– **Erma Bombeck**

If there is a group of men doing anything with a ball in a field, another group of men will watch.

– **Jasmine Birtles**

They say everyone remembers what he was doing when Kennedy was shot. I'd love to ask Lee Harvey Oswald what he was doing.

– **Paul Merton**

I don't like country music, but I don't mean to denigrate those who do. And for people who like country music, 'denigrate' means 'put down'.

– **Bob Newhart**

He dribbles a lot and the opposition don't like it – you can see it all over their faces.

– **Ron Atkinson**

I don't feel old. In fact I don't feel anything until noon. Then it's time for my nap.

– **Bob Hope**

At the Winter Olympics, why on earth don't they do those sliding things all together instead of one at a time? Then it would be a proper race and take a couple of minutes instead of a few days and it would be exciting.

– **A.A. Gill**

Married men inevitably say that their wives don't understand them, they haven't been sleeping together for ten years, they're not going to leave their wives until their children grow up and they've never felt this way about another woman. Women, who would otherwise laugh out loud at their friends were they to volunteer this same information, believe them.

– Paula Yates, TV presenter

Be kind to your parents, though they don't deserve it; remember that 'grown-up' is a difficult stage of life.

– Harold Rome

Men name their children after themselves; women don't. Have you ever met a Sally Junior?

– Rita Rudner

Merle Oberon had so much plastic surgery done that she had to sleep with her eyes open.

– James Agate

I had a job selling hearing aids door to door. It wasn't easy, because your best prospects never answered.

– Bob Monkhouse

A guy is a lump like a doughnut. So first you gotta get rid of all the stuff his mum did to him, and then you gotta get rid of all that macho crap that they pick up from the beer commercials. And then there's my personal favourite, the male ego.

– Roseanne Barr

In Junior High a boy poured water down my shirt and yelled: 'Now maybe they'll grow.'

– Pamela Anderson

Never argue with idiots. They drag you down to their level, then beat you with experience.

– Jess Brallier

Do you think policemen walk up and down the street thinking how old the public are getting these days?

– D. Tucker

My father always said, 'Never write anything down that you wouldn't want published on the front page of the New York Times.'

– Ted Kennedy

'What in the world are you doing down there?' Mom would shout down to the basement. 'Just tinkering,' would come Dad's response. He'd be happily rearranging empty paint cans, sorting rusty bent nails from not-so-rusty bent nails – and contemplating exactly where to put up a set of shelves.

– Allen Delaney

I exercise every morning without fail. Up, down! Up, down! And then the other eyelid.

– Phyllis Diller

A policeman told me he'd caught a dozen courting couples in the stand at Hartlepool and asked me what to do about it. I told them to fix the bloody fence and board them in. Best gate of the season it would have been.

– Fred Westgarth

When I watched Spencer Tracy playing in Dr Jekyll and Mr Hyde I had great difficulty deciding which of them he was portraying at any given moment.

– Somerset Maugham

A trombone is a quaint and antique drainage system applied to the face.

– Thomas Beecham

The consistent thing about all American courtroom drama is that invariably the only vaguely human being on the credits is the psycho multiple murderer.

– A.A. Gill

Musical comedy is the Irish stew of drama. Anything may be put into it with the certainty that it will improve the general effect.

– P.G. Wodehouse

It takes courage for an adult to draw as badly as I do.

– Mel Calman

My young son, Jack, asked me the dreaded question, 'Where do I come from, Daddy?' I decided not to fob him off, and gave him the full, frank explanation about sexual intercourse, orgasms and birth. 'Oh,' he said, 'I was just wondering, because the boy who sits in front of me comes from Jamaica.'

– Paul LeBec

My father never lived to see his dream come true of an all Yiddish-speaking Canada.

– David Steinberg

At the breakfast table Kingsley would look dreamy and say, 'If they shut all the hospitals in London, we could have two Trident submarines.'

– Martin Amis

If you resolve to give up smoking, drinking and loving, you don't actually live longer – it just seems longer.

– Clement Freud

You'd think with all that money, Minnie Driver could afford a bigger car.

– Bill Bailey

As St Patrick said when he was driving the snakes out of Ireland, 'Are ye alright there in the back lads?'

– Patrick Murray

One of the reasons children are such duds socially is that they say things like 'When do you think you're going to be dead, Grandma?'

– Jean Kerr

My father was a fastidious man. He dusted the chair on which the cat had been lying before occupying it himself. He ate a banana with a knife and fork.

– **Quentin Crisp**

Nicotine patches are great. Stick one over each eye and you can't find your cigarettes.

– **Bill Hicks**

Human beings are the only creatures on earth that allow their children to come back home.

– **Bill Cosby**

Contrary to what many women believe, it's easy to develop a long-term, intimate and mutually fulfilling relationship with a male. Of course, the male has to be a Labrador retriever.

– **Dave Barry**

At Christmas time, my role is to eat the food, get drunk, and fall asleep in front of the telly wearing my novelty tie and cufflinks that double as spirit levels.

– **Tony Hawks**

As I get older, I'm trying to eat healthy. I've got Gordon Ramsay's new cook book, Take Two Eggs and Fuck Off.

– **Jack Dee**

The food was so tasteless you could eat a meal of it and belch and it wouldn't remind you of anything.

– **Red Foxx**

Give a man a fish and he eats for the day. Teach him how to fish and you get rid of him for the whole weekend.

– **Zenna Schaffer**

I'm a great lover, I'll bet.

– **Emo Philips**

Did you know that Christmas trees are edible? I don't recommend it, nor do I have a suitable recipe but, apparently, the needles are a good source of vitamin C.

   – Sandi Toksvig

In spite of their real opinions of editors as parasites and literary phonies, authors should be extra polite to them at all times, remembering that in that direction lie some of the most tasty lunches available in New York.

   – Paul Fussell

I don't worry a lot about sex education in the schools. If the kids learn it like they do everything else, they won't know how.

   – Milton Berle

I've spent a fortune on my kids' education, and a fortune on their teeth. The difference is, they use their teeth.

   – Robert Orben

The appropriate age for marriage is about eighteen for girls and thirty-seven for men.

   – Aristotle

In the days of King Henry the Eighth, the authorities knew that if they made any mistakes during the funeral of the King's wife they would always have the consolation of trying again next year.

   – John Smith

My girlfriend told me I was immature emotionally, sexually and intellectually. I said, 'Yes, but in what other ways?'

   – Woody Alien

An asylum for the sane would be empty in America.

   – George Bernard Shaw

The useless piece of flesh at the end of a penis is called a man.

   – Jo Brand

Making Sense of School Prospectuses: Parental involvement encouraged = Roped in for fund-raising activities; Staff work as a team = Headmaster usually having a nervous breakdown; Extensive playing fields = Property developers please note; Modern teaching methods = Classroom riots.

   – John Koski and Mitchell Symons

You can be sure that at the end of most operas, there will be work for the undertaker.

   – St John Peskett

I don't want to get to the end of my life and find that I have just lived the length of it. I want to have lived the width of it as well.

   – Diane Ackerman

... much like sex, the Christmas event ends with a sad flatulent realization that these things are better imagined than enacted, better anticipated than performed.

   – Stephen Fry

The greatest happiness is to scatter your enemy, to drive him before you, to see his cities reduced to ashes, to see those who love him shrouded in tears, and to gather into your bosom his wives and daughters.

   – Genghis Khan

Visiting the Millennium Dome felt like an enforced six-hour stopover at a second-rate German airport.

   – Martin Amis

Ah, what an excellent Thing is an English Pudding! 'To come in Pudding time' is as much as to say, to come in the most lucky Moment in the World.

   – H. Misson, 1719

His sperm count was lower than an English cricket score.

   – A.A. Gill

At high school, I took a little English, a little math, some science, some hubcaps and some wheel covers.

– **Gates Brown**

Even if you learn to speak correct English, to whom are you going to speak it?

– **Clarence Darrow**

Players and spectators at all levels can enjoy sport better if they totally accept two simple rules. Rule One: The referee is always right. Rule Two: In the event of the referee being obviously wrong, Rule One applies.

– **Peter Corrigan**

My dear Oscar, you are not clever enough for us in Dublin. You had better run over to Oxford.

– **John Mahaffy**

... this bizarre, archetypally British form of entertainment, in which middle-aged men with hairy legs dress up as women and attractive young women in fishnet stockings impersonate lively young men. No wonder we Brits are in such a constant muddle about sex.

– **Charles Spencer**

There is only one fruitcake in the entire world and people keep sending it to each other.

– **Johnny Carson**

It isn't pollution that is harming the environment. It's the impurities in our air and water that are doing it.

– **Dan Quayle**

I had the upbringing a nun would envy. Until I was fifteen I was more familiar with Africa than my own body.

– **Joe Orton**

My therapist and I have really bonded. Even he hates my father now.

– **Terence Davies**

Next time I'm not just having an epidural for the birth, I'm having one for the conception as well.
– Sally James

When I told my daughter that Edith Evans had died, she said, 'I don't believe it. She's not the type.'
– Bryan Forbes

Dates used to be made days or even weeks in advance. Now dates tend to be made the day after. You get a phone call from someone who says, 'If anyone asks, I was out to dinner with you last night, okay?'
– P.J. O'Rourke

He's going to have to lose twenty even to get Santa Claus work come Yuletide.
– Peter De Vries

We are none of us infallible: not even the youngest of us.
– W.H. Thompson

We are in such a slump that even the ones that aren't drinkin' aren't hittin'.
– Casey Stengel

The decathlon consists of nine Mickey Mouse events and a 1500 metres.
– Steve Ovett

I've been making a comeback but nobody ever tells me where I've been.
– Billie Holiday

There are two absolute dining rules: never ever have anything to do with a man in a straw boater and never ever put anything in your mouth that has the prefix 'hearty' (this applies to women and food).
– A.A. Gill

My parents have been there for me ever since I was about seven.

   – David Beckham

All music is folk music. I ain't ever heard no horse sing.

   – Louis Armstrong

Nobody, not even in the provinces, should ever be allowed to ask an intelligent question about pure mathematics across a dinner table.

   – Oscar Wilde

The best description of Margaret Thatcher I ever heard is that she's just the sort of woman who wouldn't give you your ball back.

   – Mike Harding

I think one of the highest compliments ever paid to Australia was the imminent Japanese invasion. To think the Japanese would actually think of coming to Australia to live! They did change their mind, with a little persuasion.

   – Barry Humphries

The vol-au-vent is the single nastiest thing ever invented as a food that doesn't involve an initiation ceremony. This one was like eating a ripe camel's conjunctive eye socket.

   – A.A. Gill

How foolish to think that one can ever slam the door in the face of age. Much wiser to be polite and gracious and ask him to lunch in advance.

   – Noël Coward

The fellows in the executive boxes at Everton are the lucky ones. They can draw the curtains.

   – Stan Boardman

I don't spank my kids. I find waving the gun around gets the same job done.

   – Denis Leary

In our house, it's almost magical when, every Christmas Eve, my wife Plum pulls out a beautifully wrapped present and asks me to write on the label 'To Plum with love from Ray', not forgetting to add those three fond kisses. Presents are supposed to be a surprise, and I'm always as surprised to see what I've bought her as much as what she's bought me.

– **Ray Connolly**

All well-regulated families set apart an hour every morning for tea and bread and butter.

– **Joseph Addison**

As a child, I thought I hated everybody, but when I grew up I realized it was just children I didn't like.

– **Philip Larkin**

Abolish the retirement age. After all, if everyone had to stop working when they reached 65, Winston Churchill would not have been our wartime leader. He was 66 when he became Prime Minister. We spend our lives on the run. We get up by the clock, eat and sleep by the clock, get up again, go to work, and then we retire. And what do they give us? A bloody clock.

– **Dave Allen**

A politician is an arse upon which everyone has sat except a man.

– **e.e. cummings**

Any astronomer can predict with absolute accuracy exactly where every star in the universe will be at 11.30 tonight. He can make no such prediction about his teenage daughter.

– **James Adams**

Jesus never put up a tree and exchanged gifts, or left cookies out for Santa. He never made a harried last-minute trip to the mall, or spent Christmas Eve cursing at a toy that he couldn't put together. He celebrated Passover. So, if you want to be more like Jesus, pass the matzo.

– **Benny Hill**

Off-peak electricity is electricity which has been examined at the power station and found to be below standard. It is sold off cheaply in the evenings when people don't use so much.

– **Dave Barry**

The word 'good' has many meanings. For example, if a man were to shoot his grandmother at a range of 500 yards, I should call him a good shot, but not necessarily a good man.

– **G.K. Chesterton**

I don't know anything about Jayne Mansfield except the common gossip I heard. When it comes to men, I hear she never turns anything down except the bedcovers.

– **Mae West**

Managing Dunfermline Athletic is a great job, except for the Saturday afternoons.

– **Jocky Scott**

Zee always went naked in the house, except for the brassiere she wore when it was her turn to get dinner. Once cooking French-fried potatoes in a kettle of boiling fat, she had come within an inch of crisping her most striking features.

– **G.S. Albee**

There is nothing wrong with that car except for the fact that it is on fire.

– **Murray Walker**

The trouble with women today is their excitement over too many things outside the home. A woman's home and her children are her real happiness. If she would stay there, the world would have less to worry about the modern woman.

– **Al Capone**

The fact that boys are allowed to exist at all is evidence of a remarkable Christian forbearance among men.

– **Ambrose Bierce**

Bill Clinton is going to try to expand his lead on female voters, one at a time.

– **Alex Castellanos**

Good judgement comes from experience, and often experience comes from bad judgement.

– **Rita Mae Brown**

In spite of the 7,000 books of expert advice, the right way to discipline a child is still a mystery to most fathers. Only your grandmother and Genghis Khan know how to do it.

– **Bill Cosby**

What I like is the way that extended family Christmases take on all the traditions brought by each separate family and add them to the rest. So my wife's family like a nice cold glass of Bailey's while opening presents, while others we'll be with tomorrow will have their eye on something sparkling. Then there will be mince pies, a couple of those mini-Toblerone things, like chocolate shrapnel, and before lunch no doubt a spot of smoked salmon.

– **Alan Ayckbourn**

Lesbianism has always seemed to me an extremely inventive response to the shortage of men, but otherwise not worth the trouble.

– **Nora Ephron**

I'm very pleased to be here. Let's face it, at my age I'm pleased to be anywhere.

– **George Burns**

The charming aspect of Christmas is the fact that it expresses goodwill in a cheerful, happy, benevolent, non-sacrificial way. One says 'Merry Christmas' not 'Weep and Repent.' And the goodwill is expressed in a material, earthly form, by giving presents to one's friends or by sending them cards in token of remembrance...

– **Ayn Rand**

You're getting old if you discuss the facts of life with your children and you get slapped by your wife when you attempt to try out some of the things they told you.

— **Russell Bell**

The kilt, being a practical outdoor garment, failed him only once, and that occurred during a short-lived interest in beekeeping.

— **J.M. Bannerman**

We enjoyed Eddie 'The Eagle' Edwards' abject failures because he was, in essence, sending up Alpine sports, in a typically British way. As he plopped off the 90-metre jump with the acceleration of a week-old bread pudding, setting new records for the smallest leap, it was an eloquent raising of two fingers – or two legs in Eddie's case – to Alpine culture.

— **Stan Hey**

The Christmas tree was proof that Narnia, fairies and hobgoblins and fauns truly did exist. For the tree miraculously appeared overnight and it shed such light and a divine perfume. Being small, I could sit under it all evening with the glass baubles dancing in my face.

— **Toyah Willcox**

A golf ball can stop in the fairway, rough, woods, bunker or lake. With five equally likely options, very few balls choose the fairway.

— **Jim Bishop**

Ariana Stassinopoulos is so boring that you fall asleep halfway through her name.

— **Alan Bennett**

Before I met my husband, I'd never fallen in love, though I'd stepped in it a few times.

— **Rita Rudner**

If you can't get rid of the family skeleton, you may as well make it dance.

— **George Bernard Shaw**

My father wore the trousers in the family – at least, after the court order.

– Vernon Chapman

I would advise Zola, now that the family tree of the Rougon-Macquarts is complete, to go and hang himself from the highest branch.

– Alphonse Daudet

Secretariat and Rivia Ridge are the most famous pair of stablemates since Joseph and Mary.

– Dick Schaap

My sex life is now reduced to fan letters from an elderly lesbian who wants to borrow $800.

– Groucho Marx

I have more talent in my smallest fart than Barbra Streisand has in her entire body.

– Walter Matthau

Because of their cuisine, Germans don't consider farting rude. They'd certainly be out of luck if they did.

– P.J. O'Rourke

I read about writers' lives with the fascination of one slowing down to get a good look at an automobile accident.

– Kaye Gibbons

Drive carefully, kids. And don't forget to fasten your condoms – seatbelts, I mean seatbelts.

– George Banks, Father of the Bride

I continued to do arithmetic with my father, passing proudly through fractions to decimals. I eventually arrived at the point where so many cows ate so much grass, and tanks filled with water in so many hours. I found it quite enthralling.

– Agatha Christie

We are now approaching Washington airport. Please fasten your seat belts, adjust your watches and would Senator Kennedy return the hostess to the upright position.

– **Mort Sahl**

The mini-skirt enables young ladies to run faster and because of it, they may have to.

– **John V. Lindsay**

His neck was the width of a fat man's thigh. He looked like Lou Feringo's idiot cousin.

– **Zoë Heller**

When I was a little kid, a father was like the light in the refrigerator: every house had one, but no one really knew what either of them did once the door was shut.

– **Erma Bombeck**

Like most fathers at that time, my father wasn't there, but, in a way, that can be a blessing. Familiarity breeds contempt.

– **Jack Ford**

This is the hardest truth for a father to learn: that his children are continuously growing up and moving away from him (until, of course, they move back in).

– **Bill Cosby**

'I brought you into this world,' my father would say, 'and I can take you out. It don't make no difference to me. I'll make another one just like you.'

– **Bill Cosby**

After reading GP for twenty-five years, I feel qualified to hang out my shingle as a bogus doctor, and I could remove a fishhook from an exotic dancer's bosom in under two hours.

– **Bill Tidy**

If you have not had a good father, it is necessary to invent one.

– **Friedrich Nietzsche**

No one used revenge better than my father. I always imagined that scene in The Godfather, where some guy wakes up with a horse head next to him, was probably my dad's idea of a get-well greeting card.

– **Ruby Wax**

The turkey should be cooped up and fed well some time before Christmas. Three days before it is slaughtered it should have an English walnut forced down its throat three times a day, a glass of sherry once a day. The meat will be deliciously tender, and have a fine nutty flavour.

– **Benjamin Harrison**

I don't mind dying. Trouble is, you feel so bloody stiff the next day.

– **George Axelrod**

You know you're getting old when you feel like the day after the night before and you haven't even been anywhere.

– **Milton Berle**

Never try to make Americans or foreigners feel at home – had they wished to feel at home, they would have remained in their own country.

– **Rose Heaton**

Never wear grey. Wearing grey makes one feel grey. I was shown round Tutankhamun's tomb in the 1920s. I saw all this wonderful pink on the walls and the artefacts. I was so impressed that I vowed to wear it for the rest of my life.

– **Barbara Cartland**

You could have swung a scythe five feet six inches above the ground all around California in the 1930s and not done any damage to the head of a major motion picture company.

– **Philip French**

In the pole vault Cassidy did twenty feet but he was disqualified. He didn't come down.

– **Frank Carson**

During this terzetto, the Reverend Mr Portpipe fell asleep and accompanied the performance with rather a deeper bass than was generally deemed harmonious.

– **Thomas L. Peacock**

Playing is the only place where I've felt in touch with my sexuality, my spirituality and my emotions, and never ever, ever anywhere else. So my life is a bit tricky because when I'm not playing, I'm just trying to walk down the street.

– **Tori Amos**

I never wanted to get married. I felt it was a bad contract to get into.

– **Debbie Harry**

Why is it good that there are female astronauts? Because when the crew gets lost in space, at least the women will ask for directions.

– **Anonymous**

Speaking of rapists, even the most diehard feminist must admit that's one thing men do better than women.

– **Gabrielle Burton**

It is extremely cold here. The English fielders are keeping their hands in their pockets between balls.

– **Christopher Martin-Jenkins**

I didn't direct Mae West and W.C. Fields. I merely refereed the movie between them.

– **Eddie Cline**

Ice hockey combines the best features of figure skating and World War II.

– **Alfred Hitchcock**

My movie Assassins is an existential action film, screenplay by Sartre and dialogue by Camus.
- **Sylvester Stallone**

Ever since the baby's been born, I find I cannot take my eyes off her. Instead of television, I now watch her and it's the best show I've ever seen.
- **Dave Bernard**

When we recall Christmas past, we usually find that the simplest things - not the great occasions - give off the greatest glow of happiness.
- **Bob Hope**

Half our life is spent trying to find something to do with the time we have rushed through life trying to save.
- **Will Rogers**

A lot of people like snow. I find it an unnecessary freezing of water.
- **Carl Reiner**

There is nothing so consoling as to find that one's neighbours' troubles are at least as great as one's own.
- **George Moore**

The one thing women don't want to find in their stockings Christmas morning is their husband.
- **Joan Rivers**

Finding the virus was as difficult as finding a Volkswagen in a haystack.
- **Elaine De Freitas**

We have many homeowners who cross the fine line, in terms of illumination, between 'tasteful holiday yard display' and 'municipal airport'. You know the houses I mean: the ones with a Frosty the Snowman the size of Godzilla; the ones with so many lights in the trees that you need an umbrella to avoid being struck by the falling bodies of electrocuted squirrels.
- **Dave Barry**

What a lovely thing a bit of fine, sharp, crystallized broken snow is, held up against the blue sky catching the sun – talk of diamonds!

    – John Ruskin

The art galleries of Paris contain the finest collection of frames I ever saw.

    – Humphry Davy

I've decided life is too fragile to finish a book I dislike just because it cost $16.95 and everyone else loved it. Or eat a fried egg with a broken yolk (which I hate) when the dog would leap over the St Louis Arch for it.

    – Erma Bombeck

Hagen said that no one remembers who finished second. But they still ask me if I ever think about that putt I missed to win the 1970 Open at St Andrews. I tell them that sometimes it doesn't cross my mind for a full five minutes.

    – Doug Saunders

There are three kinds of kissers: the fire extinguisher, the mummy and the vacuum cleaner.

    – Helen Gurley Brown

Horace Greeley wrote so illegibly that a fired employee used his letter of discharge as a letter of recommendation for another job.

    – Robert Hendrickson

I would rather be governed by the first three hundred names in the Boston telephone book than by the Faculty of Harvard University.

    – William F. Buckley

Three ducks were flying over Belfast. The first duck said 'quack', the second duck said 'quack' and the third duck said 'Look, I'm going as quack as I can.'

    – Frank Carson

It's all right to drink like a fish – if you drink what a fish drinks.

    – Mary Poole

You know you're getting older when the first thing you do after you're done eating is look for a place to lie down.

– Louie Anderson

It was a non-smoker who committed the first sin and brought death into the world and all our woe. Nero was a non-smoker. Lady Macbeth was a non-smoker. Decidedly the record of the non-smokers leaves them little to be proud of.

– Robert Lynd

I remember the year I received my first 'crumb scraper'. It was fashioned from half a paper plate and a lace doily. I have never seen such shining pride from my little four-year-old girl who asked, 'You don't have one already, do you?'... I still receive gifts at Christmas. They are thoughtful. They are wrapped with care. They are what I need. But oh, how I wish I could bend low and receive a gift of cardboard and paste so that I could hear the chimes ring at Christmas just once more.

– Erma Bombeck

I have a tip that can take five strokes off anyone's golf game. It's called an eraser.

– Arnold Palmer

I wish my father wouldn't try to fix things any more, for everything he's mended is more broken than before.

– Jack Prelutsky

Last night, it was so cold, the flashers in New York were only describing themselves.

– Johnny Carson

He was dead before he hit the floor and he never regained consciousness.

– David Coleman

As I get older the years just fly by. I don't think there was an April this year.

– Jeremy Hardy

My father once took me to the floor of the set when he was shooting Casino Royale with a lot of nude girls in a bath, because he wanted me to understand how arduous an actor's life could be.

— **David Niven Jr**

If you want to say it with flowers, a single rose says: 'I'm cheap!'

— **Delta Burke**

I am the greatest golfer in the world. I just haven't played yet.

— **Muhammad Ali**

Why should Irishmen stand with their arms folded and their hands in their pockets when England called for aid?

— **Thomas Myles**

We have put more effort into helping folks reach old age than into helping them enjoy it.

— **Frank A. Clark**

Putts should be conceded only in the following circumstances: (i) When your opponent is two inches from the pin and three down; (ii) Your opponent is nine feet from the hole and is your boss; (iii) Immediately after you have holed out in one.

— **Tom Scott**

Sometimes one likes foolish people for their folly, better than wise people for their wisdom.

— **Elizabeth Gaskell**

In my day there were plenty of footballers around who would knock your bollocks off. The difference was that at the end of the match they would shake your hand and help you look for them.

— **Nat Lofthouse**

Think of me as a sex symbol for the man who doesn't give a damn.

— **Phyllis Diller**

A child hasn't a grown-up person's appetite for affection. A little of it goes a long way with them.

– **George Bernard Shaw**

Acne seems to be an occupational hazard for football strikers, as in 'Duncan Ferguson picked his spot before tucking the ball away.'

– **Tom Shields**

The method preferred by most balding men for making themselves look silly is called the 'comb-over', which is when the man grows the hair on one side of his head very long and combs it across the bald area, creating an effect that looks from the top like an egg in the grasp of a large tropical spider.

– **Dave Barry**

On many American campuses the only qualification for admission is the ability to find the campus and then discover a parking space.

– **Malcolm Bradbury**

Christmas is for children. But it is for grown-ups too. Even if it is a headache, a chore, and a nightmare, it is a period of necessary defrosting of chill and hide-bound hearts.

– **Lenora Mattingly Weber**

I would be converted to any religion for a cigar and baptized in it for a box of them.

– **H.L. Mencken**

Don't buy fur. Do you realise that for every fur coat, twenty trees have to die to make the protest placards.

– **Emo Philips**

A mother will go to the store for bread and milk, and return with enough groceries to feed Bangladesh for a year. A father will go to the store for bread and milk and return with bread, nacho-flavoured Doritos, and five dollars' worth of lottery tickets.

– **Michael Burkett**

Edwina Currie has done about as much for the Tory Party as King Herod did for babysitting.

- **Andrew MacKay**

After the ritual exchange of presents, socks for me, lavender water for Hilda, we ate enough to ensure a gentle snooze during the broadcast by Her Majesty the Queen.

- **John Mortimer, Rumpole of the Bailey**

Parcels have always exercised an odd fascination for me – one always expects something of a sensational nature, and one is always disappointed. In that respect they resemble the modern novel.

- **Peter Ackroyd**

The one thing Father always gave up for Lent was going to church.

- **Clarence Day**

I was fired from [the convent], finally, for a lot of things, among them my insistence that the Immaculate Conception was spontaneous combustion.

- **Dorothy Parker**

The race to get a Christmas present for Father usually ends in a tie.

- **Gene Shalit**

I have been going to symphony concerts for over fifty years, and I find I mind it less and less.

- **Louise Kent**

W.C. Fields has a profound respect for old age. Especially when it's bottled.

- **Gene Fowler**

If you cannot have your dear husband for a comfort and a delight, for a crosspatch, for a sofa, chair or a hotwater bottle, one can use him as a Cross to be Borne.

- **Stevie Smith**

This year I have two friends coming for lunch and this time I shall take it easy in the morning and try to remember to put some water in the saucepan of sprouts. Last year they were brown and hard and looked like roast chestnuts.

    – Jeffrey Bernard

The only reason I made a commercial for American Express was to pay for my American Express bill.

    – Peter Ustinov

My grandfather and I used to sit for hours in front of the television watching it intently. Eventually he would say, 'Will we switch it on?'

    – Kevin McAleer

I'm not senile. I've been like this for 50 years. So even if I do become senile, people will never know.

    – Martin Landis, Night Court

I had her in my bed gasping for breath and calling out my name. Obviously I didn't hold the pillow down long enough.

    – Emo Philips

Any American who is prepared to run for president should automatically, by definition be disqualified from ever doing so.

    – Gore Vidal

Oh how nice it would be, just for today and tomorrow, to be a little boy of five instead of an ageing playwright of fifty-five and look forward to all the high jinks with passionate excitement and be given a clockwork train with a full set of rails and a tunnel.

    – Noël Coward

I was asked to suggest a title for my autobiography. I said THE DEFINITIVE VOLUME ON THE FINEST BLOODY FAST BOWLER THAT EVER DREW BREATH.

    – Freddie Trueman

It's a funny kind of month, October. For the really keen cricket fan it's when you discover that your wife left you in May.

– **Dennis Norden**

There is nothing like a morning funeral for sharpening the appetite for lunch.

– **Arthur Marshall**

For every set of horseshoes people use for luck, somewhere out there there's a barefoot horse.

– **Allan Sherman**

Long ago I proposed that unsuccessful candidates for the Presidency be quietly hanged as a matter of public sanitation.

– **H.L. Mencken**

As the Bible says, it is easier for a rich man to get through the eye of a needle than for a camel to get into heaven.

– **Andy Mulligan**

If the Red Sox ever tested me for attention deficit disorder, I don't remember it.

– **Manny Ramirez**

I am at that age. Too young for the bowling green, too old for Ecstasy.

– **Rab C. Nesbitt**

You can tell the person who lives for others by the haunted look on the faces of the others.

– **Katherine Whitehorn**

It's very hard to make a home for a man if he's always in it.

– **Winifred Kirkland**

It is unforgivable to deny race-goers facilities for losing their money swiftly and painlessly.

– **Hugh McIlvanney**

I was asked to do a benefit for babies born addicted to crack. I agreed, but I think we both knew what they're going to spend the money on.

– Laura Kightlinger

He told me what I was looking for was right under my nose. I asked him if he could be more specific.

– Jimmy Durante

I gave my wife a gift certificate for Christmas. She ran out to exchange it for a bigger size.

– Milton Berle

Some men would run away to the Foreign Legion to recover from a disastrous love affair, but others ran to the Prison Service to forget that they were members of the human race.

– Charlie Richardson

This has been a foggy morning and forenoon, snowing a little now and then, and disagreeably cold... At about twelve there is a faint glow of sunlight, like the gleaming reflection from a not highly polished copper kettle.

– Nathaniel Hawthorne

My grandmother's 85 and starting to get forgetful. The family's upset about it but I don't mind because I get 8 cheques on my birthday from her. That's 40 bucks.

– Tom Arnold

I'm retired. I'm now officially a lower form of life than a Duracell battery. I've been replaced by a box. It's standard procedure apparently for a man my age. The next stage is to stick you inside one.

– Victor Meldrew, One Foot in the Grave

Few men know how to kiss well; fortunately, I've always had time to teach them.

– Mae West

The upright piano is a musical growth found adhering to the walls of most semi-detached houses in the provinces.

– **Thomas Beecham**

Last year my wife Camille and I found a summer camp that would accept our five children... We watched the bus loaded with our kids disappear, then walked back toward the house. We could hear the property. We had never heard – our property before. We noticed that the birds were coming back. My wife's face began to twitch and tremble. I said, 'Dear, are you having a stroke?' She answered serenely, 'No, I think I'm going to smile.' I asked her why. She said simply, 'Peace of mind.'

– **Bill Cosby**

When I buy cookies, I just eat four and throw the rest away. But first I spray them with disinfectant so I won't dig them out of the garbage later. Disinfectant doesn't taste all that bad though.

– **Janette Barber**

She kept up with the lads for fourteen pints, but then they started talking about football.

– **Martin Kemp**

Great restaurants are nothing but mouth-brothels.

– **Frederic Raphael**

Being Vice-President means you get all the French fries the President can't get to.

– **Al Gore**

I love Michael Jackson. He's my best friend. I buy him a handkerchief for Christmas each year. I don't know what to buy him this year. He has no nose. No nose. What do you buy a man with no nose?

– **Joan Rivers**

Love your enemies, just in case your friends turn out to be a bunch of bastards.

– **R.A. Dickson**

I remember the night me and my friends played Find the Lady by shuffling my infant triplets – only one of whom was female – on the sofa.
   – **Richard Hannon**

If I catch one of my amateur friends playing with a one-iron, he had better be putting with it.
   – **Tommy Bolt**

Singing, fishing, meeting my close and dear friends, looking at pictures and nature, shocking a few people who deserve shocking, taking my pills, writing a book and swigging Irish whiskey. These are my ways of fending off the old gent with the scythe waiting patiently to harvest me.
   – **George Melly**

When he brings home the bacon she fries it. When she brings home the bacon they eat out.
   – **Natasha Josefowitz**

I will never accept an unsigned painting from Picasso. If he doesn't sign it, I don't know which way to hang it.
   – **Auguste Rodin**

The best advice ever given me was from my father. When I was a little girl, he told me, 'Don't spend anything unless you have to.'
   – **Dinah Shore**

Honest criticism is hard to take particularly from a relative, a friend, an acquaintance or a stranger.
   – **Franklin P. Jones**

Today is the coldest day of all; frost feathers, flowers, ferns all over the windows, giving a dim clouded light inside; my pen frozen, so that I could not write with it or fill it. Then broadest sunlight pouring on to me in bed, warm, melting the frost flowers so that a steam goes up, waving, wreathing its shadow across this page as I write. I have a lot to do.
   – **Denton Welch, 1947**

The two mistakes I see most often from amateurs are lifting up and hitting the equator of the ball, sending it into the next country, or taking a divot of sand large enough to bury a cat.

– **Sam Snead**

Anybody can have one kid. But going from one kid to two is like going from owning a dog to running a zoo.

– **P.J. O'Rourke**

No diet will remove all the fat from your body because the brain is entirely fat. Without a brain you might look good, but all you could do is run for public office.

– **Covert Bailey**

A comedian has to get a laugh from the audience, just the way a prostitute has to get an orgasm from the client.

– **Camille Paglia**

I'm not sure where the notes come from sometimes. In the studio I'm like: 'I hope you save that, 'cos it ain't coming out any time again today.' Maybe they could get a dolphin in.

– **Mariah Carey**

But it is immensely cold – everything frozen solid – milk, mustard, everything.

– **D.H. Lawrence**

I don't know whether the world is full of smart men bluffing or imbeciles who mean it.

– **Morrie Brickman**

'If you don't go to other men's funerals,' Father said, 'they won't go to yours.'

– **Clarence Day**

I drink too much. Last time I gave a urine sample it had an olive in it.

– **Rodney Dangerfield**

Steve Coogan's stand-up comedy is about as funny as a hole in a parachute.

– **Bernard Manning**

Everything I buy is vintage and smells funny. Maybe that's why I don't have a boyfriend.

– **Lucy Liu**

Sometimes it's fun to sit in your garden and try to remember your dog's name.

– **Steve Martin**

I am spending delightful afternoons in my garden, watching everything living around me. As I grow older, I feel everything departing, and I love everything with more passion.

– **Emile Zola**

When two or more television presenters are gathered together, and the subject of Anne Robinson comes up, the air grows green and acrid with spite and envy.

– **Esther Rantzen**

There is nothing wrong with the younger generation which the older generation did not outgrow.

– **Gail Hammond**

One of the surest signs of Conrad's genius is that women dislike his works.

– **George Orwell**

One thing I will say for the Germans, they are always perfectly willing to give anybody's land to somebody else.

– **Will Rogers**

I must marry – if only to get to bed at a reasonable hour.

– **Benjamin Constant**

It took me 17 years to finally get round to taking my son fishing, as every father should do once in his life. Every time we'd tried to go before, everyone was throwing up on the boat so we had to turn back.

– Ozzy Osbourne

Kids are so easy to please. They get a kick out of sitting in the front seat of the car or getting the wishbone when we have roast chicken.

– Al Brown

The quickest way for a parent to get a child's attention is to sit down and look comfortable.

– Lane Olinghouse

I basically enjoy getting older because I get smarter. So what I have to say is more worth listening to, in my opinion.

– Clive James

Guinness is a great day-shortener. If you get out of bed first thing and drink a glass then the day doesn't begin until about 12.30, when you come to again, which is nice. I try to live in a perpetual snooze.

– Quentin Crisp

I have never had to try to get my act across to a non-English-speaking audience, except at the Glasgow Empire.

– Arthur Askey

I was born in Louisiana, but I get to lots of overseas places like Canada.

– Britney Spears

You know you're knocking on when you get to the top of the stairs and can't remember what you went up for. So you go back downstairs to help you remember what you went upstairs for. You finally remember what you went upstairs for so up you go again but when you find it you have forgotten why you wanted it.

– Millicent Kemp

It's always been my ambition to go get hold of a video camera and to go round to Jeremy Beadle's house disguised as a mad axe-man, just for a laugh, and kill him.

– **Paul Merton**

When I think of my dad, I get this Obi-Wan Kenobi voice in my head, but instead of giving me words of wisdom and advice, it just says things like, 'Ouch, my back!' and 'Pull my finger. Just pull it.'

– **Lori Chapman**

In the Dublin of the 1930s to get enough to eat was regarded as an achievement. To get drunk was a victory.

– **Brendan Behan**

People that are really very weird can get into sensitive positions and have a tremendous impact on history.

– **Dan Quayle**

To please my wife, I decided to get in touch with my feminine side. I caught a yeast infection.

– **Bob Delaney**

When male golfers wiggle their feet to get their stance right they look exactly like cats preparing to pee.

– **Jilly Cooper**

They say if you stop smoking you'll get your sense of smell back. I live in New York City – why do I want my sense of smell back?

– **Bill Hicks**

Get a job, your husband hates you. Get a good job, your husband leaves you. Get a stupendous job, you husband leaves you for a teenager.

– **Cynthia Heimel**

The trouble with incest is that it gets you involved with relatives.

– **George S. Kaufman**

A 3-year-old child is a being who gets almost as much fun out of a $56 set of swings as it does out of finding a small green worm.

– Bill Vaughan

Perhaps a child who is fussed over gets a feeling of destiny, he thinks he is in the world for something important and it gives him drive and confidence.

– Dr Benjamin Spock

Our children await Christmas presents like politicians getting election results; there's the Uncle Fred precinct and the Aunt Ruth district still to come in.

– Marceline Cox

There is a saying, 'Youth is a gift of nature; Age is a work of art.' If age is a work of art, the artist is one who belongs on the subway and not in the Louvre.

– Bill Cosby

Which are harder to raise, boys or girls? Has to be girls. Boys are easy. Give them a box of matches and they're happy.

– Milton Berle

I never hated a man enough to give him back his diamonds.

– Zsa Zsa Gabor

I'm already signing books for husbands to give their wives at Christmas. When I ask if I should put 'Darling Dorothy' or 'To my sweetest Elizabeth' or what exactly, they always say, 'No. To She Who Must Be Obeyed.'

– John Mortimer

The citizens of Griggsville invited me to give them a lecture on aesthetics. I began by advising them to change the name of their town.

– Oscar Wilde

I'd like to thank my parents for giving me the gift of poverty.

– Roberto Begnini, in his Oscars acceptance speech

Carl Llewellyn is so optimistic he would give himself a fifty-fifty chance after a decapitation.

– Richard Edmondson

Dust! At the very least they could give a man about to die a clean electric chair! .

– Michael Sclafoni

The only fatherly advice I have ever given is not to eat your peas off a knife.

– John Cheever

When your daughter is 12, she is given a splendidly silly article of clothing called a training bra. To train what? I never had a training jockstrap.

– Bill Cosby

The worst Christmas present I was ever given was a 'Grow Your Own Loofah Kit' from my sister.

– Sean Lock

On entering the United States I was given a form to fill in by the Immigration Authority. To the question 'Is it your intention to overthrow the government of the US by force', I gave the written answer 'Sole purpose of visit'.

– Gilbert Harding

There are all sorts of methods of giving up smoking. My aunt used to pour a gallon of petrol over herself every morning. The idea being that she couldn't light up without turning herself into a human fireball. It didn't stop her – she'd be in the living room and you'd hear a cough and a woosh. She was up to forty wooshes a day by the end of it.

– Paul Merton

You may be a redneck if you go Christmas shopping for your mom, sister and girlfriend and you need buy only one gift.

– Jeff Foxworthy

There's one thing about children: they never go around showing snapshots of their grandparents.

– Bessie & Beulah

You know you're getting old when you go on holiday and always pack a sweater.

– Denis Norden

A man who has no office to go to – I don't care who he is – is a trial of which you can have no conception.

– George Bernard Shaw

Don't you just hate those couples who go round telling everybody that they're 'trying' for a baby. We can do without the visual.

– Pete Brown

A lady, if surprised by melancholy, might go to bed with a chap, once; or a thousand times if consumed by passion. But twice, my dear fellow, twice, a lady might think she'd been taken for a tart.

– Tom Stoppard

Anyone who believes that exponential growth can go on forever in a finite world is either mad or an economist.

– Kenneth Boulding

Old is when your wife says, 'Let's go upstairs and make love,' and you answer, 'Honey, I can't do both.'

– Red Buttons

If you're going to sin, sin against God, not the bureaucracy. God will forgive you but the bureaucracy won't.

– Hyman Rickover

Faith is putting all your eggs in God's basket, then counting your blessings before they hatch.

– Ramona C. Carroll

I'm at an age where my back goes out more than I do.
- **Phyllis Diller**

In St Moritz everyone who is anyone goes around in plaster, which may be fashionable, but is damned uncomfortable. I value my legs as much as Marlene Dietrich values hers.
- **Noël Coward**

A coarse golfer is one who normally goes from tee to green without touching the fairway.
- **Michael Green**

Father's Day is the day when father goes broke giving his family money so they can surprise him with gifts he doesn't need.
- **Richard Taylor**

The menopause is the stage that woman goes through when her body, through a complex biological process, senses that the woman has reached the stage in her life where her furniture is much too nice for her to have a baby barfing on it.
- **Dave Barry**

I'm quite happy with my mistress. She goes to bed with others because she loves them, but for money, only with me.
- **Ferenc Molnar**

That son of a bitch MacArthur isn't going to resign on me. I want him fired.
- **Harry S. Truman**

Roll carpet slippers in breadcrumbs, bake until golden brown, then tell friends you're wearing Findus Crispy Pancakes.
- **H. Lloyd, Top Tip, Viz**

Most people play a fair game of golf – if you watch them.
- **Joey Adams**

One of the advantages of bowling over golf is that you very seldom lose a bowling ball.

– **Don Carter**

More lampshades were broken in Britain by golf clubs than by Hitler's bombers.

– **Val Doonican**

However unlucky you may be on the golf course it really is not fair to expect your adversary's grief for your undeserved misfortunes to be as poignant as your own.

– **Horace Hutchinson**

My son Rollo is exceedingly good at golf. He scores 120 every time, while Mr Burns, who is supposed to be one of the best players in the club, seldom manages to reach 80.

– **P.G. Wodehouse**

One way to solve the problem of golfers' slow play is to knock the ball into them. There will be a short delay while you have a hell of a fight, but from then on they'll move faster.

– **Horace Hutchinson**

From birth to 18 a girl needs good parents; from 18 to 35, she needs good looks. From 35 to 55, good personality. From 55 on, she needs good cash. I'm saving my money.

– **Sophie Tucker**

If Ron 'Chopper' Harris was in a good mood, he'd put iodine on his studs.

– **Jimmy Greaves**

People say, oh, it's not like the good old days. When were the good old days? In 1900 your doctor was also your barber. 'Say, will you take a little off the sides when you take out my spleen?'

– **Joe Ditzel**

Sex is essentially just a matter of good lighting.

– **Noël Coward**

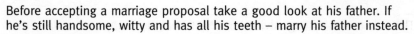

Before accepting a marriage proposal take a good look at his father. If he's still handsome, witty and has all his teeth – marry his father instead.

– **Diane Jordan**

We are here on earth to do good for others. What the others are here for I don't know.

– **W.H. Auden**

In making a sermon, think up a good beginning, then think up a good ending and finally bring these two as close together as you possibly can.

– **Frederick Temple**

The French and the English are such good enemies that they can't resist being friends.

– **Peter Ustinov**

Winter is the time for comfort, for good food and warmth, for the touch of a friendly hand and for a talk beside the fire: it is time for home.

– **Edith Sitwell**

What's the use of having a totally gorgeous body like Victoria Principal if you've got a mind like... Victoria Principal?

– **Jean Kittson**

Australia's in the big league now. We've got organized crime, racial prejudice, cable TV, AIDS, disabled toilets, and underage drug abuse, second to none.

– **Barry Humphries**

My father was so cheap. When he got engaged to my mother, he didn't buy her a diamond ring. He gave her a lump of coal and told her to be patient.

– **Cathy Ladman**

The doctor asked me if I ever got breathless after exercise. I said no, never, because I never exercise.

– John Mortimer

The only useful putting advice I ever got from my caddy was to keep the ball low.

– Chi Chi Rodriguez

If you're gonna be a boxer, you gotta prepare for memory loss. So I named all my kids George. Including the girls.

– George Foreman

One day a bachelor, the next a grampa. What is the secret of the trick? How did I get so old so quick?

– Ogden Nash

Before I went to St Andrew's, my grandmother gave me a farewell lunch. As she said goodbye, she said, 'Any good parties, invite me down.' But there was no way. I knew full well that if I invited her down, she would dance me under the table.

– Prince William

Seeing snow for the first time, my grandson jumped for joy and cried, 'Ooh, icing!'

– Alex Lacey

Gary Rhodes wants you to strain your gravy through muslin. As an alternative to spilling it over your shirt and salvaging what you can off the kitchen floor, maybe.

– Joe Joseph

The first handshake in life is the greatest of all: the clasp of an infant's fist around a parent's finger.

– Mark Beltaire

I used to think I'd like less grey hair. Now I'd like more of it.

– Richie Benaud

As our children grow, so must we grow to meet their changing emotional, intellectual, and designer-footwear needs.

— **Dave Barry**

I've always thought that very few people grow old as admirably as academics. At least books never let them down.

— **Margaret Drabble**

The Trappist monks at Our Lady of Guadalupe Abbey in Lafayette, Oregon, produce a dark, heavy fruit cake that is studded with pecan halves, chopped walnuts and candied cherries, and flavoured with 120-proof brandy. The cake has little in common with the light, flour-filled commercial varieties, and as Father Paschal Phillips... put it: 'When you slice our fruit cake and hold it up to the light, it looks like stained glass.'

— **Allison Engel**

I used to play golf with a guy who cheated so badly that he had a hole-in-one and wrote down zero on his scorecard.

— **Bob Bruce**

My dad's one of those Mr Fixit guys. Every Sunday morning he'd be locked down in the basement with the power tools. When my sister got married, we had to lead him into the church with a broken toaster.

— **Mike Rowe**

The word 'aerobics' came about when the gym instructors got together and said 'If we're going to charge ten dollars an hour, we can't call it 'jumping up and down'.

— **Rita Rudner**

My only solution for the problem of habitual accidents is to stay in bed all day. Even then, there is always the chance that you will fall out.

— **Robert Benchley**

George Kaufman had great integrity. You never had to watch him when he was dealing.

— **Harpo Marx**

Consumers genuinely prefer corny jokes, we've actually had complaints after trying to introduce more genuinely amusing gags – it seems that the British public have fond memories of groaning at a bad punchline after pulling their crackers!

   – Julian Reed, Robin Reed cracker manufacturers

My dad died in 1990 and I've had the same dream every night since. I die and go down a tunnel of light, to a room filled with light. My dad walks in and says, 'Joe! Did you leave all these lights on?'

   – Joe Ditzel

When I eventually met Mr Right, I had no idea his first name was 'Always'.

   – Rita Rudner

My recipe for perpetual youth? I've never had my face in the sun, and I have a very handsome young husband... Sex is one of the best and cheapest beauty treatments there is.

   – Joan Collins

Coffee is a pretty powerful stimulant. I had a friend who drank twenty cups a day at work. He died last month, but a week later he was still mingling in the company lounge.

   – Milton Berle

I've been travelling so much, I haven't had time to grow a beard.

   – Bob Horner

It's a pity that Marie Stopes' mother had not thought of birth control.

   – Muriel Spark

Dorothy Thompson is the only woman who had her menopause in public and got paid for it.

   – Alice Roosevelt

To say nothing especially when speaking is half the art of diplomacy.

   – Will Durant

The spectacle of twenty-two grown men with hairy legs chasing a bladder filled with air from one end of a field to another is both ludicrous and infantile.

– George Bernard Shaw

Whoever said money can't buy happiness simply hadn't found out where to go shopping.

– Bo Derek

I've been trying to grow my hair but someone came up to me and asked if I was Enya. I was so shocked, I shaved all of it off.

– Sinead O'Connor

I'm generally as busy as Germaine Greer's hairdresser, and he'd have to be busy.

– Barry Humphries

Someone said my performance in the second half of the Calcutta Cup match was a bit like J.P.R Williams. In the first half it was more like Kenneth Williams.

– Jonathan Callard

Mr Speaker, I withdraw my statement that half the cabinet are asses. Half the cabinet are not asses.

– Benjamin Disraeli

My shoes are size two and a half, the same size as my feet.

– Elaine Paige

Christmases in my house were like a Hammer horror version of Big Brother. Four mismatched individuals, with nothing more in common than a few strands of DNA, trapped under the same roof, the action fuelled by drink, paranoia and dyspepsia.

– Sarah Vine

Whenever you see a man with a handkerchief, socks and tie to match, you may be sure he is wearing a present.

– **Frank Case**

I don't know that I could have handled work, children and husband. Work and children I could have. But the husband was too much.

– **Diane von Furstenberg.**

We find delight in the beauty and happiness of children that makes the heart too big for the body.

– **Ralph Waldo Emerson**

That night in bed, the sheets were hard and slippery, unfriendly as ice. Carefully, by an act of will, Bernard made a warm place in the bed exactly the same shape as his body, thin and hunched under the covers. He extended it gradually, inch by inch, sending his toes gently into the cold until he was at last straight and comfortable.

– **Leslie Norris**

My father, Groucho Marx, has shaken hands with Presidents, danced cheek to cheek with Marlene Dietrich, played baseball with Lou Gehrig, traded backhands with Jack Kramer, strummed guitar duets with the great Segovia, and he's insulted nearly everyone worth insulting.

– **Arthur Marx**

In my mid-6os, what I find the hardest to bear is being 'safe'. After a gym session I found myself in the Jacuzzi with a gorgeous young brunette. We had a wonderful chat, laughing and joking. But it was awful. Sitting there in her skimpy bikini, she did not see me as even slightly dangerous.

– **Peter Church**

Perhaps host and guest is really the happiest relation for father and son.

– **Evelyn Waugh**

There's nothing remarkable about it. All one has to do is to hit the right keys at the right time and the instrument plays itself.

– **Johann Sebastian Bach**

The English instinctively admire any man who has no talent and is modest about it.

– **James Agee**

Mother Nature, in all her infinite wisdom, has instilled within each of us a powerful biological instinct to reproduce. This is her way of assuring that the human race, come what may, will never have any disposable income.

– **Dave Barry**

It is to be regretted that domestication has seriously deteriorated the moral character of the duck. In the wild state he is a faithful husband; but no sooner is he domesticated than he becomes polygamous, and makes nothing of owning ten or a dozen wives at a time.

– **Isabella Beaton**

No academic ever becomes chairman until he has forgotten the meaning of the word 'irrelevant'.

– **Francis Cornford**

Let no man boast himself that he has got through the perils of winter till at least the 7th of May.

– **Anthony Trollope**

I have always felt that a woman has the right to treat the subject of her age with ambiguity until, perhaps, she passes into the realm beyond 90. Then it is better that she be candid with herself and with the world.

– **Helena Rubinstein**

I see Kate Hoey, our Sports Minister, has come eleventh in the most beautiful women in sport. I'd really hate to meet the girl who came twelfth on a dark night.

– **Ken Bates**

In my heart, I think a woman has two choices: either she's a feminist or a masochist.

    – Gloria Steinem

This is an interesting circuit because it has inclines. And not just up but down as well.

    – Murray Walker

The man who invented the hokey cokey has died. His funeral was a strange affair. First, they put his left leg in...

    – Al Ferrera

A good listener is not someone who has nothing to say. A good listener is a good talker with a sore throat.

    – Katharine Whitehorn

The dawn of legibility in his handwriting has revealed his utter inability to spell.

    – Ian Hay

Duct tape is like the force. It has a light side, a dark side, and it holds the universe together.

    – Oprah Winfrey

The dumbing-down of notices on food packets has just about reached its limit. I recently bought a packet of peanuts and it said CONTAINS: PEANUTS. INSTRUCTIONS: OPEN PACKET, EAT CONTENTS.

    – Robin Young

No modern literary work of any worth has been produced in the English language by an English writer – except, of course, Bradshaw.

    – Oscar Wilde

I do benefits for all religions. I'd hate to blow the hereafter on a technicality.

    – Bob Hope

Rolf Harris is a difficult man to hate, though that doesn't mean we shouldn't try.

— A. A. Gill

When I was a teenager, I didn't have any posters over the walls because I didn't like to think I lived with my mum and dad. I liked to think I was just staying there.

— Harry Enfield

Men feel frazzled and angry if they have to answer three phone calls, and have a hard time settling back to work after the trauma. Women, on the other hand, tuck the phone in between their shoulders and their ears, hold a baby on one hip, stir a pot on the stove, all the while thinking about an idea for a story.

— Barbara Grafton

Men don't know anything about pain; they have never experienced labour, cramps or a bikini wax.

— Nan Tisdale

Racism isn't born, folks, it's taught. I have a 2-year-old son. You know what he hates? Naps. End of list.

— Denis Leary

You know you're getting older if you have more fingers than real teeth.

— Rodney Dangerfield

George Bush's problem is that the clothes have no emperor.

— Anna Quindlen

It seems to me that two people have a baby just to see what they can make, like a kind of erotic arts and crafts.

— Bill Cosby

I will not meet Swinburne because I have no wish to know anyone sitting in a sewer and adding to it.

— Thomas Carlyle

I said to my husband, my boobs have gone, my stomach's gone, say something nice about my legs. He said, 'Blue goes with everything.'
   – Joan Rivers

For the last nine million years, children have had just one guiding philosophy and it is greed: Mine! Mine! Mine!
   – Bill Cosby

From the age of 75 on, I have found my memory deteriorating and my senses getting less acute. I can mistake a reference to 'Stena Sealink' on television for 'Denis Healey'.
   – Denis Healey

Curling is the only sport where they have to speed up the action replays.
   – A.A. Gill

Turbulence is what pilots announce that you have encountered when your plane strikes an object in midair.
   – Dave Barry

God invented golf so white people would have an excuse to get dressed up like black people.
   – Stanley Morgan

The experts agree that mothers do not have a biological, psychological or natural advantage that automatically makes them better kiddie-caretakers than fathers. Clearly the experts have never watched a man change a diaper.
   – Michael Burkett

I would think the less time you have left in life, the faster you should drive. I think old people should be allowed to drive their age. If you're 80, do 80. If you're 100, do 100.
   – Jerry Seinfeld

I've married a few people I shouldn't have, but haven't we all?
   – Mamie Van Doren

We never know the love our parents have for us till we have become parents.
- **Henry Ward Beecher**

The most important thing a woman can have – next to talent of course – is her hairdresser.
- **Joan Crawford**

It is hard to tell whether Americans have become such liars because of golf or income tax.
- **Will Rogers**

If you don't want to work you have to earn enough money so that you don't have to work.
- **Ogden Nash**

The book I would most like to have with me on a desert island is Thomas's Guide to Practical Shipbuilding.
- **G.K. Chesterton**

I am 102 years of age. I have no worries since my youngest son went into an old folk's home.
- **Victoria Bedwell**

If you think you're too small to have an impact, try going to bed with a mosquito.
- **Anita Roddick, founder of The Body Shop**

One good thing about being old and having a failing memory is that I can enjoy the endless repeats of programmes like Inspector Morse, Murder She Wrote, and Midsomer Murders because I can never remember whodunit.
- **Larry Simpkins**

Having one child makes you a parent; having two you are a referee.
- **David Frost**

There's more to Inuit culture than famously having 50 words for snow, a fact that has never impressed me anyway, because, after all, the British have a thousand words for rain.

– Victor Lewis-Smith

All the unhappy marriages come from husbands having brains. What good are brains to a man? They only unsettle him.

– P.G. Wodehouse

Friends ask if there's a difference between having a son or a daughter. No doubt about it, the day my daughter was born everyone began to look like a potential molester to me... 'She's not sitting on your lap.'

– Jack Coen

Being in love with yourself means never having to say you've got a headache.

– Ellie Laine

Probably the reason we all go so haywire at Christmas time with the endless unrestrained and often silly buying of gifts is that we don't quite know how to put our love into words.

– Harlan Miller

My father had a philosophy in life. He used to say 'I brought you into being and if you do that again I'll take you out of it.'

– Adrian Walsh

Frank Lampard is a great football player. He used to be my son. Now I'm his father.

– Frank Lampard Sr

An alcoholic is a man who, when he buys his ties, has to ask if gin makes them run.

– F. Scott Fitzgerald

Even if a farmer intends to loaf, he gets up in time to get an early start.

– Edgar W. Howe

My chauffeur is a bit peculiar – he prefers to spend the weekend with his family rather than with me.

– **Michael Winner**

Beware of the man who denounces women writers – his penis is tiny and he cannot spell.

– **Erica Jongs**

Pat Jennings does actually have faults – he might be a bit vulnerable to a hard low shot from the edge of the six-yard box.

– **Don Howe**

Academic critics treated Cyril Connolly as if he were a hunting parson who had blundered into the Oriel Common Room when Newman and Keble were discussing the illapse of the Holy Ghost.

– **Noel Annan**

Dad taught me everything I know. Unfortunately, he didn't teach me everything he knows.

– **Al Unser**

He was a good family man. Everywhere he went he started a new family.

– **Liam O'Reilly**

My dad worked in a mortuary, but he was fired. He was accused of having an intimate relationship with a corpse. The family was shocked – we thought it was purely platonic.

– **Bill Hicks**

When Brahms is in extra good spirits, he sings, 'The grave is my joy'.

– **Tchaikovsky**

Man does not live by murder alone. He needs affection, approval, encouragement and, occasionally, a hearty meal.

– **Alfred Hitchcock**

An old man looks permanent, as if he had been born an old man.

– **H.E. Bates**

A James Cagney love scene is where he lets the other guy live.

– **Bob Hope**

The older a man gets, the farther he had to walk to school as a boy.

– **Henry Brightman**

A man will marry a woman because he needs a mother he can communicate with.

– **Martitt Mull**

It was a mixed marriage. I'm human, he was a Klingon.

– **Carol Leifer**

What does it profit a man if he gains the whole world and three-putts the eighteenth green?

– **Fred Corcoran**

Daddy told me that when he dies he wants his ashes scattered in Selfridges so he can be sure Mummy and I will come visit.

– **Lana Forbes-Carlton**

Saint Paul was the first golfer – he fought the good fight and finished the course.

– **Billy Graham**

Hitler – now there was a painter! He could paint an entire apartment in one afternoon. Two coats! .

– **Mel Brooks**

The umpire admitted to me afterwards that he had given me out LBW to Jim Parks because he was desperate for a pee.

– **Denis Compton**

My father 'went to the office'. What he did when he got to the office was a blank. He might have walked off the edge of the world each morning, returning at six with the Evening Standard.

– Robert Robinson

Garry Maddox has turned his life around. He used to be depressed and miserable. Now he's miserable and depressed.

– Harry Kalas

The President doesn't want yes-men around. When he says no, we all say no.

– Elizabeth Dole

Did you know that by the time he'd turned 80, Winston Churchill had coronary thrombosis, 3 attacks of pneumonia, a hernia, 2 strokes and something known as a senile itch? All the same, though often setting fire to himself, he still managed to enjoy a cigar.

– Beryl Bainbridge

The Chairman of MORI polls has died. He'll be missed by 80 per cent of his family and 35 per cent of his friends.

– Craig Kilborn

Teach your child to hold his tongue; he'll learn fast enough to speak.

– Benjamin Franklin

Jack Nicklaus isn't really a great golfer. He's just been on a thirty-year lucky streak.

– Henry Beard

When Fortune empties her chamberpot on your head, smile and say, "We are going to have a summer shower."

– John A. MacDonald

I like anything that comes under the heading, 'It's got calories and you can put it in your mouth.'

– Jo Brand

Aunt Sadie so much disliked hearing about health that people often took her for a Christian Scientist, which, indeed, she might have become had she not disliked hearing about religion even more.

   – **Nancy Mitford**

The three words you don't want to hear while making love are 'Honey, I'm home'.

   – **Ken Hammond**

A person is always startled when he hears himself called an old man for the first time.

   – **Oliver Wendell Holmes**

Remember, if Christmas isn't found in your heart, you won't find it under the tree.

   – **Charlotte Carpenter**

Forgive my not passing any opinions on heaven and hell. You see I have friends in both places.

   – **Jean Cocteau**

Dear Lord, if there is cricket in heaven, let there also be rain.

   – **Alec Douglas-Home**

Bo Derek turned down the role of Helen Keller because she couldn't remember the lines.

   – **Joan Rivers**

I dreamt last night I was in hell: It was just like a missionary meeting – I couldn't get near the fire for parsons.

   – **Samuel Wilberforce**

Music helps set a romantic mood. Imagine her surprise when you say "We don't need a stereo – I have an accordion."

   – **Martin Mull**

As an actress her only flair is her nostrils.

– Film critic Pauline Kael on Candice Bergen

If Dorothy Parker isn't more careful with her suicide attempts, one of these days she's going to hurt herself.

– Alexander Woollcott

When mom found my diaphragm, I told her it was a bathing cap for my cat.

– Liz Winston

To succeed with the opposite sex, tell her you're impotent. She can't wait to disprove it.

– Cary Grant, 72

A loving wife will do anything for her husband except to stop criticizing and trying to improve him.

– J.B. Priestley

Never date a woman whose father calls her 'Princess'. Chances are she believes it.

– Dave Marr

It is indeed fitting that we gather here today to pay tribute to Abraham Lincoln, who was born in a log cabin that he built with his own hands.

– Ronald Reagan

When he's late for dinner, I know he's either having an affair or is lying dead in the street. I always hope it's the street.

– Jessica Tandy

When the household expenses shot up very high, Father would yell his head off. He always did some yelling anyhow, merely on general principles.

– Clarence Day

And that's the third time this session he's missed his waistcoat pocket with the chalk.

— **Ted Lowe**

The rhinoceros is an animal with a hide two feet thick, and no apparent interest in politics. What a waste.

— **James Wright**

Someone threw a petrol bomb at Alex Higgins once and he drank it.

— **Frank Carson**

Little Truman Capote had a voice so high it could be detected only by a bat.

— **Tennessee Williams**

My husband has just retired. I married him for better or for worse, but not for lunch.

— **Hazel Weiss**

Prince William is wonderful. When I met him at the Queen's Jubilee Concert I said, 'I have got a daughter for you.'

— **Ozzy Osbourne**

I loved my father but I hated him, too. He was a ragman who drove a horse and wagon and couldn't read or write. But to me he was big. He was strong. He was a man. I didn't know what I was. But I wanted to be accepted by him.

— **Kirk Douglas**

There were times when Tolstoy thought of himself as God's brother, indeed God's elder brother.

— **Paul Johnson**

Winston Churchill has written four volumes about himself and called it World Crisis.

— **A.J. Balfour**

Nero renamed the month of April after himself, calling it Neroreus, but the idea never caught on because April is not Neroreus and there is no use pretending that it is.

    – Will Cuppy

Nothing buys happiness, but money can certainly hire it for short periods.

    – Irma Kurtz, agony aunt

Or consider Christmas – could Satan in his most malignant mood have devised a worse combination of graft plus bunkum than the system whereby several hundred million people get a billion or so gifts for which they have no use, and some thousands of shop-clerks die of exhaustion while selling them and every other child in the western world is made ill from overeating – all in the name of the lowly Jesus?

    – Upton Sinclair

The father is always a Republican towards his son, and his mother's always a Democrat.

    – Robert Frost

My father was always carrying me in his arms, giving me loud, moist kisses and calling me pet names like 'little sparrow' and 'little fly'. Once I ruined a tablecloth with a pair of scissors. My mother spanked me across the hand until it hurt. I cried so hard that my father came and took me by the hand – He kissed me and comforted me and quieted me down.

    – Svetlana Aliluyeva on her father, Joseph Stalin

The legend of Saint Denis, who carried his severed head for six miles after his execution, teaches us that the distance is not important; it is only the first step that is difficult.

    – Marquise Du Deffand

Every decent man carries a pencil behind his ear to write down the price of fish.

    – J.B. Morton

In 1876 the jockey Fred Archer blew his brains out at Newmarket. Knowing the place pretty well, I suspect he was trying to attract the attention of the staff in the Rutland Hotel.

   – Jeffrey Bernard

It profits a man nothing to give his soul for the whole world – but for Wales?

   – Thomas More

The Irish humour of John Ford in his Cavalry Trilogy made me wish that Oliver Cromwell had done a more thorough job.

   – James Agate

Every father should remember that one day his son will follow his example instead of his advice.

   – Anon

Disraeli is a self-made man who worships his creator.

   – John Bright

He was a self-made man who owed his lack of success to nobody.

   – Joseph Heller

I had observed Shackleton ferreting about in his bundle, out of which he presently produced a spare sock. Stored away in that sock was a small round object about the size of a cricket ball, which when brought to light, proved to be a noble plum pudding. Another dive into his lucky-bag and out came a crumpled piece of artificial holly. Heated in the cocoa, our plum pudding was soon steaming hot, and stood on the cooker-lid crowned with its decoration. Our Christmas Day had proved a delightful break in an otherwise uninterrupted spell of semi-starvation. Some days elapsed before its pleasing effects wore off.

   – Captain Robert Falcon Scott, Christmas Day 1902, during his unsuccessful attempt to reach the South Pole

Winston Churchill devoted the best years of his life to preparing his impromptu speeches.

   – F.E. Smith

Christmas is a time when everybody wants his past forgotten and his present remembered. What I don't like about office Christmas parties is looking for a job the next day.

– **Phyllis Diller**

F.E. Smith is very clever, but sometimes his brains go to his head.

– **Margot Asquith**

A Scottish lawyer was so proper in his behaviour that when mugged he pursued his assailant by shouting 'Stop alleged thief, Stop alleged thief'.

– **Ron Neil**

If you wonder where your child left his roller skates, try walking around the house in the dark.

– **Leopold Fechtner**

He's a man who likes to keep his feet on the ground – he sails a lot.

– **Alan Titchmarsh**

A father who writes birthday greetings to his daughter on the inside of an unpeeled banana must be mentally disturbed. But he must also be quite ingenious. Yes, both.

– **Jostein Gaarder**

Creep up behind a nightclub bouncer and hit him over the head with a wet fish. What follows is an example of 'response to stimuli' as well as a sojourn in the intensive care unit of your choice.

– **Russell Bell**

When Dad got mad he never actually hit me. He'd wiggle his waistband and say, 'Do I have to go for the belt?'

– **Jay Leno**

Lloyd George never saw a belt without hitting under it.

– **Margot Asquith**

I don't know who designed the Road Hole at St Andrews, but I hear he's escaped.

– Mark James

Middle age is when you're sitting at home on Saturday night and the telephone rings and you hope it isn't for you.

– Ogden Nash

I'd like to marry a nice domesticated homosexual with a fetish for wiping down formica and different vacuum cleaner attachments.

– Jenny Eclair

People are still willing to do an honest day's work. The trouble is, they want a week's pay for it.

– Joey Adams

Edward Kennedy has just gone on his honeymoon. Now he'll be able to do something he's never been able to do before – check into a hotel under his own name.

– Jay Leno

My girlfriend turns twenty-one next week. In honour of the event I'm going to stop bathing her in the sink.

– Jerry Seinfeld

It is my heart-warmed and world-embracing Christmas hope and aspiration that all of us, the high, the low, the rich, the poor, the admired, the despised, the loved, the hated, the civilized, the savage (every man and brother of us all throughout the whole earth), may eventually be gathered together in a heaven of everlasting rest and peace and bliss, except for the inventor of the telephone.

– Mark Twain

I called the book Men Without Women, hoping it would have a large sale among the fairies and old Vassar Girls.

– Ernest Hemingway

A horse show is a lot of horses showing their asses to a lot of horses' asses showing their horses.
   – **Denis Leary**

Everyone goes into an aeroplane or a hospital wondering if they'll ever get out of either alive.
   – **Richard Gordon**

I remember so clearly us going into hospital so Victoria could have Brooklyn. I was eating a Lion bar at the time.
   – **David Beckham**

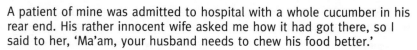

A patient of mine was admitted to hospital with a whole cucumber in his rear end. His rather innocent wife asked me how it had got there, so I said to her, 'Ma'am, your husband needs to chew his food better.'
   – **Jeff Kimball**

Never forget your photographer when visiting a hospital – there may always be a patient who can manage a smile.
   – **Virginia Bottomley**

We were so poor we had no hot water. But it didn't matter because we had no bathtub to put it in anyway.
   – **Tom Dreesen**

There was a girl knocking on my hotel room door all night last night. I finally had to let her out.
   – **Henny Youngman**

I'm not going to stay in that hotel again. The towels were so thick there I could hardly close my suitcase.
   – **Yogi Berra**

Give a man a beer, waste an hour. Teach a man to brew and waste a lifetime.
   – **Bill Owen**

I slept like a baby. Every three hours I woke up looking for a bottle.

– **Liam O'Reilly**

The judge sentenced me to a hundred hours of community work with the mentally disadvantaged. I asked him if I got credit for the time I spent in court.

– **Emo Philips**

I oppose the plan to reform the House of Lords. I will be sad, if I look down after my death and don't see my son asleep on the same benches on which I slept.

– **Lord Onslow**

Grandfather is the wisest person in the house but few of the household listen.

– **Chinese proverb**

I was three over: one over a house, one over a patio, and one over a swimming pool.

– **George Brett**

I am not the boss of my house. I don't know how I lost it. I don't know where I lost it. I don't think I ever had it. But I've seen the boss's job ... and I don't want it.

– **Bill Cosby**

My friends in Christian Coalition, no matter how rough the road may be, we can and we will never, never surrender to what is right.

– **Dan Quayle**

Dramatic art in her opinion is knowing how to fill a sweater.

– **Actor Bette Davis on Jayne Mansfield**

You can learn many things from children. How much patience you have, for instance.

– **Franklin P. Jones**

All your age says about you is how long you've been alive.

– Reverend Dianna Gwilliams

If Shakespeare had been in pro basketball he would never have had time to write his soliloquies. He would always have been in a plane between Phoenix and Kansas City.

– Paul Westhead

I grew up with six brothers. That's how I learned to dance – waiting for the bathroom.

– Bob Hope

Oh, the superb wretchedness of English food. How many foreigners has it daunted, and what a subtle glow of nationality one feels in ordering a dish that one knows will be bad and being able to eat it.

– Cyril Connolly

I miss New York. I still love how people talk to you on the street – just assault you and tell you what they think of your jacket.

– Madonna

My first copies of Treasure Island and Huckleberry Finn still have some blue-spruce needles scattered in the pages. They smell of Christmas still.

– Charlton Heston

Bobby, if you weren't my son, I'd hug you.

– Hank Hill, King of the Hill

The majority of Christmas puddings demand a huge appetite, iron constitution, indomitable will, sense of humour and dash of Christmas spirit.

– Rory Ross

I like my lovers to be female, human and alive, but in a pinch, I'll take any two out of three.

– Emo Philips

Over Christmas lunch I gave Daddy a huge present which I'd wrapped up at the flat. He opened it with glee. In it were six bottles of champagne that Leslie Grade had given me. I'd seen nothing wrong in rewrapping them for Daddy. I'd put a card inside. 'Thank you, Pussycat...' He bent forward to butt me with his forehead when his hand touched something else. He pulled out another card and read, 'To dearest Sarah. Happy Christmas! Love, Leslie Grade.' Father never let that one go.

– **Sarah Miles**

Her face was her chaperone.

– **Rupert Hughes**

If sex is such a natural phenomenon, how come there are so many books on how to?

– **Bette Midler**

Chess is the most elaborate waste of human intelligence outside an advertising agency.

– **Raymond Chandler**

People are far more sincere and good humoured at speeding their parting guests than on meeting them.

– **Anton Chekhov**

A new computer printer can produce two hundred and fifty pages a minute. It certainly cuts down on the paperwork.

– **S.J. Wilcox**

She is in love with her own husband – monstrous, what a selfish woman.

– **Jennie Churchill**

Mrs. Williams has never yet let her husband finish a sentence since his 'I will', at Trinity Church, Plymouth Dock in 1782.

– **Patrick O'Brian**

This film cost $31 million. With that I could have invaded some country.

– **Clint Eastwood**

I had a caesarean section and my husband, an Italian restaurateur, was present throughout. After it was over he whispered to me, 'Lynda, I must tell you... I saw your liver. I know I did. I recognize it from the restaurant.'

– Lynda Bellingham

'Aria' is Italian for 'a song that will not end in your lifetime'.

– Dave Barry

Now I'm over 50 my doctor says I should go out and get more fresh air and exercise. I said, 'All right, I'll drive with the car window open.'

– Angus Walker

Anyone who starts a sentence, 'Of course I can take a joke along with the best of them,' is lying and about to prove it.

– A.A. Gill

I was in a beauty contest once. I not only came in last, I was hit in the mouth by Miss Congeniality.

– Phyllis Diller

Whenever I want a really good meal, I have the most wonderful meatloaf recipe. All I have to do is mention it and my husband takes me out to eat in a terrific restaurant.

– Phyllis Diller

I didn't complain about the steak, dear. I merely said I didn't see that old horse that used to be tethered outside here.

– W.C. Fields

Things I Hate About Christmas: Presents. If I like people enough, I will give them gifts when I want to. The annual manic marathon around department stores is not my idea of heaven on earth. And in exchange for all this effort, gallons of after-shave and miles of nylon socks that take an entire year to burn, bury or otherwise divest.

– Iain Grant

Now that I am no longer President, I find that I do not win every golf game I play.

— **George Bush**

I was such an ugly kid. When I played in the sandbox, the cat kept covering me up.

— **Rodney Dangerfield**

I read Shakespeare and the Bible, and I can shoot dice. That's what I call a liberal education.

— **Tallulah Bankhead**

I think men are very funny. If I had one of those dangly things stuffed down the front of my pants, I'd sit at home all day laughing at myself.

— **Dawn French**

I did not attend his funeral, but I wrote a nice letter saying I approved of it.

— **Mark Twain**

I've never fancied being cremated or buried. I keep hoping I can hold out long enough for someone to discover some new and more suitable medium for my expiry. Evaporation through abstruse sentence, say. Interment in metaphor. Scatter me in words, O my beloved.

— **Howard Jacobson**

My problems all boil down to how I learned about sex. When I was little I asked my father, 'What is a vagina?' He said, 'It's an aerial view of geese.' But then I asked, 'What's a clitoris?' He said, 'It's mouthwash.' So I've spent the rest of my life looking for three women who, by chance, happen to be walking in formation while gargling.

— **Richard Lewis**

I shall not die of a cold. I shall die of having lived.

— **Willa Cather**

What shall I do now I'm retired? I thought I might grow a beard... give me something to do.

   – Victor Meldrew, One Foot in the Grave

I was nearly drafted. It's not that I mind fighting for my country, but they called me up at a ridiculous time: in the middle of a war.

   – Jackie Mason

I used to dread getting older because I thought I would not be able to do all the things I wanted to do, but now that I am older I find that I don't want to do them.

   – Nancy Astor, 80

All the time during the pregnancy when I was supposed to be reading baby books and taking baby classes didn't go totally to waste because I did use the time to shop for the perfect video camera.

   – Paul Reiser

I want my epitaph to be what I once read on my dry cleaning receipt: 'It distresses us to return work that is not perfect.'

   – Peter O'Toole

My father was frightened of his father. I was frightened of my father, and I am damned well going to see to it that my children are frightened of me.

   – King George V

When my screen froze, the manual suggested I reboot the computer. So I kicked it again.

   – Randy Budnikas

I'm not so good a swimmer as I used to be, thanks to evolution.

   – Emo Philips

I get along great with my parents. I still talk to them at least once a week. It's the least I can do. I still live in their house.

   – David Corrado

I married my husband out of spite. I had been let down twice and I decided the next man who asked me would get it.

– **Daisy Attridge**

People who have heard me sing say I don't.

– **Mark Twain**

Around the time I made 9½ Weeks, I was doing lots of interviews in which I talked frankly about sex. My dad sent me a can of tennis balls with this note taped to it: 'Dear Kim, when you give an interview and the feeling of being outrageous is present, place one of these balls in your mouth. If you are still able to say "oral sex" after doing this, then you are hopeless. Love from your loving father better known as Daddy.'

– **Kim Basinger**

It wasn't until I got divorced that I understood the value of money.

– **Melanie B**

Most of what I know about sex I learned from hanging around the gas station as a kid. The first couple of times I heard anyone ask, 'Getting any?' I thought they were talking about fish.

– **Lewis Grizzard**

Like any father, I have moments when I wonder whether I belong to the children or they belong to me.

– **Bob Hope**

It's not that I'm afraid to die. I just don't want to be there when it happens.

– **Woody Allen**

You have no idea how much nastier I would be if I were not a Catholic. Without supernatural aid I would hardly be a human being.

– **Evelyn Waugh**

History will be kind to me, for I intend to write it.

– **Winston Churchill**

The only thing in my life that I regret is that I once saved David Frost from drowning. I had to pull him out, otherwise nobody would have believed I didn't push him in.

– **Peter Cook**

My wife was in the bathroom and I put my Spitting Image puppet into bed and put a sheet over it and hid. She did say that it was actually more active than I was.

– **Steve Davis**

I was incredible in bed last night. I never once had to sit up and consult the manual.

– **Woody Allen**

What a wonderful life I've had! How I wish I had realized it sooner.

– **Colette**

I have a lifetime contract. That means I can't be fired during the third quarter if we're ahead and moving the ball.

– **Lou Holtz**

I am a man of regular habits. I am always in bed by four or five.

– **Oscar Wilde**

Mr Heath envies me two things. First, I have a first-class honours degree. Second, I am a gentleman.

– **Quentin Hogg**

May God defend me from my friends. I can defend myself from my enemies.

– **Voltaire**

Madam, you ask me how I compose. I compose sitting down.

– **Tchaikovsky**

My wife converted me to religion – I didn't believe in Hell until I met her.

— **Henny Youngman**

I like to melt dry ice so I can take a bath without getting wet.

— **Steven Wright**

I've had so much plastic surgery, if I have one more face-lift it will be a caesarean.

— **Phyllis Diller**

Jesus! Look at my hands. Now really, I am too young for liver spots. Maybe I can merge them into a tan.

— **Diane, in Woody Allen's *September***

I can't remember my father at all. I can remember my mother only through a child's eyes. I don't know which fact is the sadder.

— **Clive James**

I was so naïve as a kid, I used to sneak behind the barn and do nothing.

— **Johnny Carson**

When the big natural childbirth moment came, I did what came naturally: I fainted.

— **Alan Thicke**

One of the oddest things in life, I think, is the things one remembers.

— **Agatha Christie**

I became president of Fox Movies when I was 22 years old because my father gave me the studio as a birthday present.

— **Richard Zanuck**

I'm 52 years of age now but I prefer to think of myself as 11 centigrade.

— **Tom Lehrer**

A few perks of old age: things I buy now won't wear out; I enjoy hearing arguments about pensions; my secrets are safe with my friends because they can't remember them either.

– Felicity Muir

I am not part of the problem. I am a Republican.

– Dan Quayle

A lot of people criticize supermodels and I think that's very unfair, because they can't answer back.

– Jo Brand

I was so poor growing up, if I hadn't been born a boy I'd have had nothing to play with on Christmas Day.

– Rodney Dangerfield

On the television programme Call My Bluff, I was aptly nicknamed 'the portly sunbeam'.

– Arthur Marshall

I ran a respectable disorderly house – I let only gentlemen in. I never let in gunmen or convicts.

– Mary Goode

If you could see my legs when I take my boots off, you'd form some idea of what unrequited affection is.

– Charles Dickens

My obstetrician was so dumb that when I gave birth he forgot to cut the cord. For a year that kid followed me everywhere. It was like having a dog on a leash.

– Joan Rivers

I've got to stop taking Viagra because I can't zip up my trousers.

– Richard Harris

We used to terrorize our baby-sitters when I was little, except for my grandfather, because he used to read to us from his will.

– Jan Ditullio

Pancho Gonzales was the most even-tempered man I ever knew. Always mad.

– Ben Thomas

Be funny on the golf course? Do I kid my best friend's mother about her heart condition?

– Phil Silvers

Dad – who was the finest human being I have ever known, but who had the hairstyling skills and fashion flair of a lathe operator – cut my hair. This meant that I spent my critical junior high school years underneath what looked like the pelt of some very sick rodent.

– Dave Barry

Kids are great. They never know when I steal a few of their Smarties.

– Wesley Smith

What do I think about polls? Well, I have a lot of respect for them, especially the way they drink vodka.

– Thelonius Monk

I don't want to find fault, but I wonder if God ever considered having snow fall up?

– Robert Orben

Before I went to see Deep Throat, I thought it was a film about a giraffe.

– Bob Hope

My girlfriend seems to forget the money I spent on her. Christmas, for example, I bought her six pairs of stockings. And later, for her birthday, I had all the stockings darned.

– Groucho Marx

I am getting to an age when I can only enjoy the last sport left. It is called hunting for your spectacles.

– Lord Grey of Falloden

I can't listen to that much Wagner. I start getting the urge to conquer Poland.

– Woody Allen

Are you labouring under the impression that I read those memoranda of yours? I can't even lift them.

– Franklin D. Roosevelt

If I do want children it's because I love Lucy. That's the only way I can think about it. If I try to think of kids in the abstract I very quickly come up against no sleep and vomit in my personal stereo.

– Ben Elton

You've no idea what a poor opinion I have of myself – and how little I deserve it.

– W.S. Gilbert

I have days when I just feel I look like a dog.

– Michelle Pfeiffer

On quiet nights, when I am alone, I like to run our wedding video backwards, just to watch myself walk out of the church a free man.

– George Coote

I don't know who my grandfather was; I am much more concerned to know what his grandson will be.

– Abraham Lincoln

When I was young I was frightened I might bore people. Now I'm old I am frightened they will bore me.

– Ruth Adam

All right, since your parents are coming, I did the standard pre-parent sweep. Which means if you're looking for your 'neck massager' it's under the bed.

— **Jimmy Cox**

Family parties? Friends' ones? Just the same, i.e. just the same as last Yule's, give or take the odd divorce or headstone, what's your son doing, mine's doing this, how was Tuscany, Provence was great, did you change cars, nor did I, is your hernia still playing up, I must sort out this bloody cartilage, what about the Budget, then, what about QPR?

— **Alan Coren**

Most people are crazy about cars, but I'd rather have a goddamn horse. A horse is at least human, for Christ's sake.

— **J.D. Salinger**

If it wasn't for the rectal probe I'd have no sex life at all.

— **Barry Cryer**

I like dolphins. If dolphins were human, I'd like to be a dolphin.

— **Jason Donovan**

I can't wait to have a kid. I'll introduce them to classical music like Hendrix and the Rolling Stones.

— **Roger Howe**

I don't have a boyfriend right now. I'm looking for anyone with a job that I don't have to support.

— **Anna Nicole Smith**

He can run any time he wants. I'm giving him the red light.

— **Yogi Berra**

Sometimes being a father is like repossession. I'm possessed by the spirit of my late father. 'Don't do that!' All of a sudden, 'Oh, my God, I've turned into my dad.'

— **Robin Williams**

I love my dad, Steve Tyler, although I'm definitely critical of him sometimes, like when his pants are too tight. We have slumber parties, and when we can't sleep we stay up all-night trading beauty tips. He knows all about the good creams and masks.

    – Liv Tyler

Bless me father for I have sinned. I'm just in here to develop the film.

    – Emo Philips

But Dad, I've had loads of life-experience. I'm 18 years old. I've been to sleep-away camps. I had a goldfish who died. I even got on the wrong bus once.

    – Corenna, Boy Meets World

At my age, I'm often asked if I'm frightened of death and my reply is always, I can't remember being frightened of birth.

    – Peter Ustinov

With them I'm Jack Nicholson. Without them I'm fat and 60.

    – Jack Nicholson on his trademark sunglasses

I've outlived most of my body, and I'm trying so hard – oh, God, I've had so many things done to my body, when I die God won't know me.

    – Phyllis Diller

Personally I know nothing about sex because I've always been married.

    – Zsa Zsa Gabor

I don't know why it is, but I've never been able to bear with fortitude anything in the shape of a child with golden curls. Confronted with one, I feel the urge to step on him or drop things from a height.

    – P.G. Wodehouse

No, I never broke my nose playing ice hockey; but eleven other guys did.

    – Gordie Howe

He had a degree so he could ice cakes with joined-up writing.

– **Evelyn Waugh**

When they asked George Washington for his ID, he just took out a quarter.

– **Steven Wright**

Never fret for an only son. The idea of failure will never occur to him.

– **George Bernard Shaw**

Marrying for love is a very recent idea. In the old country, they didn't marry for love. A man married a woman because he needed an extra mule.

– **Woody Allen**

He who lends a book is an idiot. He who returns a lent book is an even bigger idiot.

– **Joel Rosenberg**

Politics would be a helluva good business if it weren't for the people.

– **Richard Nixon**

Ashes to ashes and clay to clay; if the enemy don't get you, your own folk may.

– **James Thurber**

What a man Balzac would have been if he had known how to write.

– **Gustave Flaubert**

I couldn't have been more besotted than if it had been the Baby Jesus himself; in fact, I fully expected the christening gifts to be gold, frankincense and myrrh.

– **Mitchell Hoyle**

I wouldn't piss down Jerry Brown's throat if his heart was on fire.

– **James Carville**

Men have higher body temperatures than women. If your heating goes out in winter, I recommend sleeping next to a man. Men are basically portable heaters that snore.

— **Rita Rudner**

I played Santa Claus many times, and if you don't believe it, check out the divorce settlements awarded my wives.

— **Groucho Marx**

They say that every snowflake is different. If that were true, how could the world go on? How could we ever get up off our knees? How could we ever recover from the wonder of it?

— **Jeanette Winterson**

Bryant Gumbel's ego has applied for statehood. If it's accepted it will be the fifth largest.

— **Willard Scott**

I play golf in the low eighties. If it's any hotter than that, I won't play.

— **Joe E. Lewis**

In football it is widely accepted that if both sides agree to cheat then cheating is fair.

— **Charles B. Fry**

During my army medical, they asked me if I was homosexual. I said I wasn't but I was willing to learn.

— **Bill Murray**

Don't talk about Michael Johnson's style. Look, if that guy ran with his fingers up his bum he could still run 42 seconds for 400 metres.

— **Roger Black**

I dislike blasphemy on purely rational grounds. If there is no God, blasphemy is stupid and unnecessary; if there is, it's damned dangerous.

— **Flann O'Brien**

You know you're on a bad date if he gets really angry when you tell him you like his Siamese twin brother better.

    – David Letterman

I wouldn't give somebody my last Rolo if they were in a diabetic coma.

    – Jo Brand

There are some sure-fire ways to tell if your date is too young for you. Can he fly for half-fare? Are his love letters to you written in crayon? Do his pyjamas have feet? When you ask him a question does he raise his hand before answering?

    – Phyllis Diller

Shopping is better than sex. At least if you're not satisfied, you can exchange it for something you really like.

    – Adrienne E. Gusoff

When you win the toss, bat first. If you are in doubt about it, think, then bat first. If you have very big doubts, consult a colleague... then bat first.

    – W.G. Grace

Playing golf with the President is handy. If you hit a ball into the rough and it drops near a tree, the tree becomes a Secret Service man and moves away.

    – Bob Hope

A bad cold wouldn't be so annoying if it weren't for the advice of our friends.

    – Kin Hubbard

After all, I'm your father. It's true if it hadn't been me it would have been someone else. But that's no excuse.

    – Samuel Beckett

I hear Joad has rediscovered God: I imagine he pronounces it with a soft G and a long O.

– Lowes Dickinson

The cure [for Christmas] is to simply ignore it. You have to put up with about four years of disgrace when you receive Christmas cards and do not send them, but after that you know that the people who send you Christmas cards are doing it to please you and that they don't expect a reply.

– Quentin Crisp

The best way to adjust – no, ignore – most of the negative thoughts about ageing is to say to yourself, with conviction, 'I am still the very same person I have been all of my adult life.' You are, you know.

– Helen Hayes

Russia's a little bit like a critically ill patient. You have to get up every day and take the pulse and hope that nothing catastrophic happened the night before.

– Condoleezza Rice

I have no sense of humour. In illustration of this fact I will say this – by way of confession – that if there is a humorous passage in the Pickwick Papers, I have never been able to find it.

– Mark Twain

It was George Hamilton who said the immortal line, 'Joan, better to be a shrewd businesswoman than a screwed actress.'

– Joan Collins

A father is something mythical and infinitely important: a protector, who keeps a lid on all the chaotic and catastrophic possibilities of life.

– Tom Wolfe

Men have children to prove they aren't impotent, or at least that some of their friends aren't.

– P.J. O'Rourke

If you imagine a Scotch commercial traveller in a Scotch commercial hotel leaning on the bar and calling the barmaid Dearie, then you will know the keynote of Burns' verse.

– A.E. Housman

The Vice-President is a man who sits in the outer office of the White House, hoping to hear the President sneeze.

– **H.L. Mencken**

The only time a woman really succeeds in changing a man is when he's a baby.

– **Natalie Wood**

Illegal aliens have always been a problem in the United States. Ask any Indian.

– **Robert Orben**

My brother-in-law must be the unluckiest man in the world. He had a kidney transplant and he got one from a bed-wetter.

– **Roy Brown**

If it must be true because it's in the newspapers, what about my horoscope?

– **George Thomas**

It has long been my belief that in times of great stress, such as a four-day vacation, the thin veneer of family wears off almost at once, and we are revealed in our true personalities.

– **Shirley Jackson**

I have not been to see Irving in Faust. I go to the pantomime only at Christmas.

– **W.S. Gilbert**

The train has been punctual for once in its life. How shocked the directors would be if they knew it, but, of course, it will be kept from them.

– **Oscar Wilde**

Sure there have been deaths and injuries in boxing, but none of them serious.

– **Alan Winter**

A truly great book should be read in youth, again in maturity and once more in old age, as a fine building should be seen by morning light, at noon and by moonlight.

– Robertson Davies

Footnotes in a book are as banknotes in the stockings of a harlot.

– Walter Benjamin

Large increases in cost with questionable increases in performances can be tolerated only in racehorses and women.

– William Thomson

By tonight my dad will be back in front of the TV in his beer-stained, flea-infested, duct-taped reclining chair, adjusting his shorts with one hand and cheering on Jean Claude Van Damme with the other.

– Frasier Crane, Frasier

We all knew Dad was the one in charge: he had control of the remote.

– Raymond Bell

Suicide is much easier and more acceptable in Hollywood than growing old gracefully.

– Julie Burchill

David Attenborough informs, entertains and educates, sometimes in the presence of unbelievable quantities of bat faeces.

– Lynne Truss

I am very fond of women, but in an orchestra, if they're not good-looking – and often they're not and they always look worse when they're blowing – it puts me off; while if they are good-looking it puts me off a damn sight more.

– Thomas Beecham

I think the husband should always be in the delivery room. Along with the child's father.

– Maureen Murphy

What have I got against having children? In the first place there isn't enough room. In the second place they seem to start by mucking up their parents' lives, and then go on in the third place to muck up their own. In the fourth place it doesn't seem right to bring them into a world like this. In the fifth place and in the sixth place I don't like them very much in the first place. OK?

– Simon Gray, Otherwise Engaged

We used to have fire drill practice in my house. Everyone had their own special duty. My dad had to get the pets, my mom took the jewellery, my brother ran to get help. They told me to save the washer and dryer.

– Ellen DeGeneres

... a few home truths about Christmas in the countryside: Contrary to Christmas card lore, it doesn't always snow on Christmas Day. Nor does a coach and horses stop outside the local pub; the large brown quadrupeds with horns are roe deer, not reindeer; a Christmas Day walk is compulsory unless it clashes with the Queen's Speech or the James Bond film; do not drink from bottles with the hand-written label 'Home Farm Sloe Gin' or similar.

– Adam Edwards

At my age I like threesomes – in case one of us dies.

– Rodney Dangerfield

As a psychiatrist, I can take comfort in the fact that without embarrassing parents, there'd be no psychology.

– Frasier Crane, Frasier

The great thing is not to believe in Santa Claus; it is to be Santa Claus.

– Pat Boone

From experience, I know that anything ending in '-os' on a restaurant menu is pronounced 'heartburn'.

– Hugh Leonard

I'd like Jennifer Lopez to play me in a film of my life.

– Kacey Ainsworth

I spend a lot of my life in the back of cars – Oops! I didn't mean that in the way it sounded. Like, hence the two kids.

– Kerry McFadden, pop singer

To get a man's attention, just stand in front of the TV and don't move. He'll talk to you, I promise.

– Tim Allen

To keep your marriage brimming, With love in the loving cup, Whenever you're wrong admit it; Whenever you're right, shut up.

– Ogden Nash

A boy does not put his hand in his pocket until every other means of gaining his end has failed.

– J.M. Barrie

There is absolutely nothing to be said in favour of growing old. There ought to be legislation against it.

– Patrick Moore

The three ages of man: he believes in Santa Claus; he doesn't believe in Santa Claus; he is Santa Claus.

– Donald Guthrie

The major achievement of the women's movement in the nineteen-seventies was the Dutch treat.

– Nora Ephron

The only lack of refinement I remember in my father was an unconscious habit he had, while reading his newspaper in his armchair, of picking his nose abstractedly and rolling the little bit of snot between his thumb and forefinger.

– J.R. Ackerley

Hospitals generally prefer people not to die in them. It disturbs the other patients and depresses the nurses.

– Germaine Greer

As you grow old, you lose interest in sex, your friends drift away, and your children often ignore you. There are other advantages, of course, but these are the outstanding ones.

– **Richard Needham**

The second sight possessed by the Highlanders in Scotland is actually a foreknowledge of future events. I believe they possess this gift because they don't wear trousers.

– **Georg C. Lichtenberg**

I found this priceless piece of advice in a childcare book dated 1595: 'A mouse roasted and given to children to eat remedieth pissing the bed.' So now you know.

– **Reg Collins**

In a 1956 production of King Lear in New York, Orson Welles, who had fractured his ankle in a fall, played the title role from a wheelchair.

– **Mark Fowler**

Dickensian Christmas: Costumed Rotarians may approach you in the street for money and won't take 'sod Victorian values' for an answer.

– **Malcolm Burgess**

Personally, I can't see where the difficulty in choosing suitable presents lies. No boy who had brought himself up properly could fail to appreciate one of those decorative bottles of liqueurs... And then, of course, there are liqueur glasses, and crystallized fruits, and tapestry curtains and heaps of other necessaries of life that make really sensible presents – not to speak of luxuries, such as having one's bills paid, or getting something quite sweet in the way of jewellery. Unlike the alleged Good Woman of the Bible, I'm not above rubies.

– **Saki**

I have never seen an old person in a new bathing suit in my life. I don't know where they get their bathing suits, but my father has bathing suits from other centuries. If I forget mine, he always wants me to wear his.

– **Jerry Seinfeld**

Vegetarians have wicked, shifty eyes and laugh in a cold, calculating manner. They pinch little children, steal stamps, drink water and grow beards.

– J.B. Morton

This afternoon I slept for two hours in the Library of the House of Commons. A House of Commons sleep – rich, deep and guilty.

– Henry Channon

Any dish that tastes good with capers in it, tastes even better with capers not in it.

– Nora Ephron

The fulminations of the missionaries about sex in Listowel will have as little effect as the droppings of an underweight blackbird on the water-level of the Grand Coulee Dam.

– Eamon Keane

The aim of the music hall is, in fact, to cheer the lower classes up by showing them a life uglier and more sordid than their own.

– Max Beerbohm

There's snow on the fields, And cold in the cottage, While I sit in the chimney nook, Supping hot pottage.

– Christina Rossetti

There are only three ages for women in Hollywood: Babe, District Attorney, and Driving Miss Daisy.

– Goldie Hawn

When Father went to church and sat in his pew, he felt he was doing enough. Any further spiritual work ought to be done by the clergy.

– Clarence Day

If you want to spend your money in a way that really shows, buy rich food.

– Beth Gurney

The police officer told me to walk in a straight line. And when I had finished he said, 'You call that a straight line?' I shouldn't have, but I replied, 'The closest you'll ever come to a straight line is if they ever do an electroencephalogram of your brainwave.'

   – Emo Philips

Although the so-called tradition of putting money in the pudding isn't really an ancient custom at all, it's just a Yuletide conspiracy dreamed up by orthodontists, who know that coins hidden in food have an unerring ability to locate and crack a weak tooth, thereby enabling emergency dentists to charge quadruple fees on Boxing Day, so they can buy that nice new BMW they've had their eye on all year...

   – Victor Lewis-Smith

When a kid turns 13, stick him in a barrel, nail the lid shut, and feed him through the knothole. When he turns 16, plug the hole.

   – Mark Twain

A male gets very, very frustrated sitting in a chair all the time because males are biologically driven to go out and hunt giraffes.

   – Newt Gingrich

Then came the war: North Africa, promoted in the field (they wouldn't let me indoors). Mentioned in dispatches: nothing positive. Just mentioned.

   – Spike Milligan

They say, 'If you want a friend in Washington, buy a dog,' but I didn't need one because I have Barbara.

   – George Bush

I always feel you can do Europe in a wheelchair.

   – Erma Bombeck

You know when you put a stick in the water and it looks like it's bent but it really isn't? That's why I don't take baths.

   – Steven Wright

The one thing you will never find in a teenager's bedroom is the floor.
– **Bruce Lansky**

I've saved enough money to pay my income tax, now all I have to do is to borrow some to live on.
– **Lou Costello**

He will lie even when it is inconvenient, the sign of the true artist.
– **Gore Vidal**

In restaurants, the hardness of the butter increases in direct proportion to the softness of the bread being served.
– **Harriet Markman**

Metaphysics is an attempt to prove the incredible by an appeal to the unintelligible.
– **H.L. Mencken**

Bookie Bob is a very hard guy indeed. In fact, the softest thing about him are his front teeth.
– **Damon Runyon**

When asked by an anthropologist what the Indians called America before the white man came, an Indian said simply 'Ours'.
– **Vine Deloira**

Snow is falling outside my window, and indoors all around me half a hundred garden catalogues are in bloom.
– **Katharine S. White**

John Barnes' problem is that he gets injured appearing on A Question of Sport.
– **Tommy Docherty**

One of the cardinal rules of travel is 'stay the hell out of Paraguay.'
– **Dave Barry**

I don't agree with all this artificial insemination. I prefer the old-fashioned way of having children. By accident.

– **Rick Stone**

I was glad to get a letter instead of a Christmas card. A Christmas card is a rather innutritious thing.

– **Oscar W. Firkins**

A criminal is a person with predatory instincts who has not sufficient capital to form a corporation.

– **Howard Scott**

A recipe is a series of step-by-step instructions for preparing ingredients you forgot to buy in utensils you don't own to make a dish the dog won't eat the rest of.

– **Henry Beard**

I took a physical for some life insurance. All they would give me was fire and theft.

– **Milton Berle**

A father is always making his baby into a little woman. And when she is a woman he turns her back again.

– **Enid Bagnold**

How do pebbles know how to get into a shoe, but never know how to get out?

– **Casper Dante**

Jocky Wilson is the minimum of mass into which a human being can be contracted.

– **Nancy Banks-Smith**

Elections are held to delude the populace into believing that they are participating in government.

– **Gerald Lieberman**

A script of Brideshead Revisited needs an intravenous dose of syrup of figs or just a bullet.

– **A.A. Gill**

I should like to see a custom introduced of readers who are pleased with a book sending the author some small cash token: anything between half-a-crown and a hundred pounds. Not more than a hundred pounds – that would be bad for my character – not less than half-a-crown – that would do no good to yours.

– **Cyril Connolly**

Practically every game played internationally today was invented in Britain, and when foreigners became good enough to match or even defeat the British, the British quickly invented a new game.

– **Peter Ustinov**

Hugh Fearnley-Whittingstall's A River Cottage Christmas Feast involves a woodcock cooked inside a pigeon, inside a pheasant, inside a duck, inside a goose, inside a turkey. This was first shown last year, so it will be a repeat, and in more senses than one for anyone reckless enough to eat this motorway pile-up of poultry.

– **Paul Hoggart**

Extremist Catholics and extremist Protestants in Northern Ireland are getting together to get rid of ecumenism.

– **Patrick Murray**

I once saw this sign on an Irish lift: 'Please do not use this when it is not working.'

– **Spike Milligan**

Grey-haired men look 'distinguished'? Surely the word is 'extinguished'. I'm so grey, I look like I'm gonna rain.

– **Julie Burchill**

My notion of a wife at 40 is that a man should be able to change her, like a bank note, for two 20s.

– **Douglas Jerrold**

The best thing about the rainforests is that they never suffer from drought.

   – Dan Quayle

The irritating thing about badly behaved children is that they so often make as orderly and valuable men and women as the other kind.

   – Mark Twain

The nice thing about being a celebrity is that if you bore people they think it's their fault.

   – Henry Kissinger

The great thing about having a kid is they never ask, 'Do these Huggies make my bum look big?'

   – Rod Lake

For all the advances in medicine, there is still no cure for the common birthday.

   – John Glenn

The most delightful advantage of being bald is that one can hear snowflakes.

   – R.G. Daniels

One of the advantages of living alone is that you don't have to wake up in the arms of a loved one.

   – Marion Smith

Loving your neighbour as much as yourself is practically impossible. You might as well have a commandment that states, 'Thou shalt fly.'

   – John Cleese

The way to beat Osama bin Laden is through humiliation. The CIA should kidnap him, give him a sex change operation and send him back to Afghanistan.

   – Sean Moncrieff

The main difference between men and women is that men are lunatics and women are idiots.

– **Rebecca West, novelist**

The only real blind person at Christmastime is he who has not Christmas in his heart.

– **Helen Keller**

One accusation you cannot throw at me is that I've always done my best.

– **Alan Shearer**

The bowling of Cunis, like his name, is neither one thing nor another.

– **John Arlott**

One of the disadvantages of having children is that they eventually get old enough to give you presents they make at school.

– **Robert Byrne**

There is no doubt... that being prepared is the secret of a more harmonious Christmas. If Joseph had booked a room in advance, Jesus would not have been born in a stable.

– **Jilly Cooper**

At seventy-eight, my favourite slow sex position is called 'The Plumber'. You stay in all day, but nobody comes.

– **John Mortimer**

If your adversary is badly bunkered, there is no rule against your standing over him and counting his strokes aloud, with increasing gusto as their number mounts up; but it will be a wise precaution to arm yourself with the niblick before doing so, so as to meet him on equal terms.

– **Horace Hutchinson**

The trouble with fighting for human freedom is that you have to spend much of your life defending sons-of-bitches.

– **H.L. Mencken**

There is a fountain of youth: it is your mind, your talents, the creativity you bring to your life and to the lives of the people you love.
— **Sophia Loren**

Honesty is a good thing but it is not profitable to its possessor unless it is kept under control.
— **Don Marquis**

The only time he tells the truth is when he admits he's lying.
— **Gene Autry**

You can tell how bad a musical is by the number of times the chorus yells "hooray".
— **John Crosby**

Have you any idea how difficult it is to be a father? Children forget that although they have no previous experience of being children, their fathers have no previous experience of being fathers.
— **Peter Ustinov**

Is my friend in the bunker or is the bastard on the green?
— **David Feherty**

The little trouble in the world that is not due to love is due to friendship.
— **E.W. Howe**

The hardest task in a girl's life is to prove to a man that his intentions are serious.
— **Helen Rowland**

If our child is a boy, he is to be named James; if a girl, it would be kinder to drown her.
— **Evelyn Waugh**

Why does a man want a child? Is it to perpetuate the species? Is the child a pet substitute? Is it to prove that he has had sex at least once?
— **Jeremy Hardy**

Lawyers should never marry other lawyers. This is called inbreeding, from which come idiot children and more lawyers.

– **Ruth Gordon**

My dad taught me, 'What you see is what you get – except in pre-packaged strawberries.'

– **H. Jackson Brown Jr**

The Marxist law of distribution of wealth is that shortages will be divided equally among the peasants.

– **John Gujtason**

The starting pay of an American pilot is $16,800. Never let somebody fly you up in the air who makes less than the kid at Taco Bell.

– **Michael Moore**

Some people's idea of keeping a secret is lowering their voice when they tell it.

– **Franklin Adams**

Next to children on a trip, there is nothing more trying than their father. He doesn't go on a trip to enjoy the scenery and relax. He's on a virtual test-run to prove his car's performance in a grinding show of speed and endurance equalled only on the salt flats testing grounds.

– **Erma Bombeck**

I've noticed that one thing about parents is that no matter what stage your child is in, the parents who have older children always tell you the next stage is worse.

– **Dave Barry**

The trouble with opera is that there is always too much singing.

– **Claude Debussy**

Going to the opera, like getting drunk, is a sin that carries its own punishment with it.

– **Hannah More**

That so many people respond to me is fabulous. It's like having a kind of Alzheimer's disease where everyone knows you and you don't know anyone.

– **Tony Curtis**

Journalism is a profession whose business it is to explain to others what it personally does not understand.

– **Lord Northcliff**

I love Christmas pudding, particularly if it is sliced and fried in butter the next day! At the end of the meal when you are all flagging, suddenly the lights go off and someone brings through a flaming pudding, it brings another 'wow!' moment.

– **Clarissa Dickson Wright**

Any money I put on a horse is a sort of insurance policy to prevent it from winning.

– **Frank Richardson**

The most popular question for small children is 'Why?' They can use it anywhere and it's usually impossible to answer: CHILD: What's that? YOU: It's a goat. CHILD: Why?

– **Dave Barry**

The only time Ray Wilkins goes forward is to toss the coin.

– **Tommy Docherty**

The thing to remember about Cyril Connolly is that he is not as nice as he looks.

– **Maurice Bowra**

I am a rock music producer. It is an honour and a privilege to be in the same business as Wagner and Elgar.

– **Pete Waterman**

Telling a teenager the facts of life is like giving a fish a bath.

– **Arnold Glasgow**

The secret of salvation in old age is this: keep sweet, keep useful, and keep busy.

– **Elbert Hubbard**

One of the signs of old age is that you have to carry your senses around in your handbag – glasses, hearing aid, dentures, etc.

– **Kurt Strauss**

How firstborns ever survive their parents' attention is beyond me. I tested the warmth of formulas from dusk to dawn, it seemed. We were so germ-conscious my wife even sterilized the skin of oranges before squeezing them.

– **Malcolm Forbes**

All that you suspect about women's friendships is true. We talk about dick size.

– **Cynthia Heimel**

Another reason girls talk earlier than boys is breastfeeding. Boys would rather breastfeed than talk because they know they won't be getting that close again for another fifteen years.

– **Paul Seaburn**

The problem with the designated driver program is that it's not a desirable job. But if you ever get sucked into doing it, have fun with it. At the end of the night, drop everybody off at the wrong house.

– **Jeff Foxworthy**

The heart of the airport security system is the metal detector, a device that shoots invisible rays into your body. According to security personnel, these rays are perfectly harmless, although you notice that THEY never go through the metal detector. In fact, when nobody's around, they use it to cook their lunch.

– **Dave Barry**

The only good thing about the theatre is that you can leave at the interval.

– **Philip Larkin**

Perhaps passing through the gates of death is like passing quietly through the gate in a pasture fence. On the other side, you keep walking, without the need to look back. No shock, no drama, just the lifting of a plank or two in a simple wooden gate in a clearing. Neither pain, nor floods of light, not great voices, but just the silent crossing of a meadow.

  – **Mark Helperin**

The really frightening thing about middle age is the knowledge that you'll grow out of it.

  – **Doris Day**

The reason grandparents and grandchildren get along so well is that they have a common enemy.

  – **Sam Levenson**

Sixty minutes of thinking of any kind is bound to lead to confusion and unhappiness.

  – **James Thurber**

My rule of thumb for Christmas-like occasions is to try to acknowledge my own ambivalent feelings, and to develop low expectations... One family I heard of had an even better suggestion. Each member was to have their own little foil-wrapped gift on the Christmas tree. In it lay a bottle of Valium.

  – **Ann Karpf**

The chief objection to playing wind instruments is that it prolongs the life of the player beyond all reasonable limits.

  – **George Bernard Shaw**

The best way to cure a hangover is to avoid alcohol the night before.

  – **Cathy Hopkins**

Having your book turned into a movie is like seeing your oxen turned into bouillon cubes.

  – **John Le Carré**

An extra trip to the DIY store is always needed to complete the job.
- **Douglas Donahue**

The time not to become a father is 18 years before a world war.
- **E.B. White**

The only man who thinks Phyllis Diller is a ten is a shoe salesman.
- **Bob Hope**

I don't know why the Yankees' record is so bad this season. I wish I knew because I'm getting tired of answering that question.
- **Yogi Berra**

There is little wife-swapping in suburbia. It is unnecessary, the females all being so similar.
- **Richard Gordon**

My only problem with the death penalty is its name. We are all going to die, so it should just be called 'the early death penalty'.
- **John Malkovich**

A Jewish man with parents still alive is a 15-year-old boy, and will remain a 15-year-old boy until they die.
- **Philip Roth**

'When I was your age...' No one is ever anyone else's age, except physically.
- **Faith Baldwin**

Perfectly managed Christmas correct in every detail is, like basted inside seams and letters answered by return, a sure sign of someone who hasn't enough to do.
- **Katharine Whitehorn**

One cannot touch a fig leaf without it turning into a price tag.
- **Saul Bellow**

My grandma told me, 'The good news is, after menopause the hair on your legs gets really thin and you don't have to shave anymore. Which is great because it means you have more time to work on your new moustache.'

– Karen Haber

Cystitis is a living death, it really is. Nobody ever talks about it, but if I was faced with a choice between having my arms removed and getting cystitis, I'd wave goodbye to my arms quite happily.

– Louise Wesner

People ask me what my favourite colour is. I'd say blue. But you certainly wouldn't want a girl to be that colour after a bout of lovemaking. Who needs that again?

– Emo Philips

To wear your heart on your sleeve isn't a very good plan; you should wear it inside, where it functions best.

– Margaret Thatcher

I went to a girls' school and it made me so stupid that I could barely remember how to breathe.

– India Knight

Whatever a man's age, he can reduce it several years by putting a bright-coloured flower in his buttonhole.

– Mark Twain

Whatever else can be said about sex, it cannot be called a dignified performance.

– Helen Lawrenson

When a man falls into his anecdotage, it is a sign for him to retire from the world.

– Benjamin Disraeli

Marriage is but for a little while. It is alimony that is forever.

   – Quentin Crisp

The older you get, the more important it is not to act your age.

   – Ashleigh Brilliant

You can be glamorous at any age. It is not the prerogative of the young. In fact, the self-confidence of experience is an added bonus.

   – Joan Collins

One problem with growing older is that it gets increasingly tougher to find a famous historical figure who didn't amount to much when he was your age.

   – Bill Vaughan

The Germans – if they can't stuff it into an animal casing, they won't eat it.

   – Tim Allen

They say Hell is hot, but is it humid? Because I can take the heat; it's the humidity I can't stand.

   – Ronnie Shakes

It's so tiring making love to women, it takes forever. I'm too lazy to be a lesbian.

   – Camille Paglia

There are many people – happy people, it usually appears – whose thoughts at Christmas always turn to books. The notion of a Christmas tree with no books under it is repugnant and unnatural to them.

   – Robertson Davies

I like Wagner's music better than anybody's. It is so loud that one can talk the whole time without other people hearing what one says.

   – Oscar Wilde

Where large sums of money are concerned, it is advisable to trust nobody.

– Agatha Christie

The worst aspect of marriage is that it makes a woman believe that other men are just as easy to fool.

– H.L. Mencken

Very few people possess true artistic ability. It is therefore both unseemly and unproductive to irritate the situation by making an effort. If you have a burning, restless urge to write or paint, simply eat something sweet and the feeling will pass.

– Fran Lebowitz

I married Frank Sinatra because what would it have looked like if I didn't?

– Ava Gardner

We lost the test through fifteen-man rugby. It was just that we didn't have the ball.

– Ian McGeechan

The trouble with the Internet is that it is replacing masturbation as a leisure activity.

– Patrick Murray

What do I think of Dustin Hoffman? It taught me never to work with any actor smaller than his Oscar.

– Larry Gelbart

Christmas is being together – gathering together. It is the time of the heart's inventory. It is the time of going home in many ways.

– William Saroyan

I think she's unpleasant, a right snob. It would be unoriginal for her to have a go at me now.

– Tara Palmer-Tomkinson on Lady Victoria Hervey

Roses are red, Violets are bluish. If it weren't for Christmas, We'd all be Jewish.

– **Tracy Ullman**

Sure the fight was fixed. I fixed it with my right hand.

– **George Foreman**

My father's technique was much harder than it looked, like most works of art. If a kid was rude to him, he was usually rude right back: 'I wouldn't take it from a grown-up; why should I take it from you?'

– **Wilfred Sheed**

It doesn't matter who my father was; it matters who I remember he was.

– **Anne Sexton**

A man and wife should never have it in their power to hang one another.

– **George Farquhar**

Parenting is like your Aunt Edna's ass. It goes on for ever and it's just as frightening.

– **Frank Buckman, Parenthood**

The people of Zaire are not thieves. It merely happens that they move things, or borrow them.

– **Sese Mobuto**

You should always be missing some buttons. It's part of your boyish bachelor charm. Many a woman has sat down on the living-room couch to sew a button and has wound up doing something more interesting on another piece of furniture elsewhere in the room.

– **P .J. O'Rourke**

Maybe, when you come to think about it, grown-ups need Father Christmas far more than children do.

– **Anon**

This door can be closed without slamming it. Try it and see how clever you are.

– **Spike Milligan**

A lovely thing about Christmas is that it's compulsory, like a thunderstorm, and we all go through it together.

– **Garrison Keillor**

Marriage is not a man's idea. A woman must have thought of it. 'Let me get this straight, honey. I can't sleep with anyone else for the rest of my life, and if things don't work out, you get to keep half of my stuff? What a great idea.'

– **Bobby Shayton**

Oh God. I can't bear Sebastian Faulks. It's just Mills and Boon with guns!

– **Isabel Wolff**

It isn't that I'm a weak father, it's just that Jane's a strong daughter! .

– **Henry Fonda**

I love Christmas in Miami. Oh, sure, it's not like Christmas up north. We don't have Jack Frost nipping at our nose; we have Harvey Heat Rash nipping at our underwear regions. And we never look outside on Christmas morning to discover that the landscape has been magically transformed by a blanket of white, unless a cocaine plane has crashed on our lawn.

– **Dave Barry**

My favourite chair is a wicker chair. It's my favourite chair because I stole it. I was at a party, a very crowded party, and when no one was looking I went over to it and I unravelled it and stuck it through the keyhole in the door. The girl who was in it was almost killed.

– **Steven Wright**

Grab the penis, it breaks the ice, it's kind of a fun friendly thing to do!

– **Cynthia Heimel**

When it's three o'clock in New York, it's still 1938 in London.

– Bette Midler

Son, when you participate in sporting events, it's not whether you win or lose, it's how drunk you get.

– Homer Simpson

I hope my phone is still tapped. It's my only remaining link with the establishment.

– Tony Benn

Methodism is not really a religion – it's just a sort of insurance policy in case there does turn out to be a God.

– Peter Barr

How do you tell a communist? Well, it's someone who reads Marx and Lenin. And how do you tell an anti-communist? It's someone who understands Marx and Lenin.

– Ronald Reagan

Marriage is a very good thing, but it's a mistake to make a habit of it.

– Somerset Maugham

A woman is the second most important item in a bedroom.

– Paul Hogan

The Miss World Contest has always had its fair share of knockers.

– Julia Morley

My friend's baby had an accident in its diaper. The mother comes over and says, 'Oh, how adorable. Brandon made a gift for Daddy.' I'm thinking this guy must be real easy to shop for on Father's Day.

– Garry Shandling

I'm a light eater. As soon as it's light I start to eat.

– Art Donovan

A boy is Truth with dirt on its face, Beauty with a cut on its finger, Wisdom with bubble gum in its hair and Hope of the future with a frog in its pocket.

– Alan Beck

Albeit snow is very beautiful when falling, its loveliness passes away very shortly afterward. The grand poetical result is merely chilblains and slush.

– Mark Twain

Christmas – that magic blanket that wraps itself about us, that something so intangible it is like a fragrance.

– Augusta E. Rundel

Why does not science, instead of troubling itself about sunspots, which nobody ever saw, or if they did, ought not to speak about, busy itself with drainage and sanitary engineering?

– Oscar Wilde

I've trusted men all my life and I've never been deceived yet – except by my husbands and they don't count.

– Mary Boland

This film wasn't released, it escaped.

– James Caan

No one loves a Christmas tree on January 1. The wonderful soft branches that the family couldn't wait to get inside to smell have turned into rapiers that jab you. The wonderful blinking lights that Daddy arranged by branch and colour have knotted themselves hopelessly around crumbling brownery and have to be severed with a bread knife. The stockings that hung by the chimney with care are hanging out of sofa cushions, and they smell like clam dip. And the angel that everyone fought to put on top of the tree can only be removed with an extension ladder that is in the garage, and no one can remember how to fit it through the door.

– Erma Bombeck

With the money I spent to have JFK elected I could have elected my chauffeur.

– Joe Kennedy

Never trust a man with testicles.

– Jo Brand

Several years ago, I was in a job that I was about to be sacked from. Right before I left, we were asked to participate in a Christmas pot-luck party to which we would bring anonymous presents to be exchanged with other presents... My contribution was a roll of toilet paper, a vodka bottle half-filled with water, a voodoo doll and a gift certificate to an adult bookstore. At least it made my parting with the company sweet.

– Andrew Gallagher

My father always told me, 'Find a job you love and you'll never have to work a day in your life.'

– Jina Fox

The only reason I would take up jogging is so I could hear heavy breathing again.

– Erma Bombeck

A prune is an experienced plum.

– John Trattner

Sex during pregnancy – sometimes the foetus joined in and jived about a bit, so it was like doing it with someone else in the room.

– Michael Rosen

This is a youth-orientated society, and the joke is on them because youth is a disease from which we all recover.

– Dorothy Fuldheim

What woman hasn't felt that her life's journey is part meat market, part catwalk?

– Barbara Ellen

The only qualities for real success in journalism are rat-like cunning, a plausible manner and a little literary ability. The capacity to steal other people's ideas and phrases – the one about rat-like cunning was invented by my colleague Murray Sayle – is also invaluable.

  – Nicholas Tomalin

Age 17 is the point in the journey when the parents retire to the observation car, when you stop being critical of your eldest son and he starts being critical of you.

  – James B. Reston

I'm a rabid sucker for Christmas. In July I'm already worrying that there are only 146 shopping days left. I'm always the Little Drummer Boy for Halloween.

  – John Waters

My teeth are all my own. I've just finished paying for them.

  – Ken Dodd

I don't have anything against work. I just figure, why deprive somebody who really enjoys it?

  – Dobie Gillis

Mona Lisa looks as if she has just been sick or is about to be.

  – Noel Coward

French nudes look as if they had just taken off their clothes; Greek nudes as if they had never put them on.

  – Sam Hall

To find the cloakroom in my penthouse, just turn right after the Picasso.

  – Jeffrey Archer

The perfect computer has been developed. You just feed in your problems and they never come out again.

  – Al Goodman

I don't approve of smacking – I just use a cattle prod.

    – Jenny Eclair

What's the point of going out? We're just going to end up back home anyway.

    – Homer Simpson

There's some sort of mother blood that just wants you to buy firearms when you have a child.

    – Courtney Love

Groucho isn't my real name – I'm just breaking it in for a friend.

    – Groucho Marx

Those signs that say 'Baby on Board' just make you want to hit the car harder.

    – Sue Kolinsky

A bottle of sleeping tablets I have just bought bears the label 'WARNING – MAY CAUSE DROWSINESS'.

    – Peter Orr

With her regular gifts of shoe-trees Aunty Kath has hitherto held the record for boring Christmas presents, but Bill shows he is no slouch in this department either when he presents me with the history of some agricultural college in New South Wales (second volume only). 'You did history, Alan. This should interest you.'

    – Alan Bennett

My son keeps complaining about headaches. I keep telling him, 'When you get out of bed, it's feet first.'

    – Henny Youngman

My mother said it was simple to keep a man. You must be a maid in the living room, a cook in the kitchen and a whore in the bedroom. I said I'd hire the first two and take care of the bedroom bit myself.

    – Jerry Hall

She believed in nothing; only her scepticism kept her from being an atheist.

– Jean-Paul Sartre

Every household has a box of odd keys. None of them will ever be found to fit any lock.

– Pam Brown

What is the advantage of having a kid at forty-nine? So you can both be in diapers at the same time?

– Sue Kolinsky

I said, 'You have got to be kidding. I am an ape and yet I am still expected to squeeze myself into one of those damn things.'

– Helena Bonham Carter

I never got along with my dad. Kids would come up to me and say, 'My dad can beat up your dad.' And I'd say, 'Okay. When?'

– Bill Hicks

I don't have to talk to my kids about taking drugs because they've seen vans, ambulances, police cars – you name it, at the house, and I've been in a whole bunch of rehabs so I think my behaviour put them off the idea.

– Ozzy Osbourne

My daughter's boyfriends? I figure if I kill the first one, word will get out.

– Charles Barkley

The children never forgave me. Oedipus only killed his father and married his mother, but I sold their Nintendo.

– Sue Arnold

My wish is to end all the killing in the world. My hobbies are hunting and fishing.

– Bryan Harvey

There are three kinds of bachelors: the kind that must be driven into matrimony with a whip; the kind that must be coaxed with sugar; and the kind that must be blindfolded and backed into the shafts.

– Helen Rowland

I seem to live permanently in some kind of godawful soap opera.

– Liz Hurley

Daddy's a litigator. Those are the scariest kind of lawyers. Daddy's so good he gets $500 an hour to fight with people. But he fights with me for free because I'm his daughter.

– Cher Horowitz, Clueless

A menopausal mother and an electric carving knife – not a good combination.

– Jenny Eclair

The best thing I have is the knife from Fatal Attraction. I hung it in my kitchen. It's my way of saying, Don't mess with me.

– Glenn Close

If it wasn't for golf, I don't know what I'd be doing. If my IQ had been two points lower, I'd have been a tree somewhere.

– Lee Trevino

I can't believe I'm 30. Do you know how much that is in gay years?

– Jack McFarland, Will and Grace

I feel cheated, never being able to know what it's like to get pregnant, carry a child and breastfeed.

– Dustin Hoffman

The FBI are looking for Osama bin Laden's financial advisor. How good can this guy be? His top client is living in a cave and driving a donkey. It doesn't sound like he is getting the best return on his investments.

– Jay Leno

Fifty per cent of the public doesn't know what 'fifty per cent' means.

— **Patricia Hewitt**

A lot of people think I don't know the meaning of the word 'hip'. But I do, and I hope to have it replaced soon.

— **Terry Wogan**

I bought a Korean kitchen knife. The label read: WARNING – KEEP OUT OF CHILDREN.

— **Robin Young**

My wife, God bless her, was in labour for 32 hours, and I was faithful to her the entire time.

— **Jonathan Katz**

Christmas is a season of such infinite labour, as well as expense in the shopping and present-making line, that almost every woman I know is good for nothing in purse and person for a month afterwards, done up physically and broken down financially.

— **Fanny Kemble**

Arnold Schwarzenegger's future mother-in-law gave him a Labrador as an engagement present. She told her daughter to watch the way he treated the dog because one day that's the way he would treat his kids. A couple of years later, he ran over the dog.

— **Jack Dee**

The difference between a diplomat and a lady is the following: when a diplomat says 'yes', he means 'perhaps'. When he says 'perhaps', he means 'no'. When he says 'no', he is not a diplomat. When a lady says 'no', she means 'perhaps'. When she says 'perhaps', she means 'yes'. But when she says 'yes', she is no lady!

— **Alfred Denning**

All babies start off looking like the last tomato in the fridge.

— **Ben Elton**

One watches Stephen Spender use the English language with the same horrified fascination as watching a Sèvres vase in the hands of a chimpanzee.

    – Evelyn Waugh

The most terrifying words in the English language are, 'I'm from the government and I'm here to help.'

    – Ronald Reagan

The great advantage of living in a large family is that early lesson of life's essential unfairness.

    – Nancy Mitford

My only profile of heaven is a large blue sky... larger than the biggest I have seen in June – and in it are my friends – every one of them.

    – Emily Dickinson

My favourite Christmas party game: take seven large bottles of vodka. Pour them into a bucket or suitable receptacle. Drink. Lie on the floor for several hours. Don't go to bed. Repeat until dead.

    – Mel Smith

The smallest hole will eventually empty the largest container, unless it is made intentionally for drainage, in which case it will clog.

    – Dave Grissom

I have no intention of uttering my last words on the stage, darling. Room service and a couple of depraved young women will do me quite nicely for an exit.

    – Peter O'Toole

The Campaign for Real Ale is the last refuge of bearded Trotskyite Morris dancers.

    – Alun Howkins

The one great principle of the English law is to make business for itself.

    – Charles Dickens

One parent or the other got up late in the night to come and see if your backside was moving up and down.

– Garrison Keillor

I always make a point of arriving later than expected in order to transform the anxiety of the chairman into extravagant relief and enthusiasm when I do appear.

– Robert Morley

The general idea in any first class laundry is to see that no shirt or collar ever comes back twice.

– Stephen Leacock

My bottom is my delinquent daughter. I lavish praise upon her cheeks when she's well-behaved and when she gets out of control, I pretend she isn't mine.

– Anna Johnson

In parts of India they have a law that if a man is married and is unfaithful to his wife, her family can take him out and publicly shoot him. There is no trial or anything – it's just their religious and state custom. If that was the custom in America, I would take every cent I make and put it into an ammunition factory.

– Will Rogers

My father wanted me to be a lawyer but I told him I was going into the theatre, which is the same job, really – but less dangerous to my fellow men.

– Peter Ustinov

During the performance of the play, I leaned forward and politely asked the lady in front if she would mind putting on her hat.

– George S. Kaufman

The purpose of studying economics is to learn how to avoid being fooled by economists.

– Joan Robinson

The wife of a man who never learnt the difference between a brassière and a brazier was granted a divorce today on two counts. First because when she wanted underwear for Christmas he gave her two big rusty tins with holes in and second because of the way he kept trying to roast his chestnuts.

– **Ronnie Barker**

All creative people should be required to leave California for three months every year.

– **Gloria Swanson**

Whatever happened to the kind of love leech that lived in his car and dropped by once a month to throw up and use you for your shower? Now all the pigs want is a commitment.

– **Judy Tenuta**

Mickey Mantle can hit them with the left and the right. He's completely amphibious.

– **Yogi Berra**

Like food eaten standing up, the food left over on your child's plate contains no calories.

– **Keith Mayer**

At Glasgow Rangers I was third choice left-back behind an amputee and a Catholic.

– **Craig Brown**

I am investigating the possibility of taking legal action to restrain the BBC from broadcasting discouraging weather forecasts for the Weston-Super-Mare area.

– **George Brenner**

Dan Quayle taught the kids a valuable lesson: if you don't study you could wind up Vice President.

– **Jay Leno**

You know you're trailer trash when you let your twelve-year-old daughter smoke at the dinner table in front of all her kids.

– Greta Garbage

Boys, to put you at your ease, let me just say that at our all-girl gatherings, we don't just talk at length... We also talk about width.

– Kathy Lette

If you want your children to improve, let them overhear the nice things you say about them to others.

– Haim Ginott

James Hunt used to write me love letters from all over the world. Well, not actually love letters. They were more like technical reports on his car.

– Taormina Rich

For a fortnight before the big day life becomes unbearable, as traffic gets worse, shops get more crowded, and habitually abstemious office girls unwisely accept a glass or six of Bailey's at the Christmas party and are later discovered in a Y-shape underneath the under-manager in the stationery cupboard, anything but stationary.

– Victor Lewis-Smith

I am absolutely sure there is no life on Mars – it's not listed on my teenage daughter's phone bills.

– Larry Mathews

There comes a time in every man's life and I've had plenty of them.

– Casey Stengel

Sex was for men, and marriage, like lifeboats, was for women and children.

– Carrie Fisher

The conclusion of your syllogism, I said lightly, is fallacious, being based upon licensed premises.

– Flann O'Brien

Michael Parkinson has a mouth on him like the wrong end of a plucked fowl and he wouldn't last ten seconds in my wife's kitchen because she'd be up his gob with a handful of sage and onions.

– **Les Patterson**

Hanging on to a bad relationship is like chewing gum after the flavour is gone.

– **Rita Rudner**

Michael Heseltine chairs a cabinet committee looking like the last hairdresser to leave Streatham Locarno before the lights are turned off.

– **Phillip Oppenheim**

In Hollywood, if a guy's wife looks like a new woman, she probably is.

– **Dean Martin**

Why is it all the things I like eating have been proven to cause tumours in white mice?

– **Robert Benchley**

Don't write a book unless it hurts like a hot turd coming out.

– **Charles Bukowski**

I do like Christmas, but I don't like all the palaver, the phoniness of it. I like the way it was; three apples and a banana in a little bag and a pair of jeans and a checked shirt which you were told was a cowboy suit.

– **Tom Murphy**

The long ball down the middle is like pouring beer down the toilet – it cuts out the middle man.

– **Jack Charlton**

He kissed her hand with a sound like a mackerel being replaced clumsily on a fishmonger's slab, and withdrew.

– **J.B. Morton**

A woman telling her true age is like a buyer confiding his final price to an Armenian rug dealer.

– **Mignon McLaughlin**

Flying the Union Jack is a bit like a eunuch being given his nuts back for a few days to wear as earrings.

– **Julie Burchill**

Joseph Heller's God Knows even looks exactly like a real book, with pages and print and dust jacket and everything. This disguise is extremely clever, considering the contents; the longest lounge act never performed in the history of the Catskills.

– **Paul Gray**

I'm glad you like my Catherine. I like her too. She ruled thirty million people and had three thousand lovers. I do the best I can in two hours.

– **Mae West**

It occurred to me that I would like to be a poet. The chief qualification, I understand, is that you must be born. Well, I hunted up my birth certificate and found I was alright on that score.

– **H.H. Munro**

Delighted you came, my dear, and I'd like you to know that you made a happy man feel very old.

– **Terry-Thomas, The Last Remake of Beau Geste**

Happiness in the older years of life, like happiness in every year of life, is a matter of choice – your choice for yourself. Happiness is to trim the day to one's own mood and feeling, to raise the window shade of your own bedroom an hour early and squander the hour in the morning sunshine, to drink your own tea from your own teacup, to practise the little wisdoms of housekeeping, to hang a picture on the wall where memories can reach out to it a dozen times a day and to sit in your kitchen and talk to your friend.

– **Harold Azine**

If Jesus Christ rode his flaming donkey like Jim Old rode that horse, then he deserved to be crucified.

– **Rod Simpson**

When I did something really bad – like lying – my father put me to bed and threatened to make me go without dinner. He never once carried out the threat about no dinner. After a while, he'd open the bedroom door and say, 'Put your clothes on and come down to dinner. I don't know why I should have to eat that dinner and not you.'

– **Arthur Marx, son of Groucho**

There are two things in life I like firm and one of them is jelly.

– **Mae West**

I hate having workmen in. I don't like people in my house even when they're invited. The only reason I let the children stay is because it's the law, and the circus hasn't come through yet.

– **Jack Dee**

Let the scintillations of your wit be like the coruscations of summer lightning, lambent but innocuous.

– **Edward Goulbum**

People who are pro-smacking children say things like, 'It's the only language they understand.' You could apply that to tourists.

– **Jack Dee**

I can do to him whatever I like. I'm allowed to torture him as much as I want. He's mine.

– **Novelist J.K. Rowling on Harry Potter**

You have to be suspicious when you line up against girls with moustaches.

– **Maree Holland**

Immature artists imitate, mature artists steal.

– **Lionel Trilling**

The last time I attempted to buy lingerie for my other half I failed miserably. Cup sizes? That's what they offer at Starbucks, isn't it? After an hour of lurching around in the undies department, I did the manly thing and opted for vouchers.

    – Rob Singh

Giving birth is like taking your lower lip and forcing it over your head.

    – Carole Burnett

Things you don't want to hear during liposuction: 1. 'Accept this sacrifice, oh Lord Beelzebub!' 2. 'Hey! Who's got the camera? Get a load of this freak of nature!' 3. 'So everyone's washed their hands right? No? Well just wipe them on your overalls – that'll do.'

    – David Letterman

Your modern teenager is not about to listen to advice from an old person, defined as a person who remembers when there was no Velcro.

    – Dave Barry

Children have never been very good at listening to their elders, but they have never failed to imitate them.

    – James Baldwin

Watching a baby being born is a little like watching a wet St Bernard coming in through the cat flap.

    – Jeff Foxworthy

My Christmas wish is that for a little while I might know and live again in the world I knew when I was ten years old.

    – Paul Gallico

The secret of staying young is to live honestly, eat slowly, and lie about your age.

    – Lucille Ball

My father didn't tell me how to live; he lived, and let me watch him do it.

    – Clarence B. Kelland

A centenarian is a person who has lived to be a hundred years of age. He never smoked or he smoked all his life. He never drank whiskey or he drank whiskey for eighty years. He was a vegetarian or he wasn't a vegetarian. Follow these rules closely and you too can become a centenarian.

– Stephen Leacock

Jesus died too soon. If he had lived to my age he would have repudiated his doctrine.

– Friedrich Nietzsche, 48

We used to play a game in Liverpool called forwards, backwards, sideways. You'd hit a fellow on the head with a shovel and guess which way he'd fall.

– Stan Boardman

The older I get the more I loathe Christmas, because now I have a horrible family of my own to add to the one who previously scarred me for life.

– Jenny Eclair

A man that would expect to train lobsters to fly in a year is called a lunatic; but a man that thinks men can be turned into angels by an election is a reformer and remains at large.

– Finley Peter Dunne

Visitors to England should be informed that London barbers are delighted to shave patrons' armpits.

– Gerard Hoffnung

Christmas is a time which can be lonely, can be sad, but it can also bring joy, laughter and light, and a time of great blessings to so many.

– Diana, Princess of Wales

The Right Honourable gentleman has sat so long on the fence that the iron has entered his soul.

– David Lloyd-George

Too many pieces of music finish too long after the end.
– Igor Stravinsky

Do not grow old, no matter how long you live. Never cease to stand like curious children before the Great Mystery into which we were born.
– Albert Einstein

Some people ask the secret of our long marriage. We take time to go to a restaurant two times a week. A little candlelight, dinner, music and dancing. She goes on Tuesdays. I go Fridays.
– Renny Youngman

Remember, hang on to your youth as long as you can. The minute you stop believing in Santa Claus, you get socks and underwear for gifts.
– Pat Williams

We want a few mad people – look where the sane ones have landed us.
– George Bernard Shaw

My grandma was like, 'Oh Christina, you look like a whore!' I explained that's the idea.
– Christina Aguilera

Graham Sutherland's portrait of me makes me look as if I were straining at stool.
– Winston Churchill

Old age realizes the dreams of youth. Look at Dean Swift: in his youth he built an asylum for the insane; in his old age he was himself an inmate.
– Søren Kierkegaard

I have reached the age when I look just as good standing on my head as I do right side up.
– Frank Sullivan

My plastic surgeon told me my face looked like a bouquet of elbows.

– **Phyllis Diller**

Some people have a wonderful way of looking at things. Like the ones who hire Negroes to baby-sit so they can go to a Ku Klux Klan meeting.

– **Dick Gregory**

I don't like people who use good looking young women in such a way that they end up at the bottom of rivers or lakes. Nor do I particularly care for people who cheat on their exams at Harvard. Nor do I particularly like obesity, but other than that I have no special feelings one way or the other about Teddy Kennedy.

– **John Simon**

When I was a kid I got lost on the beach once and a cop helped me look for my parents. 'Do you think we'll find them?' I asked him. 'I don't know, kid,' he replied. 'There are so many places they can hide.'

– **Rodney Dangerfield**

It's not good sportsmanship to pick up lost golf balls while they are still rolling.

– **Mark Twain**

I think it's really sad that a lot of women think that 'if I lose half a stone everything will be fine and everything will be perfect' but it won't – everything will be the same but you'll be a bit thinner.

– **Lorraine Kelly**

Was there ever a wider and more loving conspiracy than that which keeps the venerable figure of Santa Claus from slipping away, with all the other old-time myths, into the forsaken wonderland of the past?

– **Hamilton Wright Mabie**

I always like to associate with a lot of priests because it makes me understand anti-clerical things so well.

– **Hilaire Belloc**

A lucky model who's been given a lot of opportunities I just wish she would have done more with.

– **Jennifer Lopez on Cameron Diaz**

I'm really smart. I know a whole lot, but I just can't think of it.

– **Morey Amsterdam**

One of my theories is that men love with their eyes; women love with their ears.

– **Zsa-Zsa Gabor**

Richard Harris once told me he would love to work with me, which surprised me as we had starred together in Camelot.

– **Robert Morley**

Cells let us walk, talk, think, make love and realise the bath water is cold.

– **Lorraine Lee Cudmore, scientist**

No female director would ever fall in love with an actor. They are stupid and ignorant and don't know how to follow instructions.

– **Catherine Breillat**

The rules for fathers are but three... Love, Limit, and Let Them Be.

– **Elaine M. Ward**

It's great being blonde – with such low expectations it's easy to impress.

– **Pamela Anderson**

I'm so bad at relationships. I haven't made a holiday twice with the same person. I have a box full of pictures of Our First Christmas Together.

– **Michele Balan**

Do you know what breakfast cereal is made of? It's made of all those little curly wooden shavings you find in pencil sharpeners.

– **Roald Dahl**

The function of an advertiser is to make women unhappy with what they have.

– **Earl Puckett**

Every morning I get up and I make instant coffee and I drink it so I'll have enough energy to make regular coffee.

– **Steven Wright**

The music critic, Huneber, could never quite make up his mind about a new symphony until he had seen the composer's mistress.

– **H.L. Mencken**

Just because someone's in a wheelchair doesn't make them a better person. So in our films we usually portray them as bastards. We think that helps to humanize them.

– **Peter Farrelly**

New York: The only city where people make radio requests like, 'This is for Tina – I'm sorry I stabbed you.'

– **Carol Leifer**

The secret of successful journalism is to make your readers so angry they will write half your paper for you.

– **C.E.M. Joad**

Money is something you have got to make in case you don't die.

– **Max Asnas**

It takes a real man to wear make-up.

– **Rikki Rocket**

Instead of slaving in a hot kitchen making mince pies, brandy butter, Christmas cakes and fancy stuffing, why not buy them from a supermarket? Then you can spend your time enjoying yourself in the pub or at a party.

– **Lily Savage**

Marriage is when a woman asks a man to remove his pyjamas because she wants to send them to the laundry.

— **Albert Finney**

You can tell a lot about a man by the way he handles three things: a rainy day, lost luggage, and tangled Christmas tree lights.

— **H. Jackson Brown, Jr**

I took up a collection for a man in our office but I didn't get enough money to buy one.

— **Ruth Buzzi**

My ultimate fantasy is to entice a man to my bedroom, put a gun to his head and say, 'Make babies or die.'

— **Ruby Wax**

I'm old-fashioned. I like it when a man pays... for sex.

— **Wendy Liebman**

Whatever you may look like, marry a man your own age – as your beauty fades, so will his eyesight.

— **Phyllis Diller**

Henry Campbell-Bannerman is remembered chiefly as the man about whom all is forgotten.

— **Nicholas Bentley**

Yesterday upon the stair, I met a man who wasn't there. He wasn't there again today; I think he's from the CIA.

— **Wright Stevens**

Why are children performing 'Away in a Manger' in headlong, wondrous rush so much more affecting than in-tune King's College Choir? Dig down into bosky corner of coat pocket and find Kleenex.

— **Allison Pearson**

It's a funny thing that when a man hasn't got anything on earth to worry about he goes off and gets married.

– **Robert Frost**

My Hungarian grandfather was the kind of man that could follow someone into a revolving door and come out first.

– **Stephen Fry**

Bigamy is when you're married to one man too many. Monogamy is the same thing.

– **Erica Jong**

John Tyler has been called a mediocre man; but this is unwarranted flattery. He was a politician of monumental littleness.

– **Theodore Roosevelt**

By a sudden and adroit movement I managed to hit his fist with my left eye.

– **Artemus Ward**

When I said "You're a disgrace to mankind," I was talking to myself, not the umpire.

– **John McEnroe**

The notes I handle no better than many pianists. But the pauses between the notes – ah, that is where the art resides.

– **Artur Schnabel**

I've had so many wives and so many children I don't know which house to go to first on Christmas.

– **Mickey Rooney, eight times married**

If old people were to mobilize en masse they would constitute a formidable fighting force, as anyone who has ever had the temerity to try to board a bus ahead of a little old lady with an umbrella well knows.

– **Vera Forrester**

If there is no Hell, a good many preachers are obtaining money under false pretences.

– William Sunday

I spent four years studying mime under Marcel Marceau – unfortunately he was teaching welding at the time.

– Paul Merton

I only knew one thing for sure. Marriage was definitely the chief cause of divorce.

– Kathy Lette

It was our son who kept our marriage together: neither of us wanted custody of him.

– Chubby Brown

I have half a mind to get married – and that's all I need.

– Bob Phillips

The Extraordinary Achievement Award goes to Billy Martin for having reached the age of fifty without being murdered by someone, to the amazement of all who knew him.

– Murray Chase

The Bishop was talking to the local Master of Hounds about the difficulty he had in keeping his vicars off the incense.

– P.G. Wodehouse

We've lost seven of our last eight matches. The only team that we have beaten is Western Samoa. It's a good job we didn't play the whole of Samoa.

– Gareth Davies

Cosby's First Law of Intergenerational Perversity: no matter what you tell your child to do, he will always do the opposite.

– Bill Cosby

Age is a question of mind over matter. If you don't mind, age don't matter.

– Satchel Paige

By the time a man realizes that maybe his father was right, he usually has a son who thinks he's wrong.

– Charles Wadsworth

If there is anything more boring to me than the problems of big-busted women, it is the problems of beautiful women.

– Nora Ephron

I feel the end approaching. Quick, bring me my dessert, coffee, and liqueur.

– Pierette Brillat-Savarin

A lot of girls go out with me just to further their careers – damn anthropologists.

– Emo Philips

When I appear in public people expect me to neigh, grind my teeth, paw the ground and swish my tail – none of which is easy.

– Princess Anne

My wife finds it difficult to envisage me as the end product of millions of years of evolution.

– Bob Barnes

No man wanted me. Rapists would tap me on the shoulder and say 'Seen any girls?'

– Joan Rivers

When a woman on my show told me she had eighteen children because she loved her husband so much. I told her I loved my cigar too, but I took it out of my mouth once in a while.

– Groucho Marx

I'm grateful to my father for making me a tough son-of-a-bitch. It helps me deal with situations.

– Lana Zanocchio, daughter of Mafia godfather Anthony Graziano

Please don't retouch my wrinkles. It took me so long to earn them.

– Anna Magnani to a photographer

There is only one thing that consoles me about my exams. They cannot possibly ask everything I don't know.

– Stanisfer Ryan

There is only one thing that keeps me from being happily married: my wife.

– Henny Youngman

I didn't like school. They never gave me the present. They said they'd give me a present. They said: 'You're Laurie Lee, ain't you? Well, you just sit there for the present.' I sat there all day but I never got it. I ain't going back there again!

– Laurie Lee

My father knew the constellations. He showed me Venus, the evening star, Aries the ram, how to find the North Star if I was ever lost in the woods. I never got lost in the woods, but I loved those times and never even knew it.

– James Dodson

I don't care what is written about me so long as it isn't true.

– Dorothy Parker

As she lay there dozing next to me, one voice inside my head kept saying, 'Relax, you are not the first doctor to sleep with one of his patients,' but another kept reminding me, 'Howard, you are a veterinarian.'

– Dick Wilson

Every man I meet wants to protect me. I can't figure out from what.

– Mae West

The basic Christmas spread is the dullest meal of the year to a generation who've eaten Thai green curries in provincial pubs by the age of nine.

– **Peter York**

As a breastfeeding mother, you are basically meals on heels.

– **Kathy Lette**

Where have all the grannies gone? I mean the genuine, original, 22-carat articles who wore black shawls and cameo brooches, sat in rocking chairs and smelled of camphor?

– **Keith Waterhouse**

At my age getting a little action means your prune juice is working.

– **George Burns**

I don't think men and women are meant to live together. They are totally different animals.

– **Diana Dors**

My brother Brian has just written his memoirs. Memoirs me arse. You could write that fellow's memoirs on the back of a stamp and still have enough room left for the Koran.

– **Brendan Behan**

A compromise is an agreement between two men to do what both agree is wrong.

– **Edward Cecil**

This book is dedicated to all those men who betrayed me at one time or another, in the hopes that they will fall off their motorcycles and break their necks.

– **Diane Wakoski**

I would hope I can attract both men and women. And that when a person is attracted to me, they're not thinking about my genitals.

– **k.d. lang**

If it's natural to kill, how come men have to go into training to learn how?

    – Joan Baez

The trouble is you can't live with men, but then you can't chop them into little pieces and boil the flesh off their bones, because that would be cooking.

    – Jenny Eclair

I gave my beauty and youth to men. I am going to give my wisdom and experience to animals.

    – Brigitte Bardot

In our family we don't divorce our men. We bury them.

    – Ruth Gordon

In my prime I could have handled Michael Jordan. Of course, he would only have been twelve years old then.

    – Jerry Sloan

I hear Elvis is living now in Michigan or Minnesota. Well, we'd like him to come and be on our bench. We don't care how much he weighs.

    – Jerry Glanville

Being old is getting up in the middle of the night as often as George Clooney, but not for the same reason.

    – Mel Brooks

Florence Nightingale felt towards God as she might have felt towards a glorified sanitary engineer; and in some of her speculations she seems hardly to distinguish between the Deity and the Drains.

    – Lytton Strachey

When I was born folks came from miles around to take a look. They weren't quite sure what the little thing was.

    – W.C. Fields

I don't know much about being a millionaire but I'll bet I'd be darling at it.

– **Dorothy Parker**

I think it so kind of the mimic to tell us who he is imitating. It avoids discussion, doesn't it?

– **Oscar Wilde**

Like Albion's rich plum-pudding, famous grown, The mince-pie reigns in realms beyond his own, Through foreign latitudes his power extends, And only terminates where eating ends.

– **William Hone, Ode to the Mince-Pie**

Men aren't attracted to me by my mind. They are attracted to me by what I don't mind.

– **Gypsy Rose Lee**

When it comes to staying young, a mind-lift beats a face-lift any day.

– **Marty Bucella**

The bowler had the batsman in two minds. He didn't know whether to hit him for four or six.

– **Arthur Wood**

Do you think those triplets were really mine? After all, I did only go into hospital to have my ears pierced.

– **Victoria Wood**

I try to make each day a miniature lifetime in which I achieve something and I enjoy something.

– **Leslie Bricusse**

Voting for [Margaret Thatcher, former British Prime Minister] was like buying a Vera Lynn LP, getting it home and finding 'Never Mind the Bollocks' inside the red, white and blue sleeve.

– **Julie Burchill**

Much has been written about the Prime Minister's Madonna-and-child study with Cherie and Leo, which comes with a scrawled 'Tony and Cherie', clearly written by just one hand. To be honest, isn't sending a photograph of yourself at Christmas the height of egomania? Couldn't Cherie and Tony just have given us little Leo in a swaddling Timberland sweatshirt and stayed out of the limelight? I suspect the reason they didn't is that Christmas cards have become status symbols. It's not how many you get, but who they come from.

   – Janet Street-Porter

The editor asked me to cut fifteen minutes from my play, Ah, Wilderness!, so I decided to cut the third intermission and play it in three acts rather than four.

   – Eugene O'Neill

Meet me in the bedroom in five minutes and bring a cattle prod.

   – Woody Allen

Look, I'm not interested in agriculture – missile silos and stuff. I want to hear about the military stuff.

   – William Scott

There are too many people around who mistake a love of reading with a talent for writing.

   – Stanley Ellin

The nice thing about a gift of money is that it's so easily exchangeable.

   – Arnold Glasgow

Anybody who finds it easy to make money on the horses is probably in the dog food business.

   – Franklin P. Jones

Tony Cascarino is the biggest waste of money since Madonna's father bought her pyjamas.

   – Frank Lauder

If advertisers spent the same amount of money improving their products as they do on advertising then they wouldn't have to advertise them.

– **Will Rogers**

Arnold Palmer has won about as much money playing golf as I've paid on lessons.

– **Bob Hope**

Companies run by engineers don't make any money, but companies run by accountants don't make anything at all.

– **Peter Kruger**

It was tough asking thrifty parents for money. You had to beg your father, 'Dad, can I have a dollar?' And he'd say, 'What happened to the dollar I gave you last year?'

– **Sinbad**

Honey, anything I said seven or eight months ago is inadmissible in an argument. All comments become null and void after twenty-four hours.

– **Denis Leary**

When Neil Armstrong set foot on the moon, he found a baseball that Jimmy Fox hit off me in 1937.

– **Lefty Gomez**

Like all ruins, I look best by moonlight. Give me a sprig of ivy and an owl under my arm and Tintern Abbey would not be in it with me.

– **W. S. Gilbert**

France has neither winter nor summer nor morals – apart from these drawbacks it is a fine country.

– **Mark Twain**

Death will be a great relief. No more interviews.

– **Katharine Hepburn**

My writing is like fine wine; the more you read, the more you get from it. Reading it just once is like taking a dog to the theatre.

– **V.S. Naipaul**

Blood is thicker than water and much more difficult to get out of the carpet.

– **Woody Allen**

I'm not really a heavy smoker any more. I get through only two lighters a day now.

– **Bill Hicks**

As I lay praying in the early morning I thought I heard a sound of distant bells. It was an intense frost. I sat down in my bath upon a sheet of thick ice which broke in the middle into large pieces whilst the sharp points and jagged edges stuck all round the side of the tub like chevaux de frise, not particularly comfortable to the naked thighs and loins, because the keen ice cut like broken glass. The ice water stung and scorched like fire. I had to collect the floating pieces of ice and pile them on a chair before I could use the sponge and then I had to thaw the sponge in my hands for it was a mass of ice. The morning was most brilliant. Walked to the Sunday School with Gibbons and the road sparkled with millions of rainbows, the seven colours gleaming in every glittering point of hoar-frost. The Church was very cold in spite of two roaring fires.

– **Reverend Francis Kilvert**

True terror is to wake up one morning and discover that your high school class is running the country.

– **Kurt Vonnegut**

Friends of mine... were awoken on Christmas morning last year by howls of protest from their two sons. 'These stockings are crap!' the ten-year-old yelled. 'We're going to sue Santa Claus.'

– **Francis Wheen**

There is no use holding a post mortem on something that is dead.

– **Gordon Duddridge**

What actresses have I slept with? Well, most of my work was in westerns with donkeys and brood mares. But some of them were pretty damn attractive.

– **Robert Mitchum**

I have learned that my kids, like most kids, would rather work all night long in a salt mine than rake leaves at home.

– **Phil Donahue**

Never will a time come when the most marvellous recent invention is as marvellous as a newborn baby.

– **Carl Sandburg**

We were never a festive family. My mother still travels on Christmas Day as she gets a free glass of champagne on planes. She once looked after my flat as I escaped to sunnier climes. I rang her guiltily on Christmas Day only to be told that she was blissfully happy, had had a plate of baked beans and hadn't seen anyone all day.

– **Dom Joly**

I knew I looked awful because my mother phoned and said I looked lovely.

– **Jo Brand, after getting a makeover on TV**

My husband's not the romantic type. For Mother's Day, he gave me a George Foreman grill. For Father's Day, I gave it him back, in a sort of forceful upward motion.

– **Sandi Selvi**

I won't lie. Fatherhood isn't easy like motherhood. But I wouldn't trade it for anything. Except for some mag wheels.

– **Homer Simpson, The Simpsons**

My father considered a walk among the mountains as the equivalent of churchgoing.

– **Aldous Huxley**

Recovering from a hangover, he resolved, having moved his eyeballs, never to move them again.

– **Kingsley Amis**

Popcorn is the last area of the movie business where good taste is still a concern.

– **Mike Barfield**

Some Like it Hot was my favourite movie. Sunset Boulevard was a nice little movie too, but I didn't have a share of the gross.

– **Billy Wilder**

My parental tactics run the gamut from moving speeches on racial pride to outright bribery in the form of cold cash.

– **Bill Cosby**

It is a sobering thought that when Mozart was my age he had been dead for two years.

– **Tom Lehrer**

This book is dedicated to my mother, Mrs Frieda Seidman; to my daughters, Laurie Jo and Mona Helene; and to my wife Sylvia. All equally dear to me, but for safety's sake listed here alphabetically according to first name.

– **Gerald Lieberman**

I am a little surprised, not at Mrs Currie's indiscretion, but at a temporary lapse in Mr Major's taste.

– **Mary Archer**

It's Boxing Day and you can't take much more of this... The floor is covered with Big Brother-theme fancy paper from yesterday's orgy of unwrapping. The sofa is strewn with coils of aerosolled spaghetti. The son is inconsolable because some small cousin has walked on his Crash Bandicoot 5 Playstation disk and ruined it... You have had it up to here with tangerines. You are dyspeptic, flatulent, unshaven and grumbling. Much against your wishes, you are gradually turning into Jim Royle.

– **John Walsh**

Gwenogfran Evans declared he knew so much about Welsh poetry that he could tell by intuition when words had been added or subtracted by incompetent bards, and corrected texts at will. In one poem of just 6,300 words he made 3,400 changes and even this is not a complete list.

— **Adrian Gilbert**

Most British statesmen have either drunk too much or womanized too much. I never fell into the second category.

— **George Brown**

The Swiss are not a people so much as a neat, clean, quite solvent business.

— **William Faulkner**

Fat people don't seem to age as much as thin people, not when you get close up and inspect the damage.

— **Hunter Davies**

In a restaurant, the average Englishman would much prefer poor food, poor service and a good complaint to the manager and maybe even a letter to the Times rather than enjoy a good meal.

— **Malcolm Muggeridge**

Most of the time I don't have much fun. The rest of the time I don't have any fun at all.

— **Woody Allen**

I hate Christmas, I hate the silly music on the radio, I hate the adverts. I don't like the mince pies involved.

— **Noel Gallagher**

An unalterable and unquestioned law of the musical world requires that the German text of French operas sung by Swedish artists should be translated into Italian for the clearer understanding of English speaking audiences.

— **Edith Wharton**

Carol Channing, 82, star of the hit musical, Hello, Dolly! , wrote fondly about her high school sweetheart, Harry Kullijian, in her memoir, Just Lucky. Kullijian, 83, read the book, got in touch with Carol, and now they've got married. 'He's exactly the same now as he was when we were 12,' said Ms Channing.

– **Amy Robinson**

My family has a propensity – it must be in our genes – for dropping dead. Here one minute, gone the next. Neat. I pray that I have inherited this gene. How would I like to die? At the end of a sentence.

– **Mary Wesley**

When the chips are down, every woman must realize she is sitting on her fortune.

– **Germaine Greer**

I was wondering what dreadful things I must have done in a previous life to end up as Sports Minister in this one.

– **Tony Banks**

Actually I am a golfer. That is my real occupation. I was never an actor; ask anybody, particularly the critics.

– **Victor Mature**

I'll be spending a typical American Christmas. My tree is from Canada, the ornaments from Hong Kong. The lights come from Japan – and the idea from Bethlehem!

– **Robert Orben**

I'm looking for a guy just like my dad, who orders dentures through the mail and takes great pride in the fact that his eyebrows meet.

– **Judy Tenuta**

Marriage? I take a cold-hearted look at my parents' life and the urge passes.

– **Drew Carey**

I live with a French woman and my four daughters. I live with all these females and not one of them can cook. I'm so sick of the female sensibility. I know they have to be on the phone all the time but do they have to have all these – lipsticks and bottles everywhere? And the smells! Why can't women smell of something that isn't a smell?

    – Bob Geldof

Can technology really be the answer when my toaster has never once worked properly in four years? I followed the instructions and pushed two slices of bread down in the slots, and seconds later they rifled upwards. Once they broke the nose of a woman I loved very dearly.

    – Woody Allen

I have never been a material girl. My father always told me never to love anything that cannot love you back.

    – Imelda Marcos

I get up before anyone else in my household, not because sleep has deserted me in my advancing years, but because an intense eagerness to live draws me from my bed.

    – Maurice Goudeket

How do I feel about men? With my fingers.

    – Cher

I was the first woman to burn my bra – it took the fire department four days to put it out.

    – Dolly Parton

My dad's spending habits used to drive my mother up the wall. One moment he'd be buying her a diamond ring, the next he'd be bawling her out for not turning off the lights when she left the room.

    – Arthur Marx, son of Groucho

In every way, I wish to imitate my maker, and, like Him, I want nothing but praise.

    – Oscar Wilde

I've been married so long I'm on my third bottle of Tabasco sauce.

   – **Susan Ulss**

At 70, I'm in fine fettle for my age, sleep like a babe and feel around 12. The secret? Lots of meat, drink and cigarettes and not giving in to things.

   – **Jennifer Paterson**

I'm 80, but in my own mind, my age veers. When I'm performing on stage, I'm 40; when I'm shopping in Waitrose, I'm 120.

   – **Humphrey Lyttelton**

When I got married, I said to my therapist, 'I want to do something creative.' He said, 'Why don't you have a baby?' I hope he's dead now.

   – **Joy Behar**

A woman told me she would fulfil my ultimate fantasy for £100. I asked her to paint my house.

   – **Sean O'Bryan**

Woke up this morning, I was folding my bed back into a couch. I almost broke both my arms because it's not one of those kinds of beds.

   – **Steven Wright**

I read the newspaper avidly. It is my one form of continuous fiction.

   – **Aneurin Bevan**

If there was no other action around, my brother Chico would play solitaire – and bet against himself.

   – **Groucho Marx**

I made a terrible mistake last Christmas. My wife made me swear that I wouldn't give her a fancy gift. And I didn't.

   – **Milton Berle**

One morning I was making tea in my pyjamas. I really must get a teapot.

   – **Chic Murray**

Hell looks like the girls' gym at my high school. In hell, I am taking gym, but I also have a book due.

  – **Fran Lebowitz**

It is relaxing to go out with my ex-wife because she already knows I'm an idiot.

  – **Warren Thomas**

I always listen to *NSYNC's 'Tearin' Up My Heart'. It reminds me to wear a bra.

  – **Britney Spears**

I know one way guaranteed to make my children scatter instantly: I get up and dance.

  – **Terry Wogan**

My car absolutely will not run unless my golf clubs are in the trunk.

  – **Bruce Berlet**

I am happy with every part of my costume except the wig. I feel as if I am looking out of a yak's asshole.

  – **Coral Browne**

A couple of years ago I'd left my gift buying to the last minute, so I bought my relatives and their kids ten quids' worth of scratch cards. One of them won 17 quid, but some of the younger children didn't win anything. So that was a valuable life lesson: 'Some people are winners, some are losers.'

  – **Ricky Gervais**

The principal difference between Babe Zahanas and myself is that I hit the ball like a girl and she hits the ball like a man.

  – **Bob Hope**

More and more these days I find myself pondering on how to reconcile my net income with my gross habits.

  – **John Nelson**

It is one of the great urban myths that people get pregnant in order to have children.

    – Menzies Campbell

I only have to read Joe Louis' name and my nose starts to bleed again.

    – Tommy Farr

I gave my kids normal names, not names like Peaches and Blossom, and Autumn and Apple and Cherry – like a range of Glade plug-ins.

    – Jack Dee

Found guilty of embezzling £5,000, Mr Thanes Nark Phong, a hotel cashier from Bangkok, had his sentence reduced from 865 years to 576 years because 'his testimony proved useful'.

    – Trevor Danker

The Soviet Union will remain a one-party nation even if an opposition party were permitted – because everyone would join that party.

    – Ronald Reagan

Alan Bennett took over the job of national teddy bear after John Betjeman's death left it vacant.

    – Phil Baker

Inhabitants of underdeveloped nations and victims of natural disasters are the only people who have ever been happy to see soyabeans.

    – Fran Lebowitz

I'm at that age when everything Mother Nature gave me, Father Time is taking away.

    – George Burns

They asked me if the train passing near the final green hadn't disturbed my putting. I said 'What train?'

    – Gary Player

Power corrupts. Absolute power is kind of neat.
  – **John Lehman**

The denunciation of the young is a necessary part of the hygiene of older people, and greatly assists the circulation of their blood.
  – **Logan Pearsall Smith**

Be kind to your mother-in-law, and if necessary, pay for her board at some good hotel.
  – **Josh Billings**

I have eyes like a bullfrog, a neck like an ostrich and limp hair. You have to be good to survive with that equipment.
  – **Bette Davis**

Next time you're having a party and need some booze, don't go to the off-licence, go with your partner to the supermarket. Fill your trolley with booze, and booze alone... vodka, gin, tequila, wine, whatever. But just before you get to the checkout put in a box of nappies. Then, when you get to the till and check everything through, pretend you don't have quite enough money – and put the nappies back. Whoever's on the till just looks at you like you're scum. It's brilliant.
  – **Ed Byrne**

Man invented language to satisfy his deep need to complain.
  – **Lily Tomlin**

I never married because there was no need. I have three pets at home which answer the same purpose as a husband. I have a dog which growls every morning, a parrot which swears all afternoon, and a cat that comes home late at night.
  – **Marie Corelli**

There are many advantages of puppets. They never argue – They have no crude views about art. They have no private lives. They recognise the presiding intellect of the dramatist and have no personalities at all.
  – **Oscar Wilde**

I got all the schooling any actress needs – I learned to write enough to sign contracts.

– **Hermione Gingold**

Electricity is of two kinds, positive and negative. The difference is, I presume, that one comes a little more expensive, but is more durable; the other is a cheaper thing, but the moths get into it.

– **Stephen Leacock**

The street was in a rather rough neighbourhood. It was near the Houses of Parliament.

– **Oscar Wilde**

We have a 10ft-high fake tree because Neil is allergic to real fir trees. We are devoted to our Christmas fairy, who must be at least 55 years old. She has lost a leg but swathed in fresh tinsel and with a light on her wand she looks absolutely fine.

– **Christine Hamilton**

He is in hospital suffering from a nervous breakdown, but no doubt he will soon be better and running around like a maniac.

– **Simon Bates**

Some Rules for Being a Good Father: Never notice the whoopee cushion placed on your chair; Read out loud to your children; Never mock them; Leave child psychiatrists and writers of books to solve their own problems rather than yours.

– **Gyles Brandreth**

I've often been chased by women but never while I was awake.

– **Bob Hope**

You can't take it with you. You never see a U-Haul following a hearse.

– **Ellen Glasgow**

My greatest strength is that I have no weaknesses.

– **John McEnroe**

I was an ugly kid. My dad never took me to the zoo. He said if they wanted me, they'd come get me.

   – Rodney Dangerfield

Mexico City was not responsible for the New York Mets loss. My players can lose at any altitude.

   – Casey Stengel

Historically, marrying for passion is a relatively new phenomenon – one that just happens to correspond with the rising divorce rate.

   – Hazel McClay

My wife just told me the good news – I'm going to be a dad for the first time. The bad news is we already have two kids.

   – Brian Kiley

First the doctor told me the good news – I was going to have a disease named after me.

   – Steve Martin

There is but one way for a newspaperman to look at a politician and that is down.

   – Frank Simonds

When my kids are preparing for a night out, I give them a little fatherly advice: 'Don't get drunk or stoned tonight. I'll be fucking pissed off because I can't! And if you're gonna have sex, wear a condom.'

   – Ozzy Osbourne

Nothing gets you ready for that first night when you're out of the hospital and alone, and she's crying and won't stop and you're holding her against you while her screams rock your chest.

   – Bob Greene

Do not go gently into that good night, Old age should burn and rage at close of day...

   – Dylan Thomas

Kids think the Christmas tree looks great no matter how lousy your decorating skills.

– **Alan Parry**

Messrs Muir and Norden regret they have no machinery for the return of cheques.

– **Frank Muir**

It isn't premarital sex if you have no intention of getting married.

– **Matt Barry**

Home life as we understand it is no more natural to us than a cage is natural to a cockatoo.

– **George Bernard Shaw**

I'm not into working out. My philosophy: no pain, no pain.

– **Carol Leifer**

Were my looks ever a burden? Gaad, no! I just wish I'd kissed more boys.

– **Debbie Harry**

Housework is what a woman does that nobody notices unless she hasn't done it.

– **Evan Esar**

At 76, there is nothing nicer than nodding off while reading. Going fast asleep then being woken up by the crash of the book on the floor, then saying to myself, well it doesn't matter much. An admirable feeling.

– **A.J.P. Taylor**

At the moment I'm working on a non-fiction version of the Warren Report.

– **Woody Allen**

Here I sit, a modern Werther Original. Not telling dusty fairy stories to my 4-year-old and feeding him teeth-rotting toffees but teaching him how to work my computer so that one day soon he can teach me things.

– **Peter Preston**

The secret of a successful marriage is not to be at home too much.
— **Colin Chapman**

Beat your child every day. You may not know why, but they will.
— **Joey Adams**

Poker is a game of chance, but not the way I play it.
— **W. C. Fields**

Life is a great surprise. I do not see why death should not be an even greater one.
— **Vladimir Nabokov**

Hers was a great old age, but not a cramped one. She remained young at heart, and the young themselves sensed that.
— **Dr George Carey, Archbishop of Canterbury**

Customers in an Irish pub are asked not to throw lighted cigarette ends on the floor. People leaving have burned their hands and faces.
— **Tony Butler**

Only one part of the body must not move during an Irish dance – the bowels.
— **Jack McHale**

When I see people wearing fur, I'm not sure if I should be chucking something at them or saying something. There's no good reason for wearing fur. And it even looks crap.
— **Sophie Ellis Bextor**

Men are not stupid, or at least not too stupid to realize that if they didn't get sensitive real fast, they weren't going to get laid any more.
— **Cynthia Heimel**

People say New Yorkers can't get along. Not true. I saw two New Yorkers, complete strangers, sharing a cab. One guy took the tyres and the radio; the other guy took the engine.
— **David Letterman**

The idea of Christmas is like a note struck on glass – long ago and for ever. For each of us, this is the earliest memory of the soul... The Holy Night links up all childhoods; we return to our own – to the first music, the first pictures, the first innocent and mysterious thrill and stir.

   – Elizabeth Bowen

You ask me if I keep a notebook in which to record my great ideas. I've only ever had one.

   – Albert Einstein

If I was an employer, I'd employ nothing but fathers – they always want an excuse to work late.

   – Julie Burchill

If you put garbage in a computer nothing comes out but garbage. But this garbage, having passed through a very expensive machine, is somehow ennobled and none dare criticise it.

   – Aaron Fuegi

What if everything is an illusion and nothing exists? In that case, I definitely overpaid for my carpet.

   – Woody Allen

I've been married seven times. I know nothing about marriage, but a lot about separation.

   – Artie Shaw

I see President and Mrs Clinton are not here tonight. Probably somewhere testifying.

   – Don Imus

Alexander Hamilton started the US Treasury with nothing and that was the closest our country has ever come to being even.

   – Will Rogers

Ever since the Republican landslide on 8 November, it's been getting dark outside a little earlier every day. You notice that?

   – Mario Cuomo

Unquestionably there is progress. The average American now pays out twice as much in taxes as he formerly got in wages.

– H.L. Mencken

Age only matters when one is ageing. Now that I have arrived at a great age, I might just as well be 20.

– Pablo Picasso

I comfort myself by pretending that the number on my bathroom scales is my IQ.

– Linda Iverson

I believe every human has a finite number of heartbeats. I don't intend to waste any of mine running around exercising.

– Neil Armstrong

Any child's birthday party in which the number of guests exceeds the number of the actual age of the child for whom the party is being given will end in disaster.

– Pierre Burton

Lest O Lord this prayer be too obscure, permit thy servant to illustrate it with an anecdote.

– Allan Laing

Don't ever save anything for a special occasion. Being alive is the special occasion.

– Avril Sloe

My father said, 'If, at the end of your life, you can count all your friends – your really good friends – on just one hand, then you've been spending a lot of time alone in your room.'

– Bob Saget

When we had a little girl, all of a sudden I couldn't remember that I ever wanted to have a boy.

– Henry Louis Gates

One good thing about playing a piece of modern music is that if you make a mistake, no one notices.

– **Gordon Brown**

It is no accident that the symbol of a bishop is a crook and the symbol of an archbishop is a double-cross.

– **Gregory Dix**

I have been accused by the media of one in a bed romps.

– **Steve Davis**

I was in analysis for years because of a traumatic childhood; I was breast-fed through falsies.

– **Woody Allen**

Christmas cracker jokes are just a way of binding people together... If the joke is good and you tell it and it doesn't get a laugh, it's your problem. If the joke's bad and it doesn't get a laugh, then it's the joke's problem. My theory is that it's a way of not embarrassing people at Christmas.

– **Professor Richard Wiseman**

I regard golf as an expensive way of playing marbles.

– **G.K. Chesterton**

Riegger's Dichotomy sounded as though a pack of rats were being slowly tortured to death, while from time to time a dying cow moaned.

– **Walter Abendroth**

I never put aside the past resentment of the boy until, with my own sons, I shared his final hours, and came to see what he'd become, or always was – the father who will never cease to be alive in me.

– **Jimmy Carter**

The opening night audience is mostly friends of the cast and backers of the show, and they come to applaud their money.

– **Al Hirschfeld**

Where would we be without The Sound of Music on television at Christmas? My house.

– Jimmy Carr

I wish to be cremated. One tenth of my ashes shall be given to my agent, as written in our contract.

– Groucho Marx

A son could bear complacently the death of his father while the loss of his inheritance might drive him to despair.

– Niccolò Machiavelli

If there had been any formidable body of cannibals in the country, Harry Truman would have promised to provide them with free missionaries fattened at the taxpayer's expense.

– H.L. Mencken

So cold, so bitterly cold, and both of us so stiff, that we were medieval, and spent the day in bed.

– Sylvia Townsend Warner

An enraged cartoonist burst into the office of the editor of the New Yorker and shouted 'You never use my stuff but you publish the work of a fifth rate artist like Thurber.' The editor immediately sprang to my defence. 'Third rate,' he said.

– James Thurber

It has been calculated that Santa's team of nine reindeer would emit methane with a global warming impact equivalent to more than 40,600 tonnes of greenhouse gases on the 122-million-mile Christmas Eve dash to deliver presents around the world. That would make his marathon sleigh ride almost as environmentally damaging as an aircraft...
The methane calculations were made by Liberal Democrat transport spokesman Tom Brake. He said the best Christmas present for the environment would be if Santa took the bus... although he admitted the annual trip might take a bit longer than usual.

– Raymond Hainey

We should be careful to get out of an experience only the wisdom that is in it – and stop there; lest we be like the cat that sits down on a hot stove-lid. She will never sit down on a hot stove-lid again – and that is well; but also she will never sit down on a cold one any more.

   – **Mark Twain**

The tuba is certainly the most intestinal of instruments, the very lower bowel of music.

   – **Peter de Vries**

Irving Berlin took Christmas, took Christ out of it, and made it about the weather.

   – **Philip Roth**

How can people complain about the length of time spent waiting in Out Patients for an appointment? I've spent many happy hours in our local hospital familiarizing myself with people's ailments and afflictions.

   – **Mrs Merton**

When we were dating we spent most of our time talking about sex – why I couldn't do it, where we could do it, were her parents going to go out so we could do it. Now that we're married, we've got nothing to talk about.

   – **Daniel Stern**

She used to diet on any kind of food she could lay her hands on.

   – **Arthur Baer**

Age does not diminish the extreme disappointment of having a scoop of ice cream fall from the cone.

   – **Jim Fiebig**

I've never actually drunk the national drink of Holland, but I often sprinkle a few drops on the Y-fronts before a heavy night on the job.

   – **Les Patterson**

I used to eat quite a lot of fast food.When my daughter, Chelsea, started preschool and she was asked what her father did, she said that he worked at McDonald's.

– **Bill Clinton**

To put private enterprise into the idea of health care is a heinous crime! Much better waste it! Let it be frittered away! Let a bunch of dopes lose it!

– **Fran Lebowitz**

Use your health, even to the point of wearing it out. That is what it is for. Spend all you have before you die; do not outlive yourself.

– **George Bernard Shaw**

I often stop, flabbergasted, at the sight of this incredible thing that serves me as a face.

– **Simone de Beauvoir**

If it wasn't for Baird, the inventor of television, we'd still be eating frozen radio dinners.

– **Johnny Carson**

A famous passage found in column 1,303 of the Annual Report of the Library at Alexandria for 250 BC indicates that the disappearance, exchange, and loss of umbrellas is a phenomenon closely associated with libraries.

– **Norman Stevens**

Las Vegas is full of all kinds of gambling devices – dice tables, slot machines and wedding chapels.

– **Joey Adams**

Arnold Palmer turned golf into a game of 'Hit it hard, go find it and hit it hard again!'

– **John Schulian**

I have never got over the shock of seeing my first cricket ball. I simply couldn't believe that there was anything so dangerous loose in what up to then had seemed a safe sort of world.

— **Robert Morley**

You got to have smelt a lot of mule manure before you can sing like a hillbilly.

— **Hank Williams**

They will all have heard that story of yours before – but if you tell it well they won't mind hearing it again.

— **Thora Hird**

Court TV is holding a fantasy trial of Osama bin Laden – They got the idea a couple of years ago from the Los Angeles trial of O.J. Simpson.

— **David Letterman**

If one morning I walked on top of the water across the Potomac River, the headline that afternoon would read PRESIDENT CAN'T SWIM.

— **Lyndon B. Johnson**

So infinitesimal did I find the knowledge of art west of the Rocky Mountains, that an art patron actually sued the railroad company for damages because the plaster cast of Venus de Milo, which he had imported from Paris, had been delivered minus the arms. And what is more surprising, he gained his case and the damages.

— **Oscar Wilde**

In spite of illness, in spite even of the arch-enemy sorrow, one can remain alive long past the usual date of disintegration if one is unafraid of change, insatiable in intellectual curiosity, interested in big things, and happy in small ways.

— **Edith Wharton**

As a child I experienced the rigours of the Scottish Sabbath, where the highlight was a visit to the cemetery.

— **T.C. Smout**

I love Christmas. I receive a lot of wonderful presents I can't wait to exchange.

– **Henny Youngman**

The first cuckoo I ever heard outside of a cuckoo clock, I was surprised how closely it imitated the clock and yet, of course, it could never have heard a clock.

– **Mark Twain**

Here we are in the Holy Land of Israel – a Mecca for tourists.

– **David Vine**

A human being is a computer's way of making another computer. We are just a computer's sex organs.

– **Solomon Short**

The upper crust is just a bunch of crumbs held together by dough.

– **Joseph A. Thomas**

At 60 a man has passed most of the reefs and whirlpools. Excepting death, he has no enemies left to meet. That man has awakened to a new youth. He is young.

– **George Luks**

Sometimes a man just cannot satisfy all of a woman's desires. Which is why God invented dental floss.

– **Susanne Kollrack**

Outside of the killings, Washington has one of the lowest crime rates in the country.

– **Marion Barry, former Mayor of Washington**

A baby first laughs at the age of four weeks. By that time their eyes focus well enough to see you clearly.

– **Dr Jonathan Agnew**

The House of Lords is a model of how to care for the elderly.

– **Frank Field**

I had a love-hate relationship with one of my husbands. He loved me, I hated him.

– **Zsa-Zsa Gabor**

After Schwarzenegger, Dolph Lundgren is a bit of a disappointment. At least Arnie looks as if he comes supplied with batteries.

– **Adam Mars-Jones**

Never trust a man who speaks well of everyone.

– **John Collins**

I was introduced to a beautiful young lady as a gentleman in his 90s. Early 90s, I insisted.

– **George Burns**

He created a man who was hard of head, blunt of speech, knew which side his bread was buttered on, and above all took no notice of women. Then God sent him forth to multiply in Yorkshire.

– **Reginald Hill**

I was polishing off the last mouthful of a dish in a restaurant when I heard one waiter whisper to another, "He's actually eating it."

– **Gilbert Harding**

Only last month, one in the north of England was sacked for giving a toy gun to a child with the words, 'Take that and shoot Margaret Thatcher.'

– **Stephen Pile, 1985**

Don't bother telling people your troubles. Half of them don't care and the other half figure you probably had it coming.

– **Josh Billings**

After supper we played games – best of all – The Game – where people acted out words, or phrases, given to them by the opposing team. We specialized in book titles... The funniest one I remember was Lady Chatterley's Lover which my mother-in-law had to act out, and I would not have dreamed she had in her what emerged.

– Robertson Davies

Something in me resists the calendar expectation of happiness. Merry Christmas yourself! it mutters as it shapes a ghostly grin.

– J.B. Priestley

I hesitate to say what the functions of the modern journalist may be, but I imagine that they do not exclude the intelligent anticipation of facts before they occur.

– Lord Curzon

In 1700, Charles Seymour, the sixth Duke of Somerset, ordered his two daughters to stand guard over him while he took his afternoon nap. On waking he found one of them was sitting down, so he docked £20,000 from her inheritance. And in 1700, £20,000 really was £20,000.

– Frank Muir

The police have stated that the discovery of a woman's body in a suitcase is being treated as 'suspicious'. It is nice to see that the spirit of Sherlock Holmes lives on.

– Sydney Wilkins

I think the strangest and strongest sensation of your life will be hearing for the first time the thin cry of your own child. For a moment you have the feeling of being double; but there is something more, quite impossible to analyse – perhaps the echo in a man's heart of all the sensations felt – by all the fathers and mothers of his race at a similar instant in the past. It is very tender, but also a very ghostly feeling.

– Lafcadio Hearn

My ex-husband is suing me for custody of the kids, so now I have to go to court and fight him because my lawyer says it would look really bad if I don't.

– Roseanne Barr

Past experience indicates that the best way of dealing with my daughter is total attention and love.

– **Lyndon B. Johnson**

England played out the last half hour of the game against Brazil apparently under the impression that they were leading.

– **Tom Humphries**

The badness of the jokes is part of the Christmas tradition and I would absolutely hate it if anyone tried to modernize them.

– **Frank Muir**

Television is probably the least physically harmful of all the narcotics known to man.

– **Christopher Lehmann-Haupt**

The invention of the ball was one of the worst tragedies ever to befall mankind and to force small boys on to soggy playing fields every afternoon to kick or throw or hurl these objects at each other for a couple of hours before returning the ball to precisely where they had first found it is a near criminal waste of time, energy and childhood.

– **Robert Morley**

I never intended to be the father of two teenage daughters. If I had been asked, I might have chosen to go for something cheaper, like a stable of racehorses, or something easier to raise, like wolverines.

– **W. Bruce Cameron**

I belong to the Gérard Depardieu school of nudity: just drop 'em. Whether you are fat or old or ugly or sagging, just get it over.

– **Helen Mirren**

After my act there was a lot of booing but also a lot of clapping. But the clapping was for the booing.

– **Milton Berle**

If you want to sacrifice the admiration of many men for the criticism of one, go ahead, get married.

– **Katharine Hepburn**

I'm not going to let a group of power-mongering political men with short penises tell me what to do.

– **Doris Allen**

To impress upon us what the loss of the soul through mortal sin meant, my father would light a match, grab our hands and hold them briefly over the flame, saying, 'See how that feels? Now imagine that for all eternity.'

– **Pat Buchanan**

I knew I was in love. First of all, I was very nauseous.

– **Woody Allen**

Whether or not we watch The Sound of Music from California, we do eat an American bird, stuffed with Spanish chestnuts, garlanded with potatoes from the New World, sprouts from Brussels, a plum pudding spiced from the Orient, and we sit around an alien tree, and sing with music from Sweden about a King of Bohemia, the one who looked out on St Stephen's Day. And that other favourite carol, the one that interrupts many a silent night, is as British as sauerkraut and bratwurst.

– **Anthony Smith**

Red squirrels – you don't see many of them since they became extinct.

– **Michael Aspel**

I sometimes think we expect too much of Christmas Day. We try to crowd into it the long arrears of kindliness and humanity of the whole year. As for me, I like to take my Christmas a little at a time, all through the year. And thus I drift along into the holidays – let them overtake me unexpectedly – waking up some fine morning and suddenly saying to myself, 'Why, this is Christmas Day!'

– **David Grayson**

Sure I lost weight during twenty years of smoking. How much does a lung weigh?

– **Michael Meehan**

Mom and Pop were just a couple of kids when they got married. He was 18, she was 16 and I was 3.

– **Billie Holiday**

A man's womenfolk, whatever their outward show of respect for his merit and authority, always regard him secretly as an ass, and with something akin to pity.

– **H.L. Mencken**

I don't mind whether my crumpled sheet of A4 paper listed for the Turner Prize is art or not. It is to me.

– **Martin Creed**

Like everyone else who makes the mistake of getting older, I begin each day with coffee and obituaries.

– **Bill Cosby**

A Christmas dinner, with the middle classes of this empire, would scarcely be a Christmas dinner without its turkey; and we can hardly imagine an object of greater envy than is presented by a respected, portly paterfamilias carving, at the season devoted to good cheer and genial charity, his own fat turkey, and carving it well.

– **Mrs Isabella Beeton**

God seems to have left the phone off the hook.

– **Arthur Koestler**

Ah, the speed with which the plates of soup are placed before the customers: not a drop splashes over, but then there is never more than a drop to start with.

– **Robert Morley**

Behind almost every woman you ever heard of stands a man who let her down.

– **Naomi Bliven**

I don't need you to remind me of my age, I have a bladder to do that for me.

– **Stephen Fry**

When authorities warn you of the dangers of sex, there is an important lesson to be learned. Do not have sex with the authorities.

    – Matt Groening

The more things a man is ashamed of, the more respectable he is.

    – George Bernard Shaw

By the bye, as I must leave off being young, I find many Douceurs in being a sort of Chaperon for I am put on the Sofa near the fire & can drink as much wine as I like.

    – Jane Austen

My mother always said you could eat off her floor; you could eat off my floor too, there's so much food down there.

    – Elaine Boostler

A struggling golfer should take two weeks off and then quit the game.

    – Jimmy Demaret

I won't wear skanky clothes that show off my booty, my belly or boobs. I have a great body. I could be Britney. I could be better than Britney.

    – Avril Lavigne

Lanny Wadkins doesn't have to worry about offending his friends out here on the tour, because he doesn't have any.

    – Hal Sutton

Snow Blower for Sale. $230 or nearest offer. Only used on snowy days.

    – Classified ad in the Minnesota Echo

You end up as you deserve. In old age you must put up with the face, the friends, the health, and the children you have earned.

    – Judith Viorst

The song 'White Christmas' is like an old Christmas memory: it inspires a happy sadness in the heart.

– **Bing Crosby**

I've got to go and see the old folk.

– **The Queen Mother, 97, spotting a group of pensioners at Cheltenham Racecourse**

I refused to go on that Grumpy Old Men programme because I said, 'If I go on, I will be grumpy about grumpy old men.'

– **Stephen Fry**

One of the greatest pleasures of growing old is looking back at the people you didn't marry.

– **Elizabeth Taylor**

The woman who has a gift for old age is the woman who delights in comfort. If warmth is known as the blessing it is, if your bed, your bath, your best-liked food and drink are regarded as fresh delights, then you know how to thrive when old.

– **Florida Scott-Maxwell**

I don't know how you feel about old age, but in my case I didn't even see it coming. It hit me from the rear.

– **Phyllis Diller**

My wife's aunt is about 109 years old and has a pair of glasses for every activity you can imagine – glasses for knitting, glasses for reading, glasses for doing the crossword. But she's always losing them. 'Have you seen my glasses?' she'll say. 'Surely you have a pair of looking-for-your-glasses glasses, don't you?'

– **Jack Dee**

Ken Dodd's act is like watching an old man having constipation against the clock.

– **A.A. Gill**

We don't stop playing because we grow old, we grow old because we stop playing.

– **George Bernard Shaw**

The great thing about sex when you're older is that you don't have to worry about getting pregnant.

– **Barbra Streisand**

One thing I've learned as I get older is to just go ahead and do it. It's much easier to apologize after something's been done than to get permission ahead of time.

– **Grace Murray Hopper**

I loved my grandparents' home. Everything smelled older, worn but safe; the food aroma had baked itself into the furniture.

– **Susan Strasberg**

William Inge handles symbolism rather like an Olympic weightlifter, raising it with agonizing care, brandishing it with a tiny grunt of triumph, then dropping it with a terrible clang.

– **Benedict Nightingale**

Rehearsals can prove entertaining... a soloist insists on singing 'a whale in a manger'.

– **Maggie Clifford**

A literary collaboration is a partnership based on the false assumption that the other fellow can spell.

– **Ambrose Bierce**

Bill Gates's baby looks at the baby on the Pampers packet and thinks: 'I can buy and sell you.'

– **David Letterman**

I feel very old sometimes. I carry on and would not like to die before having emptied a few more buckets of shit on the heads of my fellow men.

– **Gustave Flaubert**

A beggar is one who has relied on the assistance of his friends.

– **Ambrose Bierce**

Most of your parishioners will meet you on only three occasions. The first and last, baptism and burial, they are not conscious at all. And the middle one, holy matrimony, they are barely half conscious, if that.

– **Kenneth Haworth**

In 1969 I published a small book on Humility. It was a pioneering work which has not, to my knowledge, been superseded.

– **Frank Longford**

Seize the moment. Remember all those women on the Titanic who waved away the dessert trolley.

– **Erma Bombeck**

Domestic Goddesses who say they get high on housework have obviously been inhaling too much cleaning fluid.

– **Kathy Lette**

His shoes are slut pumps. You put on your Manolos and you find yourself saying 'Hi, Sailor' to every man that walks by.

– **Joan Rivers**

For toddlers I suggest leaving their mittens on year-round, indoors and out. That way they can't get into aspirin bottles, liquor cabinets or boxes of kitchen matches. Also, it keeps their little hands clean for mealtimes.

– **P.J. O'Rourke**

You can tell that a marriage is on the rocks when a couple speak to each other rationally.

– **Leo Tolstoy**

Research has shown that men usually sleep on the right side of the bed. Even in their sleep they have to be right.

– **Rita Rudner**

I am prepared to offer better odds on an alien landing on earth than a Briton winning the men's singles at Wimbledon.

– **William Hill**

To consult is to seek another's advice on a course already decided upon.

– **Ambrose Bierce**

I asked her what she was doing on Saturday night and when she said "committing suicide," I asked her what she was doing on Friday night.

– **Woody Allen**

I introduced a girlfriend to my parents once and my dad said, 'Pleased to meet you – how much do you earn?'

– **Sanjeev Bhaskar**

Woman is a primitive animal who micturates once a day, defecates once a week, menstruates once a month, parturates once a year and copulates whenever she has the opportunity.

– **Somerset Maugham**

Sex and death. Two things that come once in a lifetime. But at least after death you are not nauseous.

– **Woody Allen**

Every woman needs at least three men: one for sex, one for money and one for fun.

– **Bess Myerson**

If truth is beauty, how come no one has their hair done in the library?

– **Lily Tomlin**

The most indulgent Christmas spread ever was one that my fellow 'Fat Lady', Jennifer Paterson, and I prepared for the 'cost-cutting' former head of the BBC, John Birt, as he entertained the board of governors. We watched them indulge in goose stuffed with foie gras and a Christmas pudding bombe made with vintage brandy butter.

– **Clarissa Dickson Wright**

Marriage is like having to stand on one leg for the rest of your life.
- **Philip Larkin**

Between two evils, I always pick the one I never tried before.
- **Mae West**

Sir Christopher Dilke kept his wife in one part of a very big bed and his mistress in another, and neither knew the other was there.
- **Tony O'Reilly**

I said to my wife, 'Give me one good reason why I should be in the delivery room with you while you're in labour.' She said, 'Alimony.'
- **Paul Mather**

It had never occurred to him that one foreign language could be translated into another. He had assumed that strange tongues existed only by virtue of their not being English.
- **Tom Stoppard**

There are days of oldness, and then one gets young again. It goes backward and forward, not in one direction.
- **Katharine Hathaway**

Friendship is not possible between two women, one of whom is very well-dressed.
- **Laurie Colwin**

Fathers and sons show more consideration towards one another than mothers and daughters do.
- **Friedrich Nietzsche**

I went to the United States for one purpose only; to continue my lifelong search for naked women in wet mackintoshes.
- **Dylan Thomas**

I know only two words of Spanish. One is mañana, which means tomorrow. The other is pyjama, which means tonight.

– **Woodrow Wyatt**

Don't confuse fame with success. Madonna is one; Helen Keller is the other.

– **Erma Bombeck**

If one hears bad music, it is one's duty to drown it out by one's conversation.

– **Oscar Wilde**

I left school at fifteen having passed only one test – my cervical smear test.

– **Kathy Lette**

What would I do if I had only had six months to live? I'd type faster.

– **Isaac Asimov**

Cass's expense account showed that he not only did the labour of several men at the same time; but that he often did it at several places, many hundreds of miles apart at the same time.

– **Abraham Lincoln**

If we did get a divorce, the only way my husband would find out about it is if they announced it on Wide World of Sports.

– **Joyce Brothers**

As life's pleasures go, food is second only to sex. Except for salami and eggs. Now that's better than sex, but only if the salami is thickly sliced.

– **Alan King**

The first fall of snow is not only an event but it is a magical event. You go to bed in one kind of a world and wake up to find yourself in another quite different, and if this is not enchantment, then where is it to be found?

– **J.B. Priestley**

As you grow older, you'll find the only things you regret are the things you didn't do.

– Zachary Scott

With my bum size, décolletage is my only hope. The theory is that men will be so mesmerised by my cleavage that they won't notice my bum.

– Jane Owen

Finding that the Vatican gardens were open only to the Bohemian and Portuguese pilgrims, I at once spoke both languages fluently, explaining that my English dress was a form of penance.

– Oscar Wilde

A non-technical person is someone who cannot open a childproof bottle without an axe.

– Dave Barry

It has been said that if the opening phrase of a classical minuet can be fitted to the words "Are you the O'Reilly who owns this hotel?" then it was written by Haydn; if it can't then it wasn't.

– Gervase Hughes

I do not mind what language an opera is sung in as long as I do not understand it.

– Edward Appleton

This Scottish fellow had a hip replacement operation. He asked the surgeon if he could have the bone for his dog.

– Frank Carson

It is an odd but universally held opinion that anyone who doesn't drink must be an alcoholic.

– P.J. O'Rourke

Aye, they say the new striker I'm opposing is fast – but how fast can he limp?

– Mick McCarthy

I have nothing against Nicholas Ridley's wife or family, but I think it is time he spent more time with them.

– **Philip Goodhart**

I am a big fan of Superman or anyone who can make his living in his underwear.

– **David Mamet**

How can we have any new ideas or fresh outlooks in science when ninety per cent of all the scientists who have ever lived have still not died?

– **Alan Mackay**

I swim a lot. It's either that or buy a new golf ball.

– **Bob Hope**

As well might we dance without music, or attempt to write a poem without rhythm, as to keep Christmas without a Christmas tree.

– **The Weekly Press**

Anticipator plagiarism occurs when someone steals your original idea and publishes it a hundred years before you were born.

– **Robert Merton**

Daddy, I don't want to be an orphan. I saw Annie. Orphans have to eat gruel and tap dance with mops.

– **Emily Tait**

Cancel the kitchen scraps for lepers and orphans, no more merciful beheadings, and call off Christmas!

– **Sheriff of Nottingham, Robin Hood, Prince of Thieves**

The standing ovation I got at the Oscar ceremony made up for the strip search.

– **Woody Allen**

It is said that Sir William Wilde, Oscar's father, was so patriotic that he carried a considerable portion of his country's soil about on his person.

– **Hesketh Pearson**

I went into a feminist bookstore the other day. I looked more female than anybody in there.

– **Clint Eastwood**

The grass is always greener on the other side of the fence. So if you don't want to stain your skirt, do it on this side.

– **Joan Rivers**

Astray, by Charlotte M. Yonge (and three other writers) needed four people to write it and even to read it requires assistance; all the same it is a book that can be recommended to other people.

– **Oscar Wilde**

You simply must stop taking advice from other people.

– **Melissa Timberman**

What are you supposed to do with other people's family-portrait Christmas cards, welcome as a box of Matchmakers? We make merry by drinking a lot and then uproariously deciding who is trying hardest to look successful and harmonious, and who therefore had the worst year and most arguments.

– **Gillian Ferguson**

Some women think bikinis are immodest, while others have beautiful figures.

– **Olin Miller**

At age 20, we worry about what others think of us; at 40, we don't care what they think of us; at 60, we discover they haven't been thinking of us at all.

– **Bob Hope**

I like to drive with my knees. Otherwise, how can I put on my lipstick and talk on the phone?

    – Sharon Stone

Christmas is emphatically not a festival that ought to be celebrated in shorts.

    – Zoë Heller (in southern California)

Fatherhood trumps gayness. As gay parents of our son, Erez, we tried our best: we played him Judy Garland records and showed him tapes of West Side Story but his inclinations remain resolutely heterosexual.

    – Jesse Green

There used to be a notice in our rugby club bar which read: 'We open at 9:30 am and close at 11 pm. If you still haven't had enough to drink in that time, the management feel you can't have been trying.'

    – Bill Mulcahy

Why do we get older? Why do our bodies wear out? Why can't we just go on and on, accumulating a potentially infinite number of Frequent Flier mileage points?

    – Dave Barry

Age is a product of good health. Our research shows that people who live to be 100 are as mentally and physically healthy as people 30 years younger. We've replaced the saying, 'The older you get, the sicker you get,' with the more accurate, 'The older you get, the healthier you've been.'

    – Dr Thomas Perls

The cable TV sex channels don't expand our horizons, don't make us better people, and don't come in clearly enough.

    – Bill Maher

I believe that we parents must encourage our children to become educated, so they can get into a good college that we cannot afford.

    – Dave Barry

One Christmas things were so bad in our house that I asked Santa Claus for a yo-yo and all I got was a piece of string. My father told me it was a yo.

    – Brendan O'Carroll

My parents have been divorced three times. Ours wasn't so much a broken home as a derelict one. When he left, my dad said, 'You're the head of the family now. Look after your mum and sisters.' What did he expect me to do? Pick my mum up from work on my Chopper bike?

    – Jeff Green

I have to be careful to get out before I become the grotesque caricature of a hatchet-faced woman with big knockers.

    – Jamie Lee Curtis

There isn't a child who hasn't gone out into the brave new world who eventually doesn't return to the old homestead carrying a bundle of dirty clothes.

    – Art Buchwald

The inventor of Crest passed away. Four out of five dentists came to the funeral.

    – Jay Leno

With whitened hair, desires failing, strength ebbing out of him, with the sun gone down and with only the serenity and the calm warning of the evening star left to him, he drank to Life, to all it had been, to what it was, to what it would be. Hurrah!

    – Sean O'Casey

The Welsh are not meant to go out in the sun. They start to photosynthesize.

    – Rhys Ifans

My parents used to beat the shit out of me. And, looking back on it, I'm glad they did. And I'm looking forward to beating the shit out of my own kids. For no reason whatsoever.

    – Denis Leary

Mum comes in and says 'I'm working out,' and she'll just be standing there naked doing a dance.

    – Kelly Osbourne

Old age is an excellent time for outrage. My goal is to say or do at least one outrageous thing every week.

    – Maggie Kuhn

Under twenty-one, women are protected by law; over sixty-five they're protected by nature; anything in between is fair game.

    – Cary Grant

One of the disadvantages of inviting Utrillo over for dinner was that he would disappear into the bedroom and drink all your wife's perfume.

    – Waldemar Januszczak

If I had my life to live over again, I should devote it to the arrangement of headphones and microphones or the like whereby the noises used by musical maniacs should be audible to themselves only. It should be made a felony to play a musical instrument in any other than a completely soundproof room.

    – George Bernard Shaw

If I had to live my life over again, I'd be a plumber.

    – Albert Einstein

If you had your life to live over again, you'd need lots of money.

    – Jackie Mason

If I had my life to live over, I don't think I'd have the strength.

    – Flip Wilson

If I had my life to live over, I'd live over a saloon.

    – W.C. Fields

Jules Janis once rewrote one of his own manuscripts rather than try to decipher it for the printer.

– Robert Hendrickson

Bogart's a helluva nice guy until 10.30 p.m. After that he thinks he's Bogart.

– David Chasen

They say men can never experience the pain of childbirth... they can if you hit them in the goolies with a cricket bat... for fourteen hours.

– Jo Brand

I have a very low threshold of pain. Not even a limbo dancer could get down there.

– Kathy Lette

I don't own any of my own paintings because a Picasso original costs several thousand dollars and that's a luxury I cannot afford.

– Pablo Picasso

Gelée of duck has the consistency of Pamela Anderson Lee's implants, and was so salty and horrid it was like licking an Abyssinian shotputter's armpit.

– A.A. Gill

You'll never catch a nudist with his pants down.

– David Letterman

I put things down on sheets of paper and stuff them in my pockets. When I have enough I have a book.

– John Lennon

The Daily Telegraph is top as the paper that readers specially choose to buy – but research shows they don't want their friends to know they read it.

– **Brian MacArthur**

Most of what you read in the papers is lies. And I should know, because a lot of the lies you see in the papers are mine.

– **Max Clifford**

It's hard to be nice to some paranoid schizophrenic just because she lives in your body.

– **Judy Tenuta**

My very first day of school, my parents dropped me off at the wrong nursery. I didn't know anyone. And there were lots of trees.

– **Brian Kiley**

A child supplies the power but the parents have to do the steering.

– **Dr Benjamin Spock**

One time, I was mad at my parents and I said to them, 'I hate both of you! I'm running away from home!' And my father lifted me up over his head, and said, 'How far do you want to go?' He didn't know I was THE BILL COSBY.

– **Bill Cosby**

Arnold Palmer has more people watching him park the car than I do on the course.

– **Lee Trevino**

My wife is a sound driver. When parking the car she listens for the crunch and then stops.

– **Laurence Millington**

President Johnson was a real centaur – part man and part horse's ass.

– **Dean Acheson**

We accept Cliff Richard at Christmas, he's part of it. No other time though. Father Christmas in July is annoying and so is Cliff Richard.
- **Paul Morley**

My girlfriend has lovely coloured eyes. I particularly like the blue one.
- **Harry Scott**

I wouldn't put Jimmy Carter and his party in charge of snake control in Ireland.
- **Eugene McCarthy**

I do not often attack the Labour Party. They do it so well themselves.
- **Edward Heath**

I have made good judgements in the past; I have made good judgements in the future.
- **Dan Quayle**

Shaw has the emotional range of a Pat Boone record with a scratch.
- **A.A. Gill**

The average American Southerner has the speech patterns of someone slipping in and out of consciousness.
- **Bill Bryson**

I'm not going to have some reporters pawing through our papers. We are the President.
- **Hillary Clinton**

What a mess we are in now. Peace has broken out.
- **Napoleon Bonaparte**

There is no such thing as inner peace. There is only nervousness or death.
- **Fran Lebowitz**

Faure writes the sort of music a pederast might hum when raping a choirboy.
— **Marcel Proust**

I was the first person to teach Peggy Guggenheim about painting. What a tragedy that I wasn't the last.
— **Bernard Berenson**

The sun shone all day, but the people were boring as hell.
— **Kim Catrall on California**

The war years count double. Things and people not actively in use age twice as fast.
— **Arnold Bennett**

Politicians who lose elections should be executed. People would then think twice about running for office.
— **Mike Royko**

Prior to The Golden Girls, when old people were shown on television, you could almost smell them.
— **Bea Arthur**

Euthanasia is a way of putting old people out of their family's misery.
— **Mike Barfield**

In a national survey in Britain most people thought that Lulu the singer was fictitious and that Alf Garnett was real.
— **Warren Mitchell**

What would make life better for old people? Axe that Churchill Insurance 'nodding dog' commercial on television.
— **Clement Freud**

For some reason, a glaze passes over people's faces when you say 'Canada'.
— **Sondra Gottlieb, US ambassador's wife**

A survey this week revealed that 45 per cent of people have had it away at the works Christmas do. Why? You sit opposite the plump girl for 48 weeks and it never once occurs to you that she is interesting. So how come, after one warm wine, she only needs to put on a paper hat to become Jordan?

— **Jeremy Clarkson**

I came from a long line of performers and actors. It's called the dole queue.

— **Jack Dee**

Mr Wordsworth never ruined anyone's morals, unless, perhaps, he has driven some susceptible persons to crime in a very fury of boredom.

— **Ezra Pound**

To bathe a cat takes brute force, perseverance, courage, and a cat. This last ingredient is usually the hardest to come by.

— **Stephen Baker**

If you're 0–0 down, there's no better person to get you back on terms than Ian Wright.

— **Robbie Earle**

It's God. I recognised him from Blake's picture.

— **Robert Frost**

When a person with experience meets a person with money, the person with experience will get the money and the person with the money will get some experience.

— **Leonard Lauder**

You can tell a lot about a person's personality if you know his sign; Jesus: born on 25 December; fed the 5,000; walked on water. Typical Capricorn.

— **Harry Hill**

Naomi Jacob's bold adoption of the male persona was so successful that when Paul Bailey himself served her in Harrods bookshop he mistook her for J.B. Priestley.

– Michael Arditti

My kids hate me. They keep leaving phone numbers of divorce lawyers in Mom's purse.

– David Letterman

Dissatisfied with the Faith, I took up photography at which I became so good that in moments of depression I felt I was a born photographer. Tiring of churches, I tried cows, and I discovered with pleasure that cows are very fond of being photographed, and, unlike architecture, don't move.

– Oscar Wilde

There are three kinds of pianists: Jewish pianists, homosexual pianists and bad pianists.

– Vladimir Horowitz

From my mother I learned to make piecrusts and to iron shirts. From my father I learned to catnap and to tell the time without a watch.

– Verlyn Klinkenborg

Never, under any circumstances, take a sleeping pill and a laxative on the same night.

– Dave Barry

Because Christmas is generally accepted as pleasure's pinnacle, the happiest day of the year, it causes widespread and sometimes fatal depression. Many adults look forward to it and its aftermath as to dental surgery...

– Barbara Holland, Endangered Pleasures

A note from my granddaughter's school was pinned up in my daughter's kitchen a few days ago, which read: 'Alice is an angel. Please can she wear white knickers on Tuesday.'

– **David Shamash**

If I want to be alone, some place I can write, I can read, I can pray, I can cry, I can do whatever I want – I go to the bathroom.

– **Alicia Keys**

To win a woman in the first place you must please her, then undress her, and then somehow get her clothes back on her, finally, so that she will let you leave her, you've got to antagonize her.

– **Jean Giradoux**

Some people think you should eat human placenta because that's what animals do. Well, animals also lick their own balls. Do we have to do that too?

– **Denis Leary**

If I were a cassowary On the plains of Timbuctoo, I would eat a missionary Cassock, band, and hymn-book too.

– **Samuel Wilberforce**

If Beethoven had been killed in a plane crash, it would have changed the history of music and of aviation.

– **Tom Stoppard**

I have evidence that the government is planning to have me certified by psychiatrists.

– **Ian Paisley**

Observing the ancient housekeeper wrestling with the plantlife in the garden, I occasionally point out a weed and encourage her from the deckchair.

– **Arthur Marshall**

For three hundred years flautists tried to play in tune. Then they gave up and invented vibrato.

– George Barrère

Ted Simmons didn't sound like a baseball player. He said things like 'Nevertheless' and 'If, in fact'.

– Dan Quisenberry

Ice hockey fans love the fighting. The players don't mind. The coaches like the fights. What's the big deal?

– Don Cherry

Basketball is a simple game to understand. Players race up and down a fairly small area indoors and stuff the ball into a ring with Madonna's dress hanging on it.

– Dan Jenkins

It ain't getting it that hurts my players, it's staying up all night looking for it. They got to learn that if you don't get it by midnight, you ain't gonna get it, and if you do, it ain't worth it.

– Casey Stengel

Of children, as of procreation – the pleasure momentary, the posture ridiculous, the expense damnable.

– Evelyn Waugh

Surely everyone is aware of the divine pleasures which attend a wintry fireside: candles at four o'clock, warm hearth rugs, tea, a fair tea-maker, shutters closed, curtains flowing in ample draperies to the floor, whilst the wind and rain are raging audibly without.

– Thomas De Quincey

Being ill is one of the greatest pleasures of life, provided one is not too ill and is not obliged to work until one is better.

– Samuel Butler

When you're the only pea in the pod, your parents are likely to get you confused with the Hope Diamond.

– **Russell Baker**

Reading isn't an occupation we encourage among police officers. We try to keep the paperwork down to a minimum.

– **Joe Orton**

My dog Millie knows more about foreign policy than those two bozos Clinton and Gore.

– **George W. Bush**

All the contact I have had with politicians has left me feeling as though I had been drinking out of spittoons.

– **Ernest Hemingway**

A week is a long time in politics and three weeks is twice as long.

– **Rosie Barnes**

Politics is derived from two words – poly, meaning many, and tics, meaning small blood-sucking insects.

– **Chris Clayton**

I was quite enjoying The Power of Positive Thinking, until I heard that the author had committed suicide.

– **Nick Job**

My father told me that if humanly possible one should never lend people money, as it almost inevitably made them hate you.

– **Lord Rothschild**

When I get a script in the post, I ask only two things: 'Do I get wet or have to ride a horse?' If the answer to both was in the negative, I would do the film.

– **Alice Terry**

Hoover's slogan was 'a chicken in every pot' but Gorbachev has a new slogan: a chicken in every time zone.

– Johnny Carson

In some copies of the article 'The Power of the Papacy' the Pope was described as His Satanic Majesty. This should have read The Roman Antichrist.

– Ian Paisley

My father taught me that the most powerful weapon you have is your mind.

– Andrew Young

My favourite shots in golf are the practice swing and the conceded putt. The rest can never be mastered.

– Lord Robertson

I love Wagner, but the music I prefer is that of a cat hung up by its tail outside a window and trying to stick to panes of glass with its claws.

– Charles Baudelaire

So my dear brethren which would you prefer, to be in the light with the five wise virgins or in the dark with the five foolish virgins?

– Alan Bennett

Before you have kids, you'd better have prepared your answers for some tricky questions: Dad, did you inhale?

– Roger Howe

A man with pierced ears is better prepared for marriage. He has experienced pain and bought jewellery.

– Rita Rudner

A nose job is the best Christmas present ever because you'll have it for ever. It's not like some sweater you don't like and have to take back to the store.

– Helena Rasin

Now, that just leaves little Maggie's Christmas present. Ah, a squeak toy. It says it's for dogs, but she can't read.

– **Homer Simpson**

My worst awards ceremony was when I presented the award for Best Linoleum with an Adhesive Underside.

– **Tony Hawks**

The only reason I'm not running for president is I'm afraid no woman will come forward and say she's slept with me.

– **Garry Shandling**

Calvin Coolidge slept more than any other President, whether by day or by night. Nero fiddled, but Coolidge only snored.

– **H.L. Mencken**

Merit, indeed! We are come to a pretty pass if they talk of merit for a bishopric.

– **Lord Westmorland**

A man should marry only a very pretty woman in case he ever wants some other man to take her off his hands.

– **Sacha Guitry**

The reason people blame things on the previous generation is that there's only one other choice.

– **Doug Larson**

When we attempt to buy love the price goes up, as with other commodities.

– **Ann Landers**

On television today you can say you've pricked your finger but not the other way around.

– **George Carlin**

My father was silent, austere, of high principle; ungentle of manner towards his children, but always a gentleman in his phrasing.

– **Mark Twain**

I'd be the worst possible godfather. I'd probably drop her on her head at the christening. I'd forget all her birthdays until she was 18. Then I'd take her out, get her drunk and, quite possibly, try to shag her.

– **Will, *About a Boy***

In 4 BC., they had a YOK problem – they thought that civilisation would collapse in just four years because they would run out of numbers.

– **Derek Mitchell**

The best time to tackle a minor problem is before he grows up.

– **Ray Freedman**

Buying presents for old people is a problem. I would rather like it if people came to my house and took things away.

– **Clement Freud**

Did you hear that the atheists have produced a Christmas play? It's called 'Coincidence on 34th Street'.

– **Jay Leno**

It was once a rather half-hearted consumer programme, one of those don't-read-in-bed-with-a-blow-torch consumer programmes.

– **A.A. Gill**

If builders built buildings the way computer programmers write programs, the first woodpecker that came along would destroy civilisation.

– **Reede Stockton**

Why don't they pass a constitutional amendment prohibiting anybody from learning anything? If it works as good as Prohibition did, in five years Americans would be the smartest race of people on earth.

– **Will Rogers**

Look, kid, I'm begging you, if you promise not to tell your mother what I did, I'll let you squash something.

– Mitch Hogan

God gave women intuition and femininity. Used properly, the combination easily jumbles the brain of any man I've ever met.

– Farrah Fawcett

The importance of a country is inversely proportional to the length of its national anthem.

– Allen Otter

The main difference nowadays between poetry and prose is that, dreadful though it is, poetry doesn't go on for nearly so long.

– Richard Ingrams

English Catholics are just Protestants, protesting against Protestantism.

– D.H. Lawrence

Alcohol is good for you. My grandfather proved it irrevocably. He drank two quarts of booze every mature day of his life and lived to the age of 103. I was at the cremation – the fire would not go out.

– Dave Astor

Every middle-class person in America is on Prozac. Every poor person in America is on crack. Every middle-class person who is on Prozac has tremendous contempt for the poor person on crack.

– Fran Lebowitz

I am motivated thirty per cent by public service, forty per cent by sheer egomania and thirty per cent by disapproval of swankpot journalists.

– Boris Johnson

To disagree with three-fourths of the British public on all points is one of the first elements of sanity, one of the deepest consolations in moments of spiritual doubt.

– Oscar Wilde

Granny Moon's famous plum duff is a pudding boiled in a cloth bag. Granny Moon had a secret ingredient. She'd soak it for hours in rum, then ignite it in a blinding flash. As soon as she came out of the kitchen with no eyebrows, we knew dessert was ready. To this day, the smell of burning hair puts me in the holiday spirit. Merry Christmas! .

    – Daphne Moon, *Frasier*

I was so flat I used to put x's on my chest and write 'you are here'.

    – Joan Rivers

This year, can't we do Christmas ironically, put a Christmas stocking on Tracey Emin's bed, have Richard Rogers decorate the tree, get Germaine Greer to write a panto, with Tony Parsons as Buttons and Janet Street-Porter as Prince Charming?

    – A.A. Gill

I'm preparing for the baby. I'm busy putting childproof caps on all the bottles of booze.

    – David Letterman

My father taught me the importance of quality workmanship. 'Measure twice, cut once,' was one of his many mottoes.

    – Chris Hilliard

France is a relatively small and eternally quarrelsome country in Western Europe, the fountainhead of rationalist political maniacs, militarily impotent, historically inglorious during the past century, democratically bankrupt, Communist infiltrated from top to bottom.

    – William F. Buckley

The movie business divides women into ice queens and sluts, and there have been times I wanted to be a slut more than anything.

    – Sigourney Weaver

Lawrence was not in the slightest bit queer – later in life, possibly; even then he had Nancy Astor on the back of his motorbike.

    – Lowell Thomas

One's first step to wisdom is to question everything, and one's last is to come to terms with everything.

    – Georg Christoph Lichtenberg

A woman scorned is a woman who quickly learns her way around a courtroom.

    – Colette Mann

My dad skinned and cooked my pet rabbit, Blackie, for dinner. We weren't that hard up. He just fancied a bit of rabbit.

    – Johnny Vegas

John Major is the only man who ran away from the circus to become an accountant.

    – Edward Pearce

Modern music is three farts and a raspberry, orchestrated.

    – John Barbirolli

Women should try to increase their size rather than decrease it, because I believe the bigger we are, the more space we'll take up, and the more we'll have to be reckoned with.

    – Roseanne Barr

There must be at least 500 million rats in the United States; of course, I am speaking only from memory.

    – Edgar W. Nye

What is my favourite book? I haven't read a book in ages. I have a big stack of them.

    – Albert Reynolds

Trouble is, by the time you can read a girl like a book, your library card has expired.

    – Milton Berle

President Bush didn't say that. He was reading what was given to him in a speech.

— **Richard Darman**

The whiter my hair becomes, the more ready people are to believe what I say.

— **Bertrand Russell**

I hope The Times has my obituary ready because I haven't been feeling very well recently.

— **Spike Milligan**

When I think of my father, Ronald Reagan, the memories that bubble to the surface are not of policy or politics. They are of the man who opened a child's imagination, who taught her to be a good horsewoman and to always get back on when I fell off.

— **Patti Davis**

For seven-and-a-half years I've worked alongside President Reagan. We've had triumphs. Made some mistakes. We've had some sex... uh, setbacks.

— **George Bush**

Grannies are only cute on TV. In real life they're like Oxfam shops on legs.

— **Pamela Stephenson**

The other day I ate at a real nice family restaurant. Every table had an argument going.

— **George Carlin**

An actress I met assured me her real ambition was to be a waitress at a coffeehouse.

— **Woody Allen**

Life is like chewing your Christmas pudding really carefully because you are fearful you may be the lucky one with the threepenny bit.

— **Lynne Truss**

It's widely known that one of the reasons I gave up drinking was to avoid having to go to the pub on Christmas Day. The sight of 25 men creating a sea of static electricity with their just-unwrapped, absurdly patterned sweaters is not consistent with good cheer.

– A.A. Gill

As Father Christmas on our Rotary float recently, I asked one little girl if she had written to tell me what she wanted for Christmas. She replied: "No, my computer has crashed."

– Tony Walker

My friend has a baby boy. I'm recording all the noises he makes so later I can ask him what he meant.

– Steven Wright

So, the season is over, the cards recycled, the refuse men tipped, the candle wax dug out of the Menorah, the earrings exchanged for the kitchen clock, the case-on-wheels and accompanying mother-in-law deposited on a station platform and the inflatable beds deflated. As are we all.

– Maureen Lipman

Women are not forgiven for ageing. Robert Redford's 'lines of distinction' are my 'old-age wrinkles'.

– Jane Fonda

Remember that children, marriages and flower gardens reflect the kind of care they get.

– H. Jackson Brown Jr

The only way a woman can ever reform a man is by boring him so completely that he loses all possible interest in life.

– Oscar Wilde

Mr Verhoeven and I have a love-hate relationship: he loves me and I hate him.

– Sharon Stone

I hate it at weddings when old relatives tell me, 'You'll be next, love.' I get my own back at funerals.

– **Mandy Knight**

What is so sad about all this religious censorship is that nearly every aspect of Christmas has a religious meaning. This means eventually the very celebration of Christ's birth will have to be destroyed. The New York public school system is doing just that by claiming that Christ's birth never happened! Please accept without obligation, implied or implicit, our best wishes for an environmentally conscious, socially responsible, politically correct, low-stress, non-addictive, gender-neutral, celebration of the winter solstice holiday practised within the most enjoyable traditions of the religious persuasion of your choice, or secular practices of your choice, with respect for the religious/secular persuasions and/or traditions of others, or their choice not to practise religious or secular traditions at all. We wish you a fiscally successful, personally fulfilling and medically uncomplicated recognition of the onset of the generally accepted calendar year, but not without due respect for the calendars of choice of other cultures... and without regard to the race, creed, colour, age, physical ability, religious faith, choice of computer platform, genetic secrets or sexual orientation of the wishee. By accepting this greeting you are bound by these terms: this greeting is subject to further clarification or withdrawal. Have yourselves a merry little seasonal day of enjoyment.

– **Mark Steyn**

Will all the snakes who wish to remain in Ireland please raise their right hands.

– **Brendan Behan**

The Welsh are said to be so remarkably fond of cheese, that in cases of difficulty their midwives apply a piece of toasted cheese to the janua vitae to attract and entice the young Taffy, who on smelling it makes the most vigorous efforts to come forth.

– **Francis Grose**

If you survive long enough, you're revered, rather like an old building.
– **Katharine Hepburn**

Suffice it to say this will be remembered as a season best forgotten.
– **Terry Badoo**

A diplomat is a man who always remembers a woman's birthday but never remembers her age.

— **Robert Frost**

Animal rights activists demanded that the film-makers remove a scene in which a wolf attacks a man, describing it as an 'anti-wolf statement'.

— **Simon Rose**

A Christian is a man who feels repentance on a Sunday for what he did on Saturday and is going to do on Monday.

— **Thomas Ybarra**

The world's worst piece of art is reputed to be Le Remède by Antoine Watteau. It depicts a reclining Venus about to receive an enema administered by her chambermaid.

— **Bruce Felton**

Children today are tyrants. They have no respect for their elders, flout authority and have appalling manners. What terrible creatures will they grow up into?

— **Socrates**

When I was young there was no respect for the young, and now that I am old there is no respect for the old. I missed out coming and going.

— **J.B. Priestley**

Parents should conduct their arguments in quiet, respectful tones, but in a foreign language. You'd be surprised what an inducement that is to the education of children.

— **Judith Martin**

He respects Owl, because you can't help respecting anybody who can spell TWESDAY, even if he doesn't spell it right.

— **A.A. Milne**

Why does Sea World have a seafood restaurant? I'm halfway through my fish burger and I realize, Oh my God, I could be eating a slow learner.

— **Lynda Montgomery**

I really think that it's better to retire, in Uncle Earl's terms, when you still have some snap left in your garters.

– Russell B. Long

An eighty-year-old friend of mine has just returned from his honeymoon with his eighteen-year-old bride. He described it as like trying to force a marshmallow into a piggy bank.

– Keith Waterhouse

Billy Graham described heaven as a family reunion that never ends. What could hell possibly be like? Home videos of the same reunion?

– Dennis Miller

The news of President Eisenhower's campaigning for Richard Nixon depresses me. After a clear record of eight years, I hate to see him involved in politics.

– Mort Sahl

The real beauty about having Lester Piggott ride for you in the Derby is that it gets him off the other fellow's horse.

– Vincent O'Brien

If somebody calls and says they'll be right over, throw everything down the clothes chute, including the kids.

– Phyllis Diller

A man who is angry on the right grounds and with the right people, and in the right manner and at the right moment for the right length of time, is to be praised.

– Aristotle

If you want to steal money don't rob a bank, open one.

– Bertolt Brecht

A peer condemned to death has a right to be hanged with a silken cord. It's a bit like insisting that the electric chair had to be a Chippendale.

– Charles Mosley

I got more children than I can rightly take care of, but I ain't got more than I can love.

– Ossie Guffy

When you're my age, you just never risk being ill, because then everyone says, 'Oh, he's done for.'

– John Gielgud

If we don't succeed, we run the risk of failure.

– Dan Quayle

Like many fathers, he had a favourite ritual: to put his whole family in the car and drive somewhere. It didn't matter where. What mattered was that he was behind the wheel.

– Signe Hammer

Why did the Aussie bloke cross the road?
'Cause his dick was in the chicken.

– Kathy Lette

Cher has just one expression. She makes Roger Moore look like the world gurning champion.

– Jo Brand

In Milan, traffic lights are instructions. In Rome they are suggestions. But in Naples, they are Christmas decorations.

– Antonio Martino

My father played the viola in the Royal Danish Symphony Orchestra. A lot of people don't know the difference between a violin and a viola. Unfortunately, my father was one of them.

– Victor Borge

I have consistently interpreted Law 26 of Rugby Union on 'misconduct' by awarding a serum for obscenity and a penalty for blasphemy.

– Alec Charters

One of the O'Flanagan twins who played rugby for Ireland was punched by a French forward but the other twin persuaded the referee not to send him off. However, the twins did ensure that the French forward eventually left the field – on a stretcher.

– **Richard Harris**

The first half of our lives is ruined by our parents and the second half by our children.

– **Clarence Darrow**

Finland has produced so many brilliant distance runners because back home it costs $2.50 a gallon for gas.

– **Esa Tikkannery**

That portrait of Prince Charles by some Russian woman was brilliant, wasn't it? And that cunning stunt with the sunglasses – I can never get the eyes right either.

– **Giles Coren**

Only a flaw of fate prevented Vita Sackville-West from being one of nature's gentlemen.

– **Edith Sitwell**

An elector is one who enjoys the sacred privilege of voting for the man of another man's choice.

– **Ambrose Bierce**

Before a man speaks it is always safe to assume that he is a fool. After he speaks it is seldom necessary to assume it.

– **H.L. Mencken**

Half the things I said, I never said them.

– **Yogi Berra**

They all laughed at me when I said I wanted to be a stand-up comedian, but they're not laughing at me now.

– **Joe Manning**

When I dislocated my shoulder the nurse said it was a lot less painful than having a baby. I said, 'Let's see what happens if you try to put it back again.'

   – Stuart Turner

This fellow called at my door and said, 'I'd like to read your gas meter.' I said, 'Whatever happened to the classics?'

   – Emo Philips

Those who survived the San Francisco earthquake said, 'Thank God, I'm still alive.' But of course, for those who died, their lives will never be the same.

   – Barbara Boxer

How true Daddy's words were when he said, 'All children must look after their own upbringing.'

   – Anne Frank

For 15 years, I've been playing the same character – which is myself – and I'm bored with 'myself'.

   – Elle MacPherson

Politicians are interested in people in the same way that dogs are interested in fleas.

   – P.J. O'Rourke

Fish are so underrated these days, especially sand dabs – all of them really. I could go on and on about it. I do, actually. Fishing is boring, unless you catch an actual fish, and then it's disgusting.

   – Dave Barry

Spain is a country that can be saved only by a series of earthquakes.

   – Cyril Connolly

Now that nobody believes in God, or Santa Claus, or the spirit of giving, or family values, or snow, or the whoppers that supermarkets tell us about where they get their turkeys, or sending cards, or the monarchy, or old people, or magic or home baking, there is very little left of Christmas but ritual.

– **Giles Coren**

My worst Christmas was the discovery that Santa Claus was none other than my father. Every year I made a special effort to stay awake and see Father Christmas. I'd left out the cake and glass of milk for him as usual. My parents used to have a few whiskies and talk while they waited for me to fall asleep. This year, though, I heard my father come in and say: 'I'll eat the cake but I'm not drinking the bloody milk.' It was quite a shock at the time...

– **Sara Parkin**

I was in a supermarket and I saw Paul Newman's face on the salad cream and the spaghetti sauce; I thought he was missing.

– **Bob Saget**

I wanted to be a nun. I saw nuns as superstars... When I was growing up I went to a Catholic school, and the nuns, to me, were these superhuman, beautiful, fantastic people.

– **Madonna**

Men come into the delivery room and say, 'Breathe.' Is that really a sharing experience? If I ever have a baby I want my husband to be on the table next to me, at least getting his legs waxed.

– **Rita Rudner**

I don't have a bad word to say about anybody. Even Adolf Hitler – he was the best in his field.

– **Buddy Hackett**

Things a father should know: how to say 'That's final' and not go back on it as soon as his wife's out of sight.

– **Katharine Whitehorn**

Whenever the talk turns to age, I say I am 49 plus VAT.

– Lionel Blair

The average man will bristle if you say his father was dishonest, but he will brag a little if he discovers that his great-grandfather was a pirate.

– Bern Williams

I was surprised, but like I always say, nothing surprises me in football.

– Les Ferdinand

My kids bring their friends over and say, 'We can tell how old our daddy is by counting the rings on his stomach.'

– Tony Kornheiser

My old father used to have a saying: If you make a bad bargain, hug it all the tighter.

– Abraham Lincoln

Fellows become bookmakers because they are too scared to steal and too heavy to become a jockey.

– Noel Whitcome

The great advantage of an English public school education is that no subsequent form of captivity can hold any particular terror for you. A friend who was put to work on the Burma railway once told me that he was greeted, on arrival, by a fellow prisoner-of-war who said, 'Cheer up. It's not half as bad as Marlborough'.

– John Mortimer

Psychology is in its infancy as a science. I hope, in the interests of art, it will always remain so.

– Oscar Wilde

I see the customs authorities in England searched the round-the-world fliers when they landed. I guess they thought the boys had smuggled over a couple of baby grand pianos.

– Will Rogers

I spent many years laughing at Harry Secombe's singing until somebody told me it wasn't a joke.

– **Spike Milligan**

What has happened to architecture since the Second World War that the only passers-by who can contemplate it without pain are those equipped with a white stick and dog?

– **Bernard Levin**

Every family has a secret, and the secret is that it's not like other families.

– **Alan Bennett**

Freud is a lot of nonsense. The secret of all neurosis is to be found in the family battle of wills to see who can refuse longest to help with the dishes.

– **Julian Mitchell**

When Gary was 9, we had to see the school psychologist because he kept asking girls to do handstands for him.

– **Gary's dad, Men Behaving Badly**

Never bet with a bookmaker if you see him knocking spikes in his shoes.

– **Jack Leach**

Some see the glass as half-empty; some see the glass as half-full. I see the glass as too big.

– **George Carlin**

The longer I live the more I see that I am never wrong about anything, and that all the pains that I have so humbly taken to verify my notions have only wasted my time.

– **George Bernard Shaw**

It is only rarely that one can see in a little boy the promise of a man, but one can almost always see in a little girl the threat of a woman.

– **Alexandre Dumas**

Are the angels sawing timber in heaven? See how they lift their planks in the flour-loft and shake the dust down on us; and they wear cloaks of frosty silver trimmed with coldest quicksilver.

– **Anon**

There isn't anybody who doesn't like to see an old man make a comeback. Jimmy Connors seemed like a jerk to me until he was 40. After that, I rooted for him all the time. How could you not?

– **T. Boone Pickens**

There are few things more satisfying than seeing your children have teenagers of their own.

– **Doug Larson**

I grow increasingly impatient of holidays: they seem a wholly feminine conception, based on an impotent dislike of everyday life and a romantic notion that it will all be better at Frinton or Venice.

– **Philip Larkin**

The week before Christmas, when the snow seemed to lie thickest, was the moment for carol singing; and when I think back to those nights it is to the crunch of the snow and to the lights of the lanterns on it.

– **Laurie Lee, Cider with Rosie**

To my generation, no other English poet seemed so perfectly to express the sensibility of a male adolescent as A.E. Housman.

– **W.H. Auden**

The better class of Briton likes to send his children away to school until they are old enough and intelligent enough to come home again. Then they're too old and intelligent to want to.

– **Malcolm Bradbury**

When you get to my age, life seems little more than one long march to and from the lavatory.

– **John Mortimer**

I don't know if anyone has ever seen a parson with a nose like a chicken's arse, but surely they must have hit the crossbar when they cast Karl Malden as the priest in On the Waterfront.

— **Allan Miller**

Anyone seeing women at a bargain-basement sale... sees aggression that would make Attila the Hun turn pale.

— **Estelle Ramey, physician and physiologist**

Naming our baby was a trial. I seize up when I have to name a document on my computer.

— **Jeff Stilson**

Having small hands, I was becoming terribly self-conscious about keeping the second tennis ball in a can in the car while I served the first.

— **Erma Bombeck**

The vice president simply presides over the Senate and sits around hoping for a funeral.

— **Harry Truman**

When they call the roll in the Senate, the senators do not know whether to answer 'present' or 'not guilty'.

— **Theodore Roosevelt**

From the vantage point of his wondrously serene old age, my father contemplates our lives almost as if they were books he can dip into whenever he wants. His back pages, perhaps.

— **Angela Carter**

The present state of English rugby is serious but not hopeless; the present state of Irish rugby is hopeless but not serious.

— **Noel Henderson**

Beneath the thick skin of the stronger sex lies an open wound called the Male Ego.

– Letty Cottin Pogrebin

A great way to meet the opposite sex when you're older is on the Internet, a good reason to learn to use a computer. The Internet is 70 per cent men, so the odds are definitely in a woman's favour for finding a guy.

– Joan Rivers

If you think women are the weaker sex, try pulling the blankets back to your side.

– Stuart Turner

The fact is I am not having sex. But I feel absolutely ripe for the... what would you say, plucking?

– Angelina Jolie

Infatuation is when you think he's as sexy as Robert Redford, as smart as Henry Kissinger, as noble as Ralph Nader, as funny as Woody Allen and as athletic as Jimmy Connors. Love is when you realise he's as sexy as Woody Allen, as smart as Jimmy Connors, as funny as Ralph Nader, as athletic as Henry Kissinger and nothing like Robert Redford... but you'll take him anyway.

– Judith Viorst

The true place for commemoration is in your mind, not on your mantelpiece – and if your mind's too busy planning ahead, it isn't properly there at the time.

– Victoria Coren

Look, I grew up in a goddamn shack, so I like a bit of comfort.

– Mariah Carey

The new West Stand casts a giant shadow over the entire pitch even on a sunny day.

– **Chris Jones**

At the end of this year, I shall be 63, if alive, and about the same if dead.

– **Mark Twain**

I'm taking early retirement. I want my share of Social Security before the whole system goes bust.

– **David Letterman**

My wife is an excellent creature, but she can never remember which came first, the Greeks or the Romans.

– **Benjamin Disraeli**

A woman knows everything about her children. She knows about dental appointments and football games and best friends and favourite foods and romances and secret fears and hopes and dreams. A man is vaguely aware of some short people living in the house.

– **Dave Barry**

Her house caught fire so often that she greeted the local fire brigade with a cry of 'Gentlemen, take your accustomed places'.

– **John Wells**

Once a woman has forgiven her man, she must not reheat his sins for breakfast.

– **Marlene Dietrich**

My mother could make anybody feel guilty. She used to get letters of apology from people she didn't even know.

– **Joan Rivers**

My mother is no spring chicken, although she has got as many chemicals in her as one.

– **Dame Edna Everage**

No matter how old a mother is, she watches her middle-aged children for signs of improvement.

– **Florida Scott-Maxwell**

She had finally reached the age where she was more afraid of getting old than dying.

– **Julia Phillips**

A tap-in is a putt that is short enough to be missed one-handed.

– **Henry Beard**

Easter eggs go on sale for a short period because they are basically horrible. Something happens to chocolate in the process of turning it egg shaped that makes it taste like something that has spent 20 years at the back of a cupboard. The pagan tradition is strong enough to persuade people to pay £3.99 for this experience once a year, but no way are they going to repeat it more often. By the time a year has passed they have forgotten how unpleasant Easter eggs are and they then buy them again.

– **Robert Crompton**

The reason there is such a food shortage in Russia is that the government stockpiles all the food for the army. Whatever the army doesn't use after a year, the government sells to the public.

– **Yakov Smirnoff**

I was married by a judge. I should have asked for a jury.

– **George Burns**

Because of its famous echo, British composers should all endeavour to have their works performed in the Royal Albert Hall; they will thus be assured of at least two performances.

– **Thomas Beecham**

When we grab Osama bin Laden, we should put him on my show. That would be a taste of hell.

– **Jerry Springer**

A father is a giant from whose shoulders you can see for ever.
   – Perry Garfinkel

My best chat-up line was: 'Shall I show you a few of my judo holds?'
   – Honor Blackman

I go back to Bach as a sick dog instinctively grubs at the roots and herbs that are its right medicine.
   – Pablo Casals

You will recognize, my boy, the first sign of old age: it is when you go out into the streets of London and realize for the first time how young the policemen look.
   – Seymour Hicks

To rephrase Samuel Butler, a man is simply a woman's way of making another woman.
   – Naomi Segal

The secret of my youthful appearance is simply mashed swede. As a face-mask, as a night-cap, and in an emergency, as a draught-excluder.
   – Kitty, *Victoria Wood*

Disc-jockeys are electronic lice.
   – Anthony Burgess

Vote early and often.
   – Al Capone

Quoting Ronald Reagan accurately is called mud-slinging.
   – Walter Mondale

Hollywood – climate and religious diversity notwithstanding – is a Christmas kind of place. And if one doesn't send out hundreds of Christmas cards (sample message: 'May the Joy of the Season Warm You and Your Family. A donation in your name has been made to an

Important-Sounding Charity'), send gift baskets of tiny, inedible muffins, and in general behave as if one day's generosity can somehow mitigate 364 days of cruelty and selfishness; well, then, just how does one expect to succeed in this town?

– **Rob Long**

Politics is show business for ugly people.

– **Paul Begala**

Playwriting and safe cracking are similar occupations – lonely work, tedious and tense, and not especially rewarding considering the time, effort and risk involved. And unless each job comes off to perfection the newspapers treat both the playwright and the safecracker as common criminals.

– **George Kaufman**

My boss wouldn't dare to sack me – I'm too far behind in my work.

– **Joey Adams**

I did not expect an Honorary Oscar – well, actually, I did. But not for another 25 years.

– **Federico Fellini**

I've read about foreign policy and studied – I know a number of continents.

– **George Wallace**

Gladstone has not got one redeeming defect.

– **Benjamin Disraeli**

Christmas is hell in a stupid sweater.

– **Carina Chocano**

A woman's place is in the wrong.

– **James Thurber**

The Democratic Party is like a mule – without pride of ancestry or hope of posterity.

- **Edmund Burke**

I know two kinds of audience only – one coughing and one not coughing.

- **Artur Schnabel**

John Major is marginally better than cystitis.

- **Jo Brand**

America is a mistake, a giant mistake.

- **Sigmund Freud**

Brigands demand your money or your life – women require both.

- **Samuel Butler**

I picked my nose as a child – in consultation with the plastic surgeon.

- **Emo Philips**

There is nothing on earth so savage – even a bear robbed of her cubs – as a hungry husband.

- **Fanny Fern**

Some families have skeletons in the closet – with us the skeletons have the run of the house and we live in the closet.

- **Joe McCarroll**

Arnold Palmer is the biggest crowd pleaser since the invention of the portable sanitary facility.

- **Bob Hope**

Teenagers are God's punishment for having sex.

- **Patrick Murray**

We will now sing hymn number forty-two – Holy, Holy, Holy; all the holies, forty-two.

– **Marty Feldman**

She was looser than an MFI wardrobe.

– **Roy Brown**

I myself have been in debt ever since I reached the age of discretion. To be in debt, in fact, is one of the plainest signs that the age of discretion has been reached, and those who are monotonously solvent have probably never fully grown up.

– **A.J.A. Symons**

I hope I have a young outlook. Since I have an old everything else, this is my one chance of having a bit of youth as a part of me.

– **Richard Armour**

We are not, by and large, a singing people, not since our misguided government axed choral singing in schools, but you can still experience a Cup Final sort of thrill as the Royal Albert Hall resounds to 'O Come, All Ye Faithful' sung by 6, 000 voices. Carols as social glue? Why not?

– **John Rutter**

I can't open my eyes when I'm singing because the words are written on the back of my eyelids.

– **Christy Moore**

The Catholic Church is for saints and sinners. For respectable people the Anglican Church will do.

– **Oscar Wilde**

Being a Catholic doesn't stop you from sinning. It just stops you from enjoying it.

– **Cleveland Amory**

My 3-year-old son turned to his 5-year-old sister, and said, 'Just you wait till I'm older than you!'.
  – **Wayne Lowe**

There's nothing that I like better than sitting in front of a roaring fire with a copy of War and Peace. You know a big fat book like that will feed the fire for two hours.
  – **Emo Philips**

I grew up in a big family, six kids – seven, if you count my dad. He got all the attention, being the youngest.
  – **Margaret Smith**

I couldn't hit a wall with a six-gun, but I can twirl it on my finger and it looks good on the screen.
  – **John Wayne**

I've just had a hole-in-one at the sixteenth and I left the ball in the hole just to prove it.
  – **Bob Hope**

After lovemaking, do you (a) go to sleep? (b) light a cigarette? (c) return to the front of the bus?
  – **Joan Rivers**

I do not mean to be the slightest bit critical of TV news people, who do a superb job, considering that they operate under severe time restraints and have the intellectual depth of hamsters.
  – **Dave Barry**

People are not homeless if they are sleeping in the streets of their hometowns.
  – **Dan Quayle**

Happiness is sitting down to watch some slides of your neighbour's vacation and finding out he spent two weeks in a nudist colony.

– Johnny Carson

As you get older, the pickings get slimmer, but the people don't.

– Carrie Fisher

Never, ever buy clothes you intend to slim into or – oh, the possibility of it – gain weight to fill.

– Karen Homer

There is also a place for very small and/or very cheap Christmas cards. They imply bad taste, poverty or disrespect to the recipient, and will guarantee deletion from their Christmas card list. These are particularly effective for terminating pointless long-term Christmas card exchanges with people like the Fanshaws you met in Torremolinos... and can't even remember what they look like any more – or was it Benidorm?

– William Connor

Yuppies, we knew, were greedy, shallow and small... We renamed the seven dwarves: Artsy, Fartsy, Cranky, Sleazy, Beasty, Dud and Yuppie.

– Lorrie Moore

Dad used to say, 'No matter how smart a girl is, she can't be that smart if she's dating you.'

– Artie, *The Norm Show*

A wedding is a funeral where you smell your own flowers.

– Eddie Cantor

I loved the way all the actresses smelt. I didn't realise until years afterwards that it was gin.

– Rhys Ifans

I have a daughter who goes to SMU. She could have gone to UCLA here in California, but that would have been one more letter for her to remember.

– Shecky Green

Just because your mother's nuttier than a Snickers bar doesn't mean that you should disrespect her.

– Victor Pellet, In-Laws

If it were not for the intellectual snobs who pay in solid cash, the arts would perish with their starving practitioners.

– Aldous Huxley

Laugh and the world laughs with you. Snore and you sleep alone.

– Anthony Burgess

At a certain age, you begin to snort at fashion, you stop going to the cinema and you watch the black-and-white classic on aeroplanes. You slouch into a curmudgeonly comfort culture of the old and familiar, and become a 'call that' person. Call that music/fashion/poetry/a chair?

– A.A. Gill

In January 1494 a great deal of snow fell in Florence and Piero de' Medici... wanted a statue of snow made in the middle of the courtyard. He remembered Michelangelo, sent for him and had him make the statue.

– Ascanio Condivi, assistant to Michelangelo, 1553

How do the men who drive the snow plough get to work in the morning?

– Steven Wright

Around all and beyond all, was the snow, almost exactly resembling the snow that fell in English films on top of people like Alistair Sim and Margaret Rutherford.

– Clive James on first arriving in England from Australia

Y'all are so cute and y'all talk so proper over here. I love England.

– Beyonce Knowles

What feeling in all the world is so nice as that of a child's hand in yours? What tenderness it arouses, what power it conjures. You are instantly the very touchstone of wisdom and strength.
   – **Marjorie Holmes**

Poor Mexico, so far from God and so close to the United States.
   – **Porfiris Diaz**

Consider the Vice-President, George Bush, a man so bedevilled by bladder problems that he managed, for the last eight years, to be in the men's room whenever an important illegal decision was made.
   – **Barbara Ehrenreich**

One time I had to go out, so I asked Woody Allen to watch the children. When I returned less than an hour later, he was throwing his hats and gloves into the fire. The kids were ecstatic. Woody just shrugged and said, 'I ran out of things to do.'
   – **Mia Farrow**

A broken heart is what makes life so wonderful five years later, when you see the guy in the elevator and he is fat and smoking a cigar and saying long-time – no-see. If he had not broken your heart you could not have that glorious feeling of relief.
   – **Phyllis Battelle**

One night in King Lear they coughed so much I stopped and started coughing as a sort of hint. But they didn't get it.
   – **Tom Courtenay**

As a young man Peter's ugliness was so remarkable that his fellow undergraduates formed themselves into a committee to consider what could be done for the improvement of Peter's personal appearance.
   – **Hesketh Pearson**

People laugh at Mickey Mouse because he's so human. That's the secret of his popularity.
   – **Walt Disney**

I was ashamed of being a lawyer, so now I manually masturbate caged animals for artificial insemination.

– **Virginia Smith**

The reason modern poetry is difficult is so that the poet's wife cannot understand it.

– **Wendy Cope**

I could never see why people were so happy about Dickens's A Christmas Carol because I never had any confidence that Scrooge was going to be different the next day.

– **Dr Karl Menninger**

Raising a child today is a journey so fraught with bad directions, backseat drivers, and contradicting maps, that it's a wonder we even make it out of the maternity hospital parking garage.

– **Dennis Miller**

Nobody in this world can make me so happy, or so miserable, as a daughter.

– **Thomas Jefferson**

Although He is regularly asked to do so, God does not take sides in American politics.

– **George Mitchell**

My advice to young writers is to socialize. Don't just go up to a pine cabin all alone and brood. You reach that stage soon enough anyway.

– **Truman Capote**

The high-water mark, so to speak, of Socialist literature is W.H. Auden, a sort of gutless Kipling.

– **George Orwell**

We live in far too permissive a society. Never before has pornography been this rampant. And those films are lit so badly.

– **Woody Allen**

The family is the building block of society. If it did not exist it would have to be invented.

   – William Hague

Any child can tell you that the sole purpose of a middle name is so he can tell when he's in trouble.

   – Dennis Fakes

When I feel an attack of indigestion coming on, I picture two or three princes as gainers by my death, take courage out of spite, and conspire against them with rhubarb and temperance.

   – Voltaire

If this is coffee, please bring me some tea; if this is tea, please bring me some coffee.

   – Abraham Lincoln

Health nuts are going to feel stupid some day, lying in hospitals dying of nothing.

   – Red Foxx

Seeing my kids growing up brings back some of the joys of childhood – sticky fingers, running until you're out of breath, laughing so hard that your stomach hurts.

   – Neil Layton

I wish I had the experience that some woman had killed herself for love of me. The women who have admired me have all insisted on living on, long after I have ceased to care for them.

   – George Sanders

One of Canada's most serious needs is some lesser nation to domineer over and shame by displays of superior taste.

   – Robertson Davies

I am told that the Inuit have some 60 words for snow... I have 17 words for snow – none of them usable in public.

– **Arthur Black**

I have never understood the fear of some parents about babies getting mixed up in a hospital. What difference does it make as long as you get a good one?

– **Heywood Broun**

A single woman with a dog is, somehow, nowhere near as tragic as one with a cat.

– **India Knight**

Love is just a system for getting someone to call you darling after sex.

– **Julian Barnes**

The definition of an orthopaedic surgeon is someone with the strength of an ox but half the brain.

– **John Dorgan**

I can't decide whether growing pains are something kids have – or are.

– **Jackson Cole**

At your first dinner party with your son and new daughter-in-law, it's not a good idea to tell her the way your mother used to prepare the dish.

– **David Letterman**

I'm dreaming of a white Christmas. This song could only be sung in southern California around a swimming pool. Here, at the first hint of snow British Rail runs to a standstill, the roads become impassable, and even the pavements are a danger as the salt destroys your shoes.

– **Derek Jarman**

I welcome him like I welcome cold sores. He's from England, he's angry and he's got Mad Power Disease.

– **Paula Abdul on Simon Cowell**

Knight's Biography of Rossetti is just the sort of biography Guildenstern might have written of Hamlet.

– **Oscar Wilde**

No real English gentleman, in his secret soul, was ever sorry for the death of a political economist.

– **Walter Bagehot**

The best instrument is the bag-pipes. They sound exactly the same when you have finished learning them as when you start.

– **Thomas Beecham**

When jack Benny plays the violin, it sounds as though the strings are still in the cat.

– **Fred Allen**

The Church should send a satellite into space with a bishop in it. It would draw the attention of millions towards God.

– **Alastair Graham**

Hear no evil, see no evil and speak no evil, and you'll never get a job working for a tabloid.

– **Phil Pastoret**

Saul is a frequent broadcaster who never speaks but is constantly mentioned by those who do: Goodbye from Saul here in the studio.

– **Fritz Spiegl**

I come from a long line of spectacularly brilliant cooks whose pastry came out golden every time and melted in the mouth. It is not, regrettably, a talent I inherited. So every year it's: 'Mum, why aren't your mince pies as good as Grandma's?'

– **Jenni Murray**

Christmas is a funny old time. We spend one half of the year planning for it and the other half paying for it.

– **Ilona Amos**

A play is basically a means of spending two hours in the dark without being bored.

  – Kenneth Tynan

We've got our Christmas dinner already cooking. Spent two hours trussing up that lump of corned beef.

  – Tony Hancock, Hancock's Half Hour

As a baby, I was almost perfectly spherical in shape, causing my parents frequent anxieties as they feared they had left me upside down, and forcing them to enter and re-enter rooms in which I had been left in order to check.

  – Peter Ustinov

Word has somehow got around that the split infinitive is always wrong. That is of a piece with the outworn notion that it is always wrong to strike a lady.

  – James Thurber

A truly appreciative child will break, lose, spoil or fondle to death any really successful gift within a matter of minutes.

  – Russell Lynes

I listened to a football coach who spoke straight from the shoulder. At least I couldn't detect a higher origin in anything he said.

  – Dixon Fox

Horse racing is one of the real sports that's left to us: a bit of danger and excitement, and the horses, which are the best thing in the world.

  – The Queen Mother

I've reached that awkward age for any sportsman – too old physically to carry on competing at the top level, but still too mentally alert to become a selector.

  – Sebastian Coe

For Autumn is just as nice as Spring And it's never too late to fall in love.

– **Sandy Wilson**

Teenage girls can get pregnant merely by standing downwind of teenage boys.

– **Dave Barry**

Lulubelle, it's you! I didn't recognise you standing up.

– **Groucho Marx**

My daughter was born under a lucky star. Lionel Blair had the flat upstairs.

– **Bob Monkhouse**

May you build a ladder to the stars and climb on every rung.

– **Bob Dylan**

You know you're getting old when you start to like your mum and dad again. 'Yes, mum, I'd love to come caravanning to Tenby with you. No, I'll bring a packed lunch. I'm not paying café prices.'

– **Jeff Green**

I've just become a pensioner so I've started saving up for my own hospital trolley.

– **Tom Baker**

The trouble between my wife and me started during our marriage service. When I said, 'I do,' she said, 'Don't use that tone of voice with me.'

– **Roy Brown**

Sex hasn't been the same since women started to enjoy it.

– **Lewis Grizzard**

Father preferred to begin a discussion by stating his conclusion and by calling yours nonsense, and to end the debate then and there.

– **Clarence Day**

December 10, 1777 Jas. Soaper hanged for stealing a nail. December 14, 1777 Jas. Soaper found to be innocent. December 17, 1777 Jas. Soaper dug up and removed to Consecrated Ground.

– **Michael Green**

It's only when you grow up and step back from your father, or leave him for your own career and your own home – it's only then that you can measure his greatness and fully appreciate it. Pride reinforces love.

– **Margaret Truman**

How can I be overdrawn when I've still got lots of cheques left in the book?

– **Gracie Allen**

I'm a child of the Sixties. I still wear jeans and yes, my bum looks big in them but then my bum looked big in 1965.

– **Julia Richardson**

I want women to be liberated and still be able to have a nice ass and shake it.

– **Shirley MacLaine**

My baby used to put up a stink any time we put her in the car seat to take her for a ride. We found that howling like wolves made her curious enough to stop crying and listen to the strange sounds we were making.

– **Genuine advice in a baby manual**

My son, take care to have your stocking well gartered up, and your shoes well-buckled; for nothing gives a more slovenly air to a man than ill-dressed legs.

– **Lord Chesterfield**

Statistically, there has not been anyone who stole more books of such obviously high quality from more libraries than Stephen Blumberg.

– **William Moffett**

I haven't read Karl Marx. I got stuck on that footnote on page two.

– **Harold Wilson**

You know you're getting old when you stoop to tie your shoelaces and wonder what else you can do while you're down there.

– **George Burns**

It's easy to beat Brazil. You just stop them getting twenty yards from your goal.

– **Bobby Charlton**

Modern art is what happens when painters stop looking at girls and persuade themselves they have a better idea.

– **John Ciardi**

An expert is a man who has stopped thinking. Why should he think? He is an expert!

– **Frank Lloyd Wright**

You can tell it's the Christmas season. Stores are selling off their expired milk as eggnog. The Advocaat doesn't 'arf make me sleepy.

– **David Letterman**

That miss on the red will go straight out of my head as soon as I collect my pension book.

– **John Parrott**

If you are ever attacked in the street do not shout 'help!', shout 'fire!'. People adore fires and always come rushing. Nobody will come if you shout 'help'.

– **Jean Trumpington**

Almost everyone when age, disease or sorrows strike him, inclines to think there is a God, or something very like Him.

– **Arthur Hugh Clough**

A piano is a parlour utensil for subduing the impenitent visitor. It is operated by depressing the keys of the machine and the spirits of the audience.

– **Ambrose Bierce**

What makes a sane and rational person subject himself to such humiliation? Why on earth does anyone want to become a football referee?

– Roy Hattersley

Most journalists of my generation died early, succumbing to one or other of the two great killers in the craft – cirrhosis or terminal alimony.

– John Hepworth

Small wonder that Manchester United is in such a pickle when the star player talks in a squeak so high-pitched only dogs can hear him, and the manager speaks goat.

– Jeremy Clarkson

My son does not appreciate classical musicians such as the Rolling Stones; he is more into bands with names like 'Heave' and 'Squatting Turnips'.

– Dave Barry

Father is the thoughtful man who will suggest putting vodka in a baby's bottle when he's crying.

– Joan Rivers

Sometimes I wonder if men and women suit each other. Perhaps they should live next door and just visit now and then.

– Katherine Hepburn

One can always count on Gilbert and Sullivan for a rousing finale, full of words and music, signifying nothing.

– Tom Lehrer

Now I'm getting older I take health supplements: geranium, dandelion, passionflower, hibiscus. I feel great, and when I pee, I experience the fresh scent of potpourri.

– Sheila Wenz

I was watching what I thought was sumo wrestling on the television for two hours before I realised it was darts.

— **Hattie Hayridge**

Good days are to be gathered like sunshine in grapes, to be trodden and bottled into wine and kept for age to sip at ease beside the fire. If the traveller has vintaged well, he need trouble to wander no longer; the ruby moments glow in his glass at will.

— **Freya Stark**

I behaved badly only because I felt superior to all who surrounded me.

— **Sarah Bernhardt**

Because he has such respect for your superior wisdom and technical know-how, he is constantly asking questions like 'Does this kid need a sweater?' or 'Is the baby wet?'

— **Jean Kerr**

A run of good luck is a sure sign of bad luck.

— **Walt Kelly**

Money cannot buy you everything, but it sure puts you in a great bargaining position.

— **Doug Larson**

'Twas a good dinner enough, to be sure, but it was not a dinner to ask a man to.

— **Samuel Johnson**

A crowded police court docket is the surest of all signs that trade is brisk and money plenty.

— **Mark Twain**

If in the paddock the owner is surrounded by a herd of young children, don't back his horse. But if the owner is accompanied by a beautiful lady, plunge to the hilt.

— **Robert Morley**

Truth is so precious it must be surrounded by a bodyguard of lies.

– **Winston Churchill**

It is said that no actor can survive playing opposite a child or a dog. It is just as lethal playing opposite the Irish Abbey Players. Apart from being able to act you off the stage, they can also drink you under the table.

– **Sidney Gilliat**

As long as there are sex-mad teenagers swimming in the nude at night, there will be a Friday the 13th movie.

– **Simon Rose**

We had political discussions around the dinner table. Once I said, 'Dad, what we need is an effective third political party.' He said, 'I'd settle for a second.'

– **Robin Philips**

Don't be put off by the Formica tabletops; the chef used to cook for Onassis before he took to the bottle.

– **Robert Morley**

She was a singer who had to take every note above A with her eyebrows.

– **Montague Glass**

I took the day off work to take care of my son. First we did finger-painting, then we played Snakes and Ladders, then we read a story, then we watched a video, then we played Snakes and Ladders again, then we sang nursery rhymes, then we played football, and by that time it was nearly nine o'clock... in the morning.

– **Simon Wilson**

This is the last time I will take part as an amateur.

– **Daniel François Esprit Auber, 76, at a funeral**

A man is not old until regrets take the place of your dreams.

– **John Barrymore**

Shop crowded with people, who seemed to take up the cards rather roughly, and after a hurried glance at them, throw them down again. I remarked to one of the young persons serving, that carelessness appeared to be a disease with some purchasers. The observation was scarcely out of my mouth, when my thick coat-sleeve caught against a large pile of expensive cards in boxes one on top of the other, and threw them down. The manager came forward, looking very much annoyed...

    – George Grossmith, The Diary of a Nobody

The secret in the rough is to take a few dozen practice swings with a 2-iron. (A scythe is good too.)

    – Tom Callahan

There is one thing women can never take away from men. We die sooner.

    – P.J O'Rourke

At an examination we were allowed to take into the examination anything we could carry. I gave a piggyback to a postgraduate student.

    – Dirk Mollett

David Leadbetter wanted me to change my takeaway, my backswing, my downswing and my follow-through. He said I could still play right-handed.

    – Brad Bryant

I'm at the age when food has taken the place of sex in my life. In fact, I've just had a mirror put over my kitchen table.

    – Rodney Dangerfield

People always ask me how long it takes to do my hair. I don't know, I'm never there.

    – Dolly Parton

Politics has become so expensive that it takes a lot of money even to be defeated.

    – Will Rogers

What would bug a guy from the Taliban more than seeing a gay woman in a suit surrounded by Jews?

– **Ellen DeGeneres**

Ice skating is a sport where you talk about sequins, earrings and plunging necklines – and you are talking about the men.

– **Christine Brennan**

The telephone is a good way to talk to people without having to offer them a drink.

– **Fran Lebowitz**

You know you're old when your family talk about you in front of you. What are we going to do with Pop? We have company tonight.

– **Rodney Dangerfield**

I went to see my doctor to talk to him about this menopause thing, because I don't know if I really want to do it.

– **Jane Condon**

During sex, my wife often wants to talk to me. Just the other night she called me from a motel.

– **Rodney Dangerfield**

There is nothing sadder than hearing someone talking to their cat as if it were a real human being with a brain and a Marks and Spencer's charge card.

– **Jenny Eclair**

If your kid wants to get a tattoo or a piercing just say, 'Great idea! As a matter of fact, let's both go get tattoos and nose rings!'

– **David Letterman**

My idea of fatherhood is sending a telegram from Abyssinia saying 'Have you had your child yet, and what have you called it?'

– **Evelyn Waugh**

Washington couldn't tell a lie, Nixon couldn't tell the truth and Reagan couldn't tell the difference.

– **Mort Sahl**

A diplomat is a person who can tell you to go to hell in such a way that you actually look forward to the trip.

– **Caskie Stinnett**

If you have anything of importance to tell me, for God's sake begin at the end.

– **Sara Duncan**

The most hated vegetable in the land? Tell that to the good folk of Diss in Norfolk whose 6,600 residents buy 54,000 sprouts a week – 75 times the national average. That compares with a paltry 720 in West Bromwich in the Midlands, the sprout-hating capital of Britain.

– **Lisa Jones**

I can't imagine what my kids will tell their kids they had to do without.

– **Alex Blake**

I truly believe that if we keep telling the Christmas story, singing the Christmas songs, and living the Christmas spirit, we can bring joy and happiness and peace to this world.

– **Norman Vincent Peale**

Some rules about late fatherhood: don't be tempted to grow a 'youthful' pony-tail (the rule is: if it hangs, someone will swing on it); don't ask the children from your first marriage to baby-sit – they'll only compare birthday presents; do try to take it on the chin when the other mums and dads at school mistake you for grandpa.

– **Phil Hogan**

I started reading War and Peace over ten years ago. Now I have to go back to the beginning again because I have forgotten how it starts.

– **Terry Wogan**

There's a new service that lets you test your IQ over the phone. It costs $3.75 a minute. If you make the call at all, you're a moron. If you stay on hold for over three minutes, you're a complete idiot.

– Jay Leno

Of course, travelling is much easier today than it used to be. A hundred years ago, it could take you the better part of a year to get from New York to California; whereas today, because of equipment problems at O'Hare, you can't get there at all.

– Dave Barry

Things are more like they are now than they have ever been before.

– Dwight D. Eisenhower

I've given my memoirs far more thought than any of my marriages. You can't divorce a book.

– Gloria Swanson

Love is much nicer to be in than an automobile accident, a tight girdle, a higher tax bracket or a holding pattern over Philadelphia.

– Judith Viorst

If man is only a little lower than the angels, then the angels should reform.

– Mary W. Little

A nuclear power plant is infinitely safer than eating because three hundred people choke to death on food every year.

– Dixy Lee Ray

The only thing that scares me more than space aliens is the idea that there aren't any space aliens. We can't be the best creation has to offer.

– Ellen DeGeneres

Lawyers are said to be more honourable than politicians, but less honourable than prostitutes. This is an exaggeration.

– Alexander King

The trouble with a folk song is that once you have played it through there is nothing much you can do except play it over again and play it rather louder.

– **Constant Lambert**

A puck is a hard rubber disc that ice hockey players strike when they can't hit each other.

– **Jimmy Cannon**

The great thing about Glasgow now is that if there's a nuclear attack it'll look exactly the same afterwards.

– **Billy Connolly**

The only difference about being married is that you don't have to get out of bed to fart.

– **Jimmy Goldsmith**

The unique thing about Margaret Rutherford is that she can act with her chin alone.

– **Kenneth Tynan**

The lovely thing about being forty is that you can appreciate twenty-five-year-old men more.

– **Colleen McCullough**

One good thing about getting older is that if you're getting married, the phrase 'till death do you part' doesn't sound so horrible. It only means about 10 or 15 years and not the eternity it used to mean.

– **Joy Behar**

Not all coppers are bastards, but those that are make a very good job of it.

– **Charlie Kray**

Cockroaches and socialites are the only things that can stay up all night and eat anything.

– **Herb Caen**

The only real argument for marriage is that it remains the best method for getting acquainted.

– Heywood Brown

Christmas is a box of tree ornaments that have become part of the family.

– Charles M. Schulz

The difference between Christianity and Communism is that Christians believe in life after death whereas Communists believe in posthumous rehabilitation.

– Timothy Ash

The advantages of dating younger men is that on them everything, like hair and teeth, is in the right place as opposed to being on the bedside table or bathroom floor.

– Candace Bushnell

Nothing is more distasteful to me than that entire complacency and satisfaction which beam in the countenances of a new married couple.

– Charles Lamb

The trouble with eating Italian food is that five or six days later you're hungry again.

– George Miller

We're so busy flicking channels these days that we miss the best programmes. The same can certainly be said for our relationships.

– Mariella Frostrup

We are ready for any unforeseen event that may or may not occur.

– Dan Quayle

Fred Astaire was great, but don't forget that Ginger Rogers did everything that he did, backwards and in high heels.

– Bob Thaves

Any mother with half a skull knows that when Daddy's Little Boy becomes Mommy's Little Boy, the kid is so wet that he's treading water.

– **Erma Bombeck**

The Democratic Party has succeeded so well that many of its members are now Republicans.

– **Tip O'Neill**

My new son has a face like that of an ageing railway porter who is beginning to realize that his untidiness has meant that he'll never get that ticket-collector's job he's been after for twenty years.

– **Kingsley Amis**

My true friends have always given me that supreme proof of devotion; a spontaneous aversion for the man I loved.

– **Colette**

A mini series is an Australian fillum that doesn't know when to stop.

– **Barry Humphries**

Things children should know – but don't: that Mummy and Daddy don't actually do all that just to make a baby.

– **Katharine Whitehorn**

As Lavinia, Miss Leigh receives the news that she is about to be ravished on her husband's corpse with little more than the mild annoyance of one who would have preferred foam rubber.

– **Kenneth Tynan**

We were so long shooting the film that when anyone asked my children what their father did for a living, they invariably replied Spartacus.

– **Peter Ustinov**

Never give a loved one a gift that suggests they need improvement.

– **H. Jackson Brown, Jr**

Advice to expectant mothers: you must remember that when you are pregnant, you are eating for two. But you must remember that the other one of you is about the size of a golf ball, so let's not go overboard with it. A lot of pregnant women eat as though the other person they're eating for is Orson Welles.

– **Dave Barry**

The difference between mums and dads is that mums work at work and work at home, and dads just go to work to work.

– **Jack, aged 8**

What's nice about my dating life is that I don't have to leave my house. All I have to do is read the paper: I'm marrying Richard Gere, dating Daniel Day-Lewis... and even Robert De Niro was in there for a day.

– **Julia Roberts**

The secret of my piano playing is that I always make sure that the lid over the keyboard is open before I start to play.

– **Artur Schnabel**

Childlessness has many obvious advantages. One is that you need not spend $200,000 to send anyone to college. But the principal advantage of the nonparental life-style is that on Christmas Eve, you need not be struck dumb by the three most terrifying words that the government allows to be printed on any product:'Some assembly required.'

– **John Leo**

Dying is one of the few things that can be done just as easily lying down.

– **Woody Allen**

Buy a pair of red flannel pyjamas that you wear only on Christmas Eve.

– **H. Jackson Brown, Jr**

I just heard on the radio yesterday that people are giving dogs Prozac. Well, there is a really good use of the gross national product. Cheering up dogs.

– **Fran Lebowitz**

As life goes on, don't you find that all you need is about two real friends, a regular supply of books, and a Peke?
  – **P.G. Wodehouse**

One difference between outlaws and in-laws is that outlaws don't promise to pay it back.
  – **Kin Hubbard**

The trouble with quotes about death is that 99.99 per cent of them are made by people who are still alive.
  – **Joshua Burns**

The difference between reality and fiction is that fiction has to make sense.
  – **Tom Clancy**

Why is the slum set so dirty? That set cost a lot of money. It shouldn't look like just an ordinary dirty slum.
  – **Samuel Goldwyn**

Minister Michael Smith's solemn intonation is like that of a monsignor on a bad line from Medjugorje.
  – **Pat Rabbitte**

All women are stimulated by the news that any wife has left her husband.
  – **Anthony Powell**

Jimmy Connors was such an out-and-out 'personality' that he managed to get into a legal dispute with the president of his own fan club.
  – **Martin Amis**

If you had suggested to primitive man that they should watch women having babies, they would have laughed and tortured you for three or four days.
  – **Dave Barry**

A husband should tell his wife everything that he is sure she will find out anyway and before anybody else does.
– **Thomas Dewar**

Growing old is no more than a bad habit which a busy man has not time to form.
– **André Maurois**

I have all the answers, it's just that none of them are right.
– **Rich Hall**

My trouble on the golf course is that I stand too close to my shots after I've hit them.
– **Bob Hope**

I excessively hate to be forty. Not that I think it a bad thing to be – only I'm not ready yet!
– **Edith Wharton**

One pleasure attached to growing older is that many things seem to be growing younger; growing fresher and more lively than we once supposed them to be.
– **G.K. Chesterton**

It has begun to occur to me that life is a stage I'm going through.
– **Ellen Goodman**

I don't want to sound paranoid, but that electronic line judge knows who I am.
– **John McEnroe**

A low voter turnout is an indication that fewer people are going to the polls.
– **Dan Quayle**

Of all the unbearable nuisances, the ignoramus that has travelled is the worst.

– **Kin Hubbard**

My dad always used to tell me that if they challenge you to an after-school fight, tell them you won't wait, you can kick their butt right now.

– **Cameron Diaz**

The music of Wagner imposes mental tortures that only algebra has the right to inflict.

– **Paul de Saint-Victor**

Son, I don't want you to do that because I don't want Mom to worry, all right? When she worries she starts saying things like, 'I told you so,' or 'Stop doing that, I'm asleep.'

– **Peter Griffin, Family Guy**

Hoover, if elected, will do one thing that is almost incomprehensible to the human mind: he will make a great man out of Coolidge.

– **Herbert Hoover**

A glass of wine with lunch? Is that wise? You know you have to reign all afternoon.

– **The Queen Mother to Queen Elizabeth II**

The only thing wrong with immortality is that it does tend to go on a bit.

– **Herb Caen**

Over a season, you'll get goals disallowed that are good and you'll get goals that are good disallowed.

– **Kevin Keegan**

My parents waited ten years for me; that's the way they always put it, as if I were a late train to a place they desperately wanted to go.

– **Kitty Florey**

Kids do say the darndest things, but that's once in a blue moon, and in between it's a lot of drivel.

– Bill Maher

My dad was the town drunk. Usually that's not so bad, but New York City?

– Henny Youngman

When Clinton says 'Attorney General', he means the first semi-qualified woman he could find without a criminal record.

– Mort Sahl

The years between 50 and 70 are the hardest. You are always being asked to do things, and you are not yet decrepit enough to turn them down.

– T.S. Eliot

Our house was a singing house during the holidays. Although the boys are getting big for it now, we used to go out – the five of us – singing Christmas carols around the neighbourhood. Those we serenaded asked us in for refreshments, and there were cookies for the youngsters and a few shiny coins for all of us.

– Bing Crosby

Let's be honest: a wedding is absolutely the worst way to start married life.

– Caitlin Moran

The wisdom of a single snowflake outweighs the wisdom of a million meteorologists.

– Sir Francis Bacon

I'm convinced there's a small room in the attic of the Foreign Office where future diplomats are taught to stammer.

– Peter Ustinov

For certain people, after fifty, litigation takes the place of sex.

– Gore Vidal

A family is a social unit where the father is concerned with parking space, the children with outer space, and the mother with closet space.

– **Evan Esar**

Redemption, I was able to meet with the person that you all know by name, Ali Agca, who in the year 1981 on the 13th of May made an attempt on my life. But Providence took things in its own hands, in what I would call an extraordinary way, so that today... I was able to meet my assailant and repeat to him the pardon I gave him immediately.

– **Pope John Paul II**

When I was about six I received the following letter from Father Christmas on Christmas Day: 'If you don't eat your greens I shall not be coming next year.'

– **John Paxton**

I love everything about Christmas. I savour the opening of each little door of my Advent calendar (what's wrong with having an Advent calendar at the age of 36?). I usually burst into tears when I see the town centre Christmas lights for the first time and my favourite sound in the world is our old wind-up Nativity scene which plays 'Silent Night' at an ever-decreasing pace.

– **Mel Giedroyc**

The important thing about Christmas is not the gifts. The important thing is having your family around resenting you.

– **Reno Goodale**

Once at the airport I leaped onto the conveyor belt just as the luggage was coming through. When the airport police arrived I said to them, 'Just one more round and I promise to get off. I've always wanted to do this, all my life.'

– **Spike Milligan**

All sorts of allowances are made for the illusions of youth; and none for the disenchantments of old age.

– **Robert Louis Stevenson**

A true friend always stabs you in the front.

– **Oscar Wilde**

John Kenneth Galbraith and Marshall McLuhan are the two greatest modern Canadians that the US has produced.

– **Anthony Burgess**

I can close any boxing cut in the world in fifty seconds, so long as it ain't a total beheading.

– **Adolph Ritacco**

Henry VIII perhaps approached as nearly to the ideal standard of perfect wickedness as the infirmities of human nature will allow.

– **James Mackintosh**

A man is as old only as the woman he feels.

– **Groucho Marx**

Did you know babies are nauseated by the smell of a clean shirt?

– **Jeff Foxworthy**

I'd love to be a mole on the wall in the Liverpool dressing room at half time.

– **Kevin Keegan**

There can hardly be a town in the South of England where you could throw a brick without hitting the niece of a bishop.

– **George Orwell**

It would have been a birdie if the ball hadn't stopped before it reached the hole.

– **David Coleman**

When I was born, they threw away the mould. Of course some of it grew back.

– **Emo Philips**

Any American citizen can become President of the United States, just as long as he's a millionaire.

– Patrick Murray

None of us can boast much about the morality of our ancestors: the records do not show that Adam and Eve were married.

– Edgar Howe

Who says doing Christmas shopping early avoids the crush? Last year, I did mine a full twelve months in advance, and the shops were just as busy as ever.

– Gavin McKernan

In London after Christmas you always get the great New Clothes Parades in the parks! Families go out together, and they are all wearing their new Christmas pullovers – even staid old businessmen! I love it. And another thing I like about this time of year is the smell of damp wool – mittens and scarves gently steaming on the radiators after wet or snowy afternoon perambulations.

– Thora Hird

Most of my contemporaries at school entered the World of Business, the logical destiny of bores.

– Barry Humphries

The art of conversation is really within the reach of almost everyone except those who are morbidly truthful.

– Oscar Wilde

My dad never did a thing around the house. He used to just sit in his chair threatening people. That was his job. Clipping people round the ear as they walked by, and saying, 'Just get on with something, will you?'

– Jeff Green

I would never do anything to deride the profession of politics – although I think it is a form of madness.

– Alec Douglas-Home

Perfect love sometimes does not come till the first grandchild.

– Welsh proverb

How come the dove gets to be the peace symbol? How about the pillow? It has more feathers than the dove, and it doesn't have that dangerous beak.

– Jack Handey

Rose late – dull and drooping – the weather dripping and dense. Snow on the ground, and sirocco above in the sky, like yesterday. Roads up to the horse's belly, so that riding (at least for pleasure) is not very feasible. Read the conclusion for the fiftieth time (I have read all W. Scott's novels at least fifty times), of the third series of Tales of My Landlord – grand work – Scotch. Clock strikes – going out to make love. Somewhat perilous, but not disagreeable...

– Lord Byron

It is no exaggeration to say that the undecideds could go one way or the other.

– George Bush

I have to exercise very early in the morning before my brain figures out what I'm doing.

– Ruby Wax

I've got a family and children and the best part of it is giving presents. It's also the time of year when I can replenish my socks and ties.

– A.C. Grayling

One day my father came running into the room waving a five-pound note, saying, 'Look what I got for you, son!' He'd sold me.

– Ken Dodd

I refused to have an operation on the grounds that I already had two operations and found them painful. They were having my hair cut and sitting for my portrait.

– Richard Brinsley Sheridan

No one can feel as helpless as the owner of a sick goldfish.

– **Kin Hubbard**

I've posed nude for a photographer in the manner of Rodin's Thinker, but I looked merely constipated.

– **George Bernard Shaw**

You've got to get up early in the morning to catch me peeking through your bedroom window.

– **Emo Philips**

I did not get a life sentence. The judge gave me ninety-nine years.

– **Clarence Carnes**

The hand of God, reaching down into the mire, couldn't elevate a newspaperman to the depths of degradation.

– **Ben Hecht**

I wanted to have children to continue the family name. Now I've got children, there are times when I beg them not to give their full name.

– **Rod Lake**

Three things have helped me successfully through the ordeals of life: an understanding husband, a good analyst, and millions of dollars.

– **Mary Tyler Moore**

My drinking days, I think, are over. The human liver, unless it is Graham Greene's, can take so much and no more.

– **Anthony Burgess**

My girlfriend and I almost didn't have the second date because on the first date I didn't open the car door for her. I just swam to the surface.

– **Emo Philips**

After a man is married he has the legal right to deceive only one woman.

– **Edgar Howe**

As a housewife, I feel that if the kids are still alive when my husband gets home from work, then hey, I've done my job.

– Roseanne Barr

It's a good idea to obey all the rules when you're young just so you'll have the strength to break them when you're old.

– Mark Twain

If I die I'm sorry for all the bad things I did to you. And if I live I'm sorry for all the bad things I'm going to do to you.

– Roy Schneider

Ice lay hidden in the green of the Brussel sprouts that we gathered for dinner.

– George Sturt

Only one fellow in ten thousand understands the currency question, and we meet him every day.

– Kin Hubbard

No other British institution can quite touch the hotel in its single-minded devotion to the interests of those who work there and its complete indifference to those who are guests there.

– Kingsley Amis

As Margaret Thatcher is partly responsible for the Channel tunnel, why not erect her statue at the French end? If that doesn't deter immigrants, nothing will.

– R. Smith

The first child is made of glass, the second porcelain, the rest of rubber, steel and granite.

– Richard Needham

Any child who is anxious to mow the lawn is too young to do it.

– Bob Phillips

The trouble with jogging is that by the time you realize you're not in shape for it, it's too far to walk back.

– Franklin Jones

If Stalin had learned to play cricket, the world would now be a better place to live in.

– Robert Downey

Vita Sackville-West looked like Lady Chatterley above the waist, and the gamekeeper below.

– Cyril Connolly

The Protestant Church looks after you from the womb to the tomb, but the Catholic Church looks after you from erection to resurrection.

– Brendan Behan

You hear a lot of dialogue on the death of the American family. Families aren't dying. They're merging into big conglomerates.

– Erma Bombeck

Macbeth and Lady Macbeth stand out as the supreme type of all that a host and hostess should not be.

– Max Beerbohm

When Dad helped make a chocolate cake the kitchen ended up looking like Willy Wonka had been murdered in there.

– Robin Elms

A man with male pattern baldness ain't the blues. A woman with male pattern baldness is.

– Paul Cloutman

Even in civilized mankind faint traces of the monogamous instinct can sometimes be perceived.

– Bertrand Russell

My daughter told me she'd been learning the alphabet at school. 'What letter comes after T?' I asked. Without hesitation she replied, 'V.'

– Ian Rose

Grandchildren don't make me feel old. It's the knowledge that I'm married to a grandmother.

– Norman Collie

I have enough money to last me the rest of my life – unless I have to buy something.

– Jackie Mason

I've told my mother that it's called The Geneva Monologue and thats it's about women in banking.

– Maureen Lipman

A triumph of my father's salesmanship was the time he sold a Mexican both an ice pack and a hot water bottle, neither of which he came in for.

– Richard Armour

Everything you ever need to know about the Germans' innate sense of romance, lyricism, eroticism and indeed their tender feelings for the fairer sex is encapsulated in their word for nipple. The German word is brustwarze, a breast wart.

– A.A. Gill

Men have simple needs. They can survive the whole weekend with only three things: beer, boxer shorts, and batteries for the remote control.

– Diana Jordan

Although Rupert Brooke never succeeded in becoming the first modern poet, he may deserve to be called the first modern undergraduate, a title of comparable significance.

– Michael Levenson

Ballesteros is the No. 1. He hits the ball further than I go on my holidays.

– Lee Trevino

I have on occasion asked for whom the bell tolled and found it was not for me.

– **Robert Morley**

Oh the wonder of this Christmas day... The tree touched the ceiling and was heavy with tinsel and snow and candles – but who can describe a Christmas tree? The scent of pine, the cheery mystery of the packages below, the charm of the very top star, the flickering little candles...

– **Anaïs Nin**

The best part of married life is the fights. The rest is so-so.

– **Thornton Wilder**

Posterity is full of men who seized the day, while the women were planning for a fortnight on Tuesday.

– **Allison Pearson**

My dad adopted one of those Save the Children, and now he compares me to his adopted child. 'Why can't you be more like your sister Keekee? Keekee dug an irrigation ditch for her entire village.'

– **Corey Kahane**

A Christian is one who believes that the New Testament is a divinely inspired book, admirably suited to the spiritual needs of his neighbours.

– **Ambrose Bierce**

Fifteen years ago one could have bought the Federal Steel Company for twenty million dollars. And I let it go.

– **Stephen Leacock**

Do we want one? Good God no! The day Freud came up with penis envy, I think his brains had to have been out to lunch.

– **Helen Gurley Brown**

An accuser is one's former friend, particularly the person for whom one has performed some friendly service.

– **Ambrose Bierce**

I was an only child. Raised in the country. Each autumn, my father would gather in the harvest. I never really understood why because he was an accountant by profession.

– **Harry Hill**

Too often, the opportunity knocks, but by the time you push back the chain, push back the bolt, unhook the two locks and shut off the burglar alarm, it's too late.

– **Rita Coolidge**

We had gone out there to pass the beautiful day of high summer like true Irishmen – locked in the dark snug of a public house.

– **Brendan Behan**

After washing twelve pairs of such feet, the crucifixion must have been a pushover.

– **Alan Bennett**

I wonder if people in Australia call the rest of the world 'Up Over'.

– **George Carlin**

Women are a problem, but they are the kind of problem I enjoy wrestling with.

– **Warren Beatty**

If they can put a man on the moon... why can't they put them all there?

– **Anonymous**

When things get really tough there are the final, most potent words of wisdom a father can have, 'Go ask your mother.'

– **Frank Lancaster**

The most famous recipe in racing is the one for Lester Piggott's breakfast: a cough and a copy of the Sporting Life.

– **Simon Barnes**

Man is the second strangest sex in the world.

   – **Philip Barry**

Married! I can see you now, in the kitchen, bending over a hot stove, but I can't see the stove.

   – **Groucho Marx**

In baseball I see no reason why the infield should not try to put the batter off his stride at the critical moment, by neatly timed disparagements of his wife's fidelity and his mother's respectability.

   – **George Bernard Shaw**

My dad would spend ages tinkering under the bonnet of his Capri. Then it would invariably have to be towed to a garage to have the damage he'd caused repaired.

   – **Robert Greenway**

If more than ten per cent of the population likes a painting, it should be burned, for it must be bad.

   – **George Bernard Shaw**

The key to tennis is to win the last point.

   – **Jim Courier**

Caesarean section? Isn't that the part of the Roman Colosseum where the emperors sat?

   – **George Carlin**

The story goes that I first had the idea for The Hitchhiker's Guide to the Galaxy while lying drunk in a field in Innsbruck (or 'Spain' as the BBC TV publicity department has it, probably because it's easier to spell).

   – **Douglas Adams**

You're getting old when the girl you smile at thinks you're one of her father's friends.

   – **Arthur Murray**

The Christmas spirit that goes out with the dried-up Christmas tree is just as worthless.

– Thomas Tusser

Someone once said that nobody murders Troon. The way I played the Open there they couldn't even arrest me for second degree manslaughter.

– Lee Trevino

Los Angeles is the plastic asshole of the world.

– William Faulkner

I got married the second time in the same way that when a murder is committed, crackpots turn up at the police station to confess the crime.

– Delmore Schwartz

One doesn't forget the rounded wonder in the eyes of a boy as he comes bursting upstairs on Christmas morning and finds the two-wheeler or the fire truck of which for weeks he scarcely dared dream.

– Max Lerner

Marriage always demands the greatest understanding of the art of insincerity possible between two human beings.

– Vicki Baum

For six years the profound silence of the Coolidge administration was mistaken for profound wisdom.

– Alben Barkley

I'm 42 around the chest, 52 around the waist, 92 around the golf course and a nuisance around the house.

– Groucho Marx

Army generals say the biggest threat to the entertainer Wayne Newton when he arrives in Afghanistan is friendly fire.

– Jimmy Fallon

My wife got the house, the car, the bank account, and if I marry again and have children, she gets them too.

– **Woody Allen**

Tree-trimming parties get the halls decked and the boughs filled with baubles while providing a chance to see friends. If you are very brave or have far too many friends, you can do it as an afternoon eggnog party. If you haven't already got one, borrow or rent a large silver punch bowl, fill it with that rich and potent punch, set out platters of tea sandwiches and Christmas cookies and hope the tree gets trimmed... The tree should be up and the lights wound 'round before the guests arrive.

– **Susan Dooley**

You grow up the day you have the first real laugh at yourself.

– **Ethel Barrymore**

To an adolescent, there is nothing in the world more embarrassing than a parent.

– **Dave Barry**

It took me three weeks to stuff the turkey. I stuffed it through the beak.

– **Phyllis Diller**

The closest sound to Roseanne Barr's singing the National Anthem was my cat being neutered.

– **Johnny Carson**

When it comes to little girls, God the father has nothing on father, the god. It's an awesome responsibility.

– **Frank Pittman**

You learn not to make jokes at the European Parliament. Otherwise you find the Germans getting it ten minutes after the Swedes.

– **Glenys Kinnock**

When I go to the dentist, he's the one that has to have the anaesthetic.

– **Phyllis Diller**

I am sorry to have to introduce the subject of Christmas... It is an indecent subject; a cruel, gluttonous subject; a drunken, disorderly subject; a wasteful, disastrous subject; a wicked, cadging, lying, filthy, blasphemous, and demoralizing subject.

– George Bernard Shaw

I had occasion to read the Bible the other night and believe me it is a lesson in how not to write for the movies. The worst kind of overwriting. Whole chapters that could have been said in one paragraph. And the dialogue!

– Raymond Chandler

Virginia Woolf subscribed to the theory that the pen was mightier than the sword; and I once saw the mighty Evelyn Waugh reel under a savage blow from her Parker 51.

– Alan Bennett

When you come to a fork in the road, take it.

– Yogi Berra

Do you want to feel insecure? Count the number of Christmas cards you sent out, and then count those you received.

– Milton Berle

There are two types of doctor – the specialist who has trained his patients to become ill only during office hours, and the general practitioner who may be called off the golf course at any time.

– Ambrose Bierce

I was so ugly at birth that the midwife took one look at me, turned, and slapped my father.

– Joan Rivers

A lady came up to me on the street and pointed to my suede jacket. 'You know a cow was murdered for that jacket?' she sneered. I replied in a psychotic tone, 'I didn't know there were any witnesses. Now I'll have to kill you too.'

– Jake Johanson

She was growing up, and that was the direction I wanted her to take. Who wants a daughter that grows sideways?

– **Spike Milligan**

My girlfriends are usually making 'Who lit the fuse on your tampon?' taunts by now.

– **Kathy Lette**

W.C. Fields was fond of playing the golf course sideways with his pal Oliver Hardy. He liked being in the trees where he could drink without scandalising the natives.

– **Jim Murray**

Gaxton, I am watching your performance from the rear of the house. Wish you were here.

– **George Kaufman**

In a moment, we hope to see the pole vault over the satellite.

– **David Coleman**

Third class mail. What's that? They strap the letter to a crazy person and he wanders at random?

– **Richard Lewis**

During the caesarean, when the doctor cauterized the veins and smoke started billowing from Heather's stomach, I got queasy. But I had confidence that this was all routine for the doctors when I heard them discussing the college football game.

– **Richie Sambora**

At a time when religion needs all the help it can get, John Huston's The Bible may have set its cause back a couple of thousand years.

– **Rex Reed**

My father died when I was 15. The advice I remember the most, he'd always say, 'Be a man,' which meant 'Take it. Take it like a man.'

– **Billy Crystal**

The only man who makes money following the horses is one who does it with a broom and shovel.

— **Elbert Hubbard**

If Freud had worn a kilt in the prescribed Highland manner, he might have had a very different attitude to genitals.

— **Anthony Burgess**

No pleasure is worth giving up for the sake of two more years in a geriatric home in Weston-super-Mare.

— **Kingsley Amis**

Only a fool would attempt to predict the score of a Rangers-Celtic match. I think it will be a score draw.

— **Hughie Taylor**

If somebody could write a book for the people who never read they would make a fortune.

— **Nancy Mitford**

I credit my youthfulness at 80 to the fact of a cheerful disposition and contentment in every period of my life with what I was.

— **Oliver Wendell Holmes**

Once rugby players have succeeded in getting their boots on the right feet, the mental challenge of the game is largely over.

— **Derek Robinson**

Some publishers are honest and never rob their clients of more than 200 per cent.

— **Miles Franklin**

You'd be amazed how many teenagers get their first car by asking for a motorcycle.

— **James Varley**

Those characters in the Bible who rent their garments – wouldn't it have been less expensive to buy them in the first place?

— **Paul Merton**

Family values? I'm sick of hearing about them. The reason most people are in therapy is because of their families.

— **Judy Carter**

Americans do not rear children, they incite them: they give them food and shelter and applause.

— **Randall Jarrell**

Men are the only animals who devote themselves assiduously to making one another unhappy. It is, I suppose, one of their godlike qualities.

— **H.L. Mencken**

Blessed are they who can laugh at themselves, for they shall never cease to be amused.

— **Fulton J. Sheen**

Women inspire men to great undertakings and then distract us from carrying them out.

— **Oscar Wilde**

It is indeed a burning shame that there should be one law for men and another law for women. I think there should be no law for anybody.

— **Oscar Wilde**

My father invented a cure for which there was no disease, and unfortunately, my mother caught it and died of it.

— **Victor Borge**

Never talk about yourself as being old. There is something in Mind Cure, after all, and, if you continually talk of yourself as being old, you may perhaps bring on some of the infirmities of age.

— **Hannah Smith**

If you don't believe you can win, there is no point in getting out of bed at the end of the day.
   – Neville Southall

Ever since Eve gave Adam the apple, there has been a misunderstanding between the sexes about gifts.
   – Nan Robertson

He's got the icepack on his groin there so it's possibly not the old shoulder injury.
   – Ray French

If they call it 'downhill skiing', is there an uphill event we don't know about?
   – Ian Johns

How the hell would I know why there were Nazis? I don't even know how a can opener works.
   – Woody Allen

I love giving the kids a bath. There's great satisfaction in it. They get so dirty.
   – Curtis Black

He's got a wonderful head for money. There's a long slit on the top.
   – David Frost

Despite the fact you have done nothing these nine months, the baby is 50 per cent you. Some mothers never forgive the father for this.
   – Marcus Berkmann, Fatherhood: The Truth

The great thing about kids is that they never get sick of beans on toast.
   – Graham Olson

One reason people get divorced is that they run out of gift ideas.
   – Robert Byrne

Banks are really aggressive with their marketing these days, aren't they? A guy robbed a bank of $5,000 last week and they tried to talk him into opening a savings account with it.

– Henny Youngman

When people say "You're breaking my heart", they do in fact mean that you're breaking their genitals.

– Jeffrey Bernard

The English are a pacifist race – they always hold their wars in someone else's country.

– Brendan Behan

What is the age people reach when they decide, when they back out of the driveway, they're not looking anymore? You know how they do that? They just go, 'Well, I'm old, and I'm backing out. I survived, let's see if you can.'

– Jerry Seinfeld

Women dress alike all over the world; they dress to be annoying to other women.

– Elsa Schiaparelli

I was into animal husbandry – until they caught me at it.

– Tom Lehrer

If the subjects are living in splendour they can clearly afford to pay their taxes. If they are living frugally, they must be hiding money away and can also afford to pay their taxes.

– Cardinal Morton

The upper-middle classes are never satisfied – they always take things back to shops and demand to have the sales assistant beaten.

– Jenny Eclair

The Rolling Stones are on tour again. They were gonna call the tour 'Hey! You! Get Offa My Stairlift!'

– **David Letterman**

Lichtenstein and Luxembourg are not European nations. They are minor characters in William Shakespeare's famous play Hamlet II: The Next Day.

– **Dave Barry**

Objects are lost because people look where they are not instead of where they are.

– **Henry Miller**

Irishmen are so busy being Irish that they don't have any time to be anything else.

– **Beverley Nichols**

People are startled by my books because they think, how can an old woman write about sex? The idea that people go on being sexy all their life is little explored in fiction. What do people think 'happy ever after' means? It goes on and on; it doesn't end.

– **Mary Wesley**

Those who love deeply never grow old; they may die of old age, but they die young.

– **Benjamin Franklin**

My con-victims may have been respectable but they were never any good. They wanted something for nothing and I gave them nothing for something.

– **Joseph Weil**

We have women in the military, but... they don't know if we can fight, if we can kill. I think we can. All the general has to do is walk over to the women and say, 'You see the enemy over there? They say you look fat in those uniforms.'

– **Elayne Boosler**

Anyone living in Los Angeles who says they don't need a psychiatrist, needs a psychiatrist.

– **Kathy Lette**

Foreign tourists should realize that in England they are encouraged to take a piece of fruit, free of charge, from any open-air stall or display.

– **Michael Lipton**

My racehorses look remarkably healthy. That's because they don't sit up all night playing cards and drinking vodka.

– **Fred Winter**

Have you ever smelt a rain forest? They stink. They stink worse than a 13-year-old's bedroom.

– **A.A. Gill**

The trouble with the French is that they don't have any word for entrepreneur.

– **George W. Bush**

As lousy as things are now, tomorrow they will be somebody's good old days.

– **Gerald Barzan**

Sailors ought never to go to church. They ought to go to hell, where it is much more comfortable.

– **H.G. Wells**

Fortunately my parents were intelligent, enlightened people. They accepted me for exactly what I was: a punishment from God.

– **Dave Steinberg**

Be nice to your children. After all, they are going to choose your nursing home.

– **Steven Wright**

The thing to remember about fathers is, they're men. A girl has to keep it in mind: they are dragon-seekers, bent on improbable rescues. Scratch any father, you find someone chock-full of qualms and romantic terrors, believing change is a threat – like your first shoes with heels on, like your first bicycle it took such months to get.

    – Phyllis McGinley

My parents have a very good marriage. They've been together forever. They've passed their silver and gold anniversaries. The next one is rust.

    – Rita Rudner

Men are amused by almost any idiot thing – that is why professional ice hockey is so popular.

    – Dave Barry

If you are inserting a suppository last thing at night, always take your socks off first and if you are inserting a suppository in the morning, always ensure that your socks are on first. Bending over can cause the thing to fly out with great velocity and there is always the danger of a ricochet. Once I broke a holy statue.

    – Hugh Leonard

Poets are terribly sensitive people and the thing they are most sensitive about is money.

    – Robert Warren

My memory's starting to go. The only thing I still retain is water.

    – Alex Cole

Men are amused by almost any idiot thing... But you should never buy them clothes. Men believe they already have all the clothes they will ever need, and new ones make them nervous. For example, your average man has 84 ties, but he wears, at most, only three of them.

    – Dave Barry

Golf and sex are about the only things you can enjoy without being good at it.

    – Jimmy Demaret

Oh, come on, Dad, do you really think what I did was that bad? You grew up in the sixties. I've seen the photo album. Those clothes had to have some pharmaceutical explanation.

– Darlene Conner, Roseanne

You look at Ernest Borgnine and you think to yourself was there anybody else hurt in the accident?

– Don Rickles

Just because I'm in a wheelchair they think they can push me around... I coped when a bull mastiff tried to mate with my left-side tyre.

– Maud Grimes, Coronation Street

When a referee is in doubt, I think he is justified in deciding against the side that makes the most noise.

– A.H. Almond

Trust yourself. You know more than you think you do... What good mothers and fathers instinctively feel like doing for their babies is the best of all.

– Dr Benjamin Spock

When I can no longer bear to think of the victims of broken homes, I begin to think of the victims of intact ones.

– Peter de Vries

He accused me of the thing men think is the most insulting thing they can accuse you of – wanting to be married.

– Nora Ephron

A test for paranoia: if you cannot think of anything that's your fault, you've got it.

– Robert Hutchins

If you think you're in love just think of him sitting on the lavatory. If you still love him, marry him.

– Jean Baht

Broken promises don't upset me. I just think, Why did they believe me?

– **Jack Handey**

If you want to know what God thinks of money, just look at the people he gave it to.

– **Dorothy Parker**

God is love – but Satan is thirty and two sets to one up.

– **Don Geddis**

The great thing about golf – and this is the reason why a lot of health experts like me recommend it – you can drink beer and ride in a cart while you play.

– **Dave Barry**

I'm 43, and for the first time this year I have felt older. I'm slowly becoming more decrepit. I think you just move to the country and wear an old fleece.

– **Jennifer Saunders**

I don't feel I really belong to this life. I am hovering like a seagull.

– **Isak Dinesen**

'The Snowman' does it for me because this is the supreme Christmas masterpiece of our age. A boy's snowman comes to life and takes him flying over snow-covered fields to a party with Father Christmas where they feast and dance until night ends. Celebrating children, innocent happiness, winter snow, Santa Claus, communal pleasure and the miracle of regeneration when the snow thaws and day replaces night, this has got it all. My wife and I can re-enact the whole thing and used to fly the children, held aloft at arm's length, over the back of the sofa.

– **Stephen Pile**

I believe that more unhappiness comes from this source than from any other – the attempt to prolong family connections unduly and to make people hang together artificially who would never naturally do so.

– **Samuel Butler**

One of the most difficult things in this world is to convince a woman that even a bargain costs money.

– **Edgar Howe**

The greatest unsolved problem in science is this – how can you be sitting on a damp towel for half an hour and not realize it until you stand up?

– **Patrick Murray**

Nothing is faster than light. To prove this to yourself, try opening the refrigerator door before the light comes on.

– **Aaron Fuegi**

I've even heard that some people save this year's cards to display again next year, anyway. All I'm saying is that's what I've heard.

– **Deborah Ross**

In the beginning, the universe was created. This has made a lot of people very angry, and is generally considered to be have been a bad move.

– **Douglas Adams**

A Dublin marriage proposal often goes like this: would ya like to go halves on a baby?

– **Brendan Behan**

I am always glad when one of those poets dies for then I know I have all of his works on my shelf.

– **George Crabbe**

I used to hate weddings – all those old dears poking me in the stomach and saying, 'You're next.' But they stopped all that when I started doing the same to them at funerals.

– **Gail Flynn**

Don't spend your life trying to please those who won't cry at your funeral.

– **Gerald Brooks**

Edith Evans took her curtain calls as though she had just been un-nailed from the cross.

– Noël Coward

I once asked a man what he thought would happen to him after he died. He replied that he believed he would inherit eternal bliss, but he didn't wish to talk about such unpleasant subjects.

– F.W. Myers

Never feel remorse for what you have thought about your wife; she has thought much worse things about you.

– Jean Rostand

I used to go to the office three times a week for an hour a day, but I have since struck off one of the days.

– Oscar Wilde

We came back powdered with snow, all three of us – the little bull-dog, the Flemish sheepdog and I... Snow had got into the folds of our coats, I had white epaulettes, an impalpable sugar was melting in the wrinkles of Poucette's blunt muzzle, and the Flemish sheepdog sparkled all over... sheepdog – 'steaming like a footbath... listens to the whispering of the snow against the shut blinds'.

– Colette

The sport of skiing consists of wearing three thousand dollars' worth of clothes and equipment and driving two hundred miles in the snow in order to stand around at a bar and get drunk.

– P.J. O'Rourke

My grandmother's ninety. She's dating. He's ninety-three. It's going great. They never argue. They can't hear each other.

– Cathy Ladman

The way to a man's heart is through his heart, and it helps if it hurts. Hurts him, not you.

– Doris Lilly

'Twas the day after Christmas, and all through the house, the Spirit had ended; it had all been doused. The ornaments were yanked from the tree with despair, while Dad vacuumed pine needles from his rump.

> – Pete Wrigley

Every morning I get up and look through the Forbes list of the richest people in America. If I'm not there, I go to work.

> – Robert Orben

Old age is like a plane flying through a storm. Once you are aboard there is nothing you can do about it. So one might as well accept it calmly, wisely.

> – Golda Meir

Before Josh and Rebecca, I merely strode through the world like a man. Now I crawl, hunker, scramble, hop on one foot, often see the world from my hands and knees.

> – Hugh O'Neill

Son, three little sentences will get you through life: Number 1: Cover for me. Number 2: Oh, good idea, Boss! Number 3: It was like that when I got here.

> – Homer Simpson

Congressmen are so damned dumb, they could throw themselves on the ground and miss.

> – James Traficant

I'm going to memorize your name and throw my head away.

> – Oscar Levant

There are some people who want to throw their arms round you simply because it is Christmas; there are other people who want to strangle you simply because it is Christmas.

> – Robert Lynd

She was a freelance castrator.

– James Thurber

We sometimes wonder why the City Government tilts so vigorously at the snow. The first flake has hardly fluttered down when every infernal machine in town is rushing to do battle... Is snow such poisonous stuff? Our own feeling is that it is something to be honoured and preserved, and we would like to see all citizens provided with little tinkling bells so that they would make merry sounds as they plodded about their business, in high rubber boots.

– E.B. White

I shall be 70 in two months' time and feel exactly as I did when I was 20. I was idle and indolent then, and little has changed in the past 50 years except that perhaps now I am better at getting away with it.

– Arnold Thomson

I have no A-levels, and the last time I asked for directions in Paris, I inadvertently gave the man my mother's recipe for baked Alaska.

– Jeremy Clarkson

I wouldn't be marrying for the fifth time if it wasn't for keeps.

– Joan Collins

Canadians are cold so much of the time that many of them leave instructions to be cremated.

– Cynthia Nelms

Three phrases fill the air at Christmas time: 'Peace on Earth', 'Goodwill to all Men' and 'Batteries Not Included'.

– Tony Deyal

I've been up and down so many times that I feel as if I'm in a revolving door.

– Cher

'God bless us every one,' said Tiny Tim, the last of all.

– Charles Dickens, A Christmas Carol

Each of us creates our own special times at Christmas. We find our special ornaments, hang the mistletoe, and place the star as we have done before. There is a comforting certainty in the sameness – a promise of continuity.

– Lady Bird Johnson

We love our kids, but there are times when we don't really like them, or at least we can't stand what our children are doing. But most of us keep those feelings to ourselves, as if it's a dirty little secret. It doesn't fit in with our images of what we should do or feel.

– Lawrence Kutner

I've lost the same half-stone so many times my cellulite's got déjà vu... I don't need a diet. What I need is a tapeworm.

– Sue Margolis

Anton Bruckner wrote the same symphony nine times (ten, actually) trying to get it right. He failed.

– Edward Abbey

Jerry Lee Lewis has been married twenty times. He gets married on a Tuesday, they find his wife dead in a swimming pool on Thursday. Maybe if you married someone who's old enough to swim next time, OK, Jerry?

– Denis Leary

Never throw away the Radio or TV Times. They'll come in handy next year.

– Harold Wilson

A father's job is not to get tired of what he has a right to get tired of: for example, small people who keep doing things that you tell them not to do, and when you ask them why they keep doing these things, they reply, 'I don't know.'

– Bill Cosby

I've never known a person who lives to 110 who is remarkable for anything else.

– Josh Billings

When I was a teenager, I used to try to make my head explode by holding my breath, thinking that if I blew up my head, my mom and dad would be sorry.

– Kurt Cobain

If you have a burning restless urge to paint, simply eat something sweet and the feeling will pass.

– Fran Lebowitz

I have an antipathy towards shy people to this day, because I think it's lazy and dull.

– Jenny Eclair

Be suspicious of any doctor who tries to take your temperature with his finger.

– David Letterman

If there is anything that we wish to change in the child, we should first examine it and see whether it is not something that could be better changed in ourselves.

– Carl Jung

My divorce came as a complete surprise to me. That will happen when you haven't been home in eighteen years.

– Lee Trevis

I get up at 7 a.m. each day to do my exercises – after I have first put on my make-up. After all, La Loren is always La Loren.

– Sophia Loren, 70

The music performed at amateur concerts seemed to have been designed to make those who play it happy and drive those who listen to despair.

– Adolphe Adam

I'm going to attach a pine cone to my vibrator and have a really merry Christmas!

– Bobbi Markowitz, The Stepford Wives

Austin Powers was born out of trying to celebrate my father's life. He loved to be silly. When I would bring friends home to play table hockey in the basement, if my dad didn't think they were funny, he wouldn't let them in the house.

– **Mike Myers**

Never work before breakfast; if you have to work before breakfast, eat your breakfast first.

– **Josh Billings**

I hate fruit cake because it sticks to the knife when you cut it and breaks when you try to pick it up and whatever you do pick up sticks to all your fingers together and each finger separately. And then sticks to your lips so they stick together for hours afterward...

– **Jim Quinn**

Maybe all one can do is hope to end up with the right regrets.

– **Arthur Miller**

Two days before C-day, there isn't anything to eat in the house apart from bananas and Vegemite; I have six more people to buy presents for and no time; everything needs vacuuming; and I can't stop yawning from my two-hour shopping trip to a surprisingly crowded Hamleys at 11.30 p.m.

– **India Knight**

Ladies of the choir, I want you to sound like twenty-two women having babies without chloroform.

– **John Barbirolli**

Every year on Christmas Day I like to tell my mother that I'm a lesbian, even though I'm not. It just gets everything going.

– **Jenny Eclair**

Some people seem compelled by unkind fate to parental servitude for life. There is no form of penal service worse than this.

– **Samuel Butler**

A young boy down the road tried to help me across the road this afternoon. I gave him a swift cuff round the ear. Only be a matter of time before they're forcing me on a day trip to Eastbourne.

– Victor Meldrew, One Foot in the Grave

It is much easier for a Scotsman to be a genius than to be an artist.

– Oscar Wilde

I can always find plenty of women to sleep with me but the kind of woman that is really hard for me to find is a typist who can read my writing.

– Thomas Wolfe

I don't kill flies but I like to torture them psychologically. I hold them above a globe. They freak out and think, 'Whoa, I'm way too high.'

– Bruce Baum

The great thing for an actor is to be homosexual. Then nobody can say anything about you – it virtually guarantees discreet press coverage. However, it is too late for me to change my sexual proclivities. Far too late.

– Rex Harrison

I've no time for broads who want to rule the world alone. Without men, who'd do up the zipper on the back of your dress?

– Bette Davis

In early January friendly Christmas cards continue to arrive, struggling gamely home like the last few stragglers in a London marathon.

– Arthur Marshall

Life is a funny thing that happens to you on the way to the grave.

– Quentin Crisp

I would have given my right arm to have been a pianist.

– Bobby Robson

When a professional golfer hits the ball to the right it's called a fade. When an amateur hits it to the right, it's called a slice.

– Peter Jacobson

In Church your grandsire cut his throat; To do the job too long he tarry'd, He should have had my hearty vote, To cut his throat before he married.

– Jonathan Swift

The Increasingly Desperate Guy Shopper is trying to find something for that Special Someone in his life, who has made it clear that this year she'd like something a little more personal than what he got her last year, which was a trailer hitch.

– Dave Barry

The PGA tour has a simple test to see if a player is on drugs: if Isao Aoki speaks and the player understands him, the player is on something.

– Bob Hope

A real woman has a special attitude to money. If she earns money, it is hers; if her husband earns it, it is theirs.

– Joyce Jillsons

If your husband has difficulty in getting to sleep, the words, 'We need to talk about our relationship', may help.

– Rita Rudner

I have not heard from the Ambassador to Spain for over two years. If I do not hear from him in the next year, I intend to write him a letter.

– Thomas Jefferson

It is the height of bad taste to have anything business-related in your briefcase. Briefcases are for taking the contents of the stationery cupboard home with you at the end of the day. Only photocopier repairmen have their work in their briefcases – 15 different screwdrivers, a copy of the Sun and a list of exotic, faraway locations where the vital missing part will have to be supplied from.

– Guy Browning

It's important for husbands to know when to change a diaper. I figure every three days is about right.

— **Alan Thicke**

Excuse me, everybody, I have to go to the bathroom. I really have to telephone, but I'm too embarrassed to say so.

— **Dorothy Parker**

In the mid-Eighties I had breast enlargement to quiet that noise in my head and fill the gaping hole in my self-esteem.

— **Iman**

Yes, I'm 100. I put it down to 30 years of safe sex and boneless fish.

— **Annie Miller**

He's a perfectionist. If he was married to Raquel Welch, he'd expect her to cook.

— **Don Meredith**

Country manners. Even if somebody phones up to tell you your house is on fire, first they ask you how you are.

— **Alice Munro**

There's nothing sadder in this world than to awake on Christmas morning and not be a child.

— **Erma Bombeck**

I was left in no doubt as to the severity of the hangover when a cat stamped into the room.

— **P.G. Wodehouse**

The easiest job in the world has to be a pathologist. You perform surgery on dead people. What's the worst thing that could happen? Maybe once in a while you'd get a pulse.

— **Dennis Miller**

To enjoy Christmas in LA, you have to accept the fact that you're going to be listening to Nat King Cole crooning 'Chestnuts Roasting on an Open Fire' next to an infinity pool surrounded by palm trees.

– **Sarah Standing**

Being a woman is of interest only to aspiring male transsexuals. To actual women, it is simply a good excuse not to play football.

– **Fran Lebowitz**

Having a kid is a great excuse to go to the garden centre and buy a Venus fly trap. And yes, feeding it flies does count as gardening.

– **Mick Rhodes**

Predicting the future is easy. It's trying to figure out what's going on now that's hard.

– **Fritz Dressler**

A coarse golfer is one who has to shout 'Fore' when he putts.

– **Michael Green**

If a person is not talented enough to be a novelist, not smart enough to be a lawyer, and his hands are too shaky to perform operations, he becomes a journalist.

– **Norman Mailer**

A Jiffy Bag is an envelope used to alert Post Office employees to damage opportunities.

– **Mike Barfield**

If I had known I was going to win a Bafta award I would have bleached my moustache.

– **Eileen McCallum**

If I had known I was going to live so long, I would have taken better care of myself.

– **George Burns**

I'm 78. The late Ronnie Scott used to ask people their age and would respond, in his hard-edged way: 'Really! You don't look a day over (in my case) 79!' A good corrective, which I resort to when I feel sorry for myself.

    – George Melly

Margaret Beckett looks like a woman resigned to walk home alone to an empty bedsit after Grab-a-Granny night at the local disco.

    – Richard Littlejohn

Opposites attract, but like is much easier to be married to.

    – Diana Douglas Darrid

When I was little, my father used to make me stand in a closet for five minutes without moving. He said it was elevator practice.

    – Steven Wright

I attribute my long and healthy life to the fact that I never touched a cigarette, a drink, or a girl until I was 10 years old.

    – George Moore

There's nothing like looking at vacation pictures to put guests in a travelling mood.

    – Dan Bennett

We must never lower the voting age to 14. That's when they think they know everything.

    – John Goodwin

The name Big Mac is generally supposed to have come about because it is a big McDonald's burger, but in fact it was named after a big raincoat whose taste it so closely resembles.

    – Jo Brand

The energy which makes a child hard to manage is the energy which afterward makes him a manager of life.

    – Henry Ward Beecher

Talking with a man is like trying to saddle a cow. You work like hell, but what's the point?

– **Gladys Upham**

I asked the manager for a ball to train with. He couldn't have looked more horrified if I'd asked for a transfer. He told me they never used a ball at Barnsley. The theory was we'd be hungry for it on Saturday if we didn't see it for the rest of the week. I told him that, come Saturday, I probably wouldn't recognize a ball.

– **Danny Blanchflower**

I love being married. It's so great to find the one special person you want to annoy for the rest of your life.

– **Rita Rudner**

Cyril Connolly's lost masterpieces give a piquancy to his criticism, as childless women make the best babysitters and impotent men the most assiduous lovers.

– **Malcolm Muggeridge**

He was so mean it hurt him to go to the bathroom.

– **Britt Ekland on Rod Stewart**

In Blues, 'adulthood' means being old enough to get the electric chair if you shoot a man in Memphis.

– **Paul Cloutman**

March is the month that God designed to show those who don't drink what a hangover is like.

– **Garrison Keillor**

Some of mankind's most esteemed inventions seem to have no purpose other than boredom. For example, there is the dinner party for more than two, the epic poem and the science of metaphysics.

– **H.L. Mencken**

Father Christmas advertisements must now be open to both male and female applicants. However, a female appointee must have whiskers, a deep voice, a big belly and a clearly discernible bosom. Children would be terrified of such a woman.

    – Simon De Bruxelles

The first rule of consumerism is never to buy anything you can't make your children carry.

    – Bill Bryson

The toughest part of parenthood has nothing to do with putting food on the table, clothes in the closet, or tuition money in the bank. The toughest part of parenthood is never knowing if you're doing the right thing.

    – D.L. Stewart

My first rule of travel is never to go to a place that sounds like a medical condition, and Critz is clearly an incurable disease involving flaking skin.

    – Bill Bryson

As I grow older, I have learned to read the papers calmly and not to hate the fools I read about.

    – Edmund Wilson

Women are like ovens. We need 5 to 15 minutes to heat up.

    – Sandra Bullock

David Steel has passed from rising hope to elder statesman without any intervening period whatsoever.

    – Michael Frost

Home is the place, when you have to go there, they have to take you in.

    – Robert Frost

It is a politician's right to refuse to speak to a journalist though he may afterwards find ways of penalising you.

    – Gerald Kaufman

How is it possible for Bob Dylan to play the harmonica, professionally, for thirty years and still show no sign of improvement?

   – David Sinclair

My wife is pregnant but she refuses to give up smoking. She says she's smoking for two now.

   – Mervin Allen

The principle of procrastinated rape is said to be the ruling one in all the great best-sellers.

   – V.S. Pritchett

78,000 Christmas puddings have been given to staff.

   – Eighty Things About Queen Elizabeth II, 2006

When one has reached 81, one likes to sit back and let the world turn by itself, without trying to push it.

   – Sean O'Casey

Christmas: A day set apart and consecrated to gluttony, drunkenness, maudlin sentiment, gift-taking, public dullness and domestic behaviour.

   – Ambrose Bierce

These greens are so fast I have to hold my putter over the ball and hit it with the shadow.

   – Sam Snead

A Canadian is someone who knows how to make love in a canoe.

   – Pierre Berton

My generation thought fast food was something you ate during Lent, a Big Mac was an oversized raincoat and 'crumpet' was something you had for tea. 'Sheltered accommodation' was a place where you waited for a bus, 'time-sharing' meant togetherness and you kept 'coke' in the coal house.

   – Joan Collins

It is extremely tacky for a friend to mention a friend's weight to her face. Behind her back is a different thing altogether.

- **Cynthia Heimel**

If I could take just two books to a desert island, I'd take a big inflatable book and 'How to make oars out of sand'.

- **Ardal O'Hanlon**

I'm so unlucky that if I was to fall into a barrel of nipples I'd come out sucking my thumb.

- **Freddie Starr**

The most important thing in acting is to be able to laugh and cry. If I have to cry, I think of my sex life. If I have to laugh, I think of my sex life.

- **Glenda Jackson**

With my winnings this year, I intend to buy the Alamo and give it back to Mexico.

- **Lee Trevino**

You don't have to be certifiably insane to be a jump jockey but it does give you the edge over the competition.

- **Graham Sharpe**

A good way to threaten somebody is to light a stick of dynamite. Then you call the guy and hold the burning fuse up to the phone. 'Hear that?' you say. 'That's dynamite, baby.'

- **Jack Handey**

It is useless to hold a person to anything he says while he's in love, drunk or running for office.

- **Shirley MacLaine**

The doctor said to me, 'You're going to live till you're 60.' I said, 'I am 60.' He said, 'What did I tell you?'

- **Henny Youngman**

The best way to tell gold is to pass a nugget around in a crowded bar. If it comes back, it's not gold.

– Lennie Lower

The best way to get a husband to do anything is to suggest that he is too old to do it.

– Shirley MacLaine

Edible adj: good to eat, and wholesome to digest, as a worm to a toad, a toad to a snake, a snake to a pig, a pig to a man, and a man to a worm.

– Ambrose Bierce

If there are two or more ways to do something, and one of those ways can result in a catastrophe, then someone will do it.

– Edward Murphy

If this is what viral pneumonia does to one, I really don't think I shall bother to have it again.

– Gladys Cooper

People are terrified when I ask them to come with me into a small room.

– Martha Lane Fox

The only people who have the right to use the editorial 'we' are presidents, editors and people with tapeworm.

– Mark Twain

The reason your wife pays more attention to the baby than you is because the baby is a blood relation of your wife – he's her son. You're just some guy she met in a bar.

– Garry Shandling

If you're so worried that you have to cut your face up to make yourself happier, you're with the wrong guy.

– Jerry Hall

Religion is when you kill each other to see who has the best imaginary friend.

– Steven Wright

Don't worry that your kids never listen to you. Worry that they are always watching you.

– Robert Fulghum

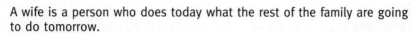

A wife is a person who does today what the rest of the family are going to do tomorrow.

– Marilyn Morris

I should go and see my doctor today, but I don't like to because I am not feeling very well. I care to see doctors only when I am in perfect health; then they comfort one, but when one is ill, they are most depressing.

– Oscar Wilde

My wife and I tried to breakfast together but we had to stop or our marriage would have been wrecked.

– Winston Churchill

Girls, you can learn to work the toilet seat: if it's up, put it down. And yes, pissing standing up is more difficult than peeing from point blank range. We're bound to miss sometimes.

– Denis Leary

My husband only got it when I told him we'd be downloading some new software in nine months' time.

– Laura Greene

My dog was my only friend. I told my wife that every man needs at least two friends, so she bought me another dog.

– Henny Youngman

I have no sex appeal. A Peeping Tom saw me and pulled down the shade.

– Phyllis Diller

A liberal is a man who is too broadminded to take his own side in an argument.

– **Robert Frost**

Never fear spoiling children by making them too happy. Happiness is the atmosphere in which all good affections grow.

– **Thomas Bray**

I'm too old for a paper round, too young for social security and too tired for an affair.

– **Erma Bombeck**

It's clear that most American children suffer too much mother and too little father.

– **Gloria Steinem**

When I was a boy, my family took great care with our snapshots. We posed in front of expensive cars, homes that weren't ours. We borrowed dogs. Almost every family picture taken of us when I was young had a different borrowed dog in it.

– **Richard Avedon**

The night of our honeymoon my husband took one look and said, "Is that all for me?".

– **Dolly Parton**

Men who claw their way to the top don't get chastised for it. But look at the grief they gave Joan Rivers for clawing her way to the middle.

– **Ruth Batchelor**

My orchestra are just assassins.

– **Arturo Toscanini**

As I grow older and older and totter towards the tomb, I find that I care less and less who goes to bed with whom.

– **Dorothy L. Sayers**

Madam, there's no such thing as a tough child. If you boil them first for a few hours, they always come out tender.

– W.C. Fields

Haven't we got all the fools in town on our side? And ain't that a big enough majority in any town?

– Mark Twain

After conducting a concert in a small town, I once received the following note from a farmer who had attended the performance: "Dear Sir, I wish to inform you that the man who played the long thing you pull in and out only did so during the brief periods you were looking at him. " .

– Arturo Toscanini

My parents raised me in the Jewish tradition. I was taught never to marry a Gentile woman, shave on Saturday and, most especially, never to shave a Gentile woman on Saturday.

– Woody Allen

Tradition. That's what you associate with Christmas: tradition. And drink-driving. And despair and loneliness. And Argos. But mainly tradition.

– Charlie Brooker

I think the delivery room should have traffic noise and pollution. The baby should then have the option to go back in.

– Rita Rudner

It always rains on tents. Rainstorms will travel thousands of miles against the prevailing winds for the opportunity to rain on a tent.

– Dave Barry

Whatever you choose, however many roads you travel, I hope that you choose not to be a lady.

– Nora Ephron

The only time a woman has a true orgasm is when she is shopping.

– Joan Rivers

Air travel efficiency would improve if more travellers started going to less popular places.

— **Dan Quayle**

Although so far there is no known treatment for death's crippling effects, still everyone can acquaint himself with the three early warning signs of death: one, rigor mortis; two, a rotting smell; three, occasional drowsiness.

— **Henry Gibson**

Then some friends came round for a tree-decorating party. I had envisaged this occasion as a glowy, WASPy sort of thing, with people in woolly jumpers standing around, clinking glasses of eggnog with each other. But it wasn't like that at all. It was just a bunch of grumpy Jews ordering takeaway Thai food and arguing about the rights and wrongs of a war with Iraq, while the children stamped up and down on the fairy lights and got bauble splinters in their hands.

— **Zoë Heller**

I believe we are on an irreversible trend towards more freedom and democracy. But that could change.

— **Dan Quayle**

When my wife was giving birth, she tried the breathing exercises and they were really effective for, oh, I'd say 15, even 20, seconds. Then she switched to the more traditional method, which is screaming for drugs.

— **Dave Barry**

I have always thought that the initial trouble between me and my father was that he couldn't see the slightest purpose in my existence.

— **Laurence Olivier**

My father once said, 'Nearly half the troubles you have in life are caused by what goes in and what comes out of your mouth.'

— **Arthur Reubens**

I'm all into self improvement – I turn my underwear inside out once a week.

— **Richard Crowley**

I have often wanted to drown my troubles, but I can't get my wife to go swimming.

– Roy Brown

One should never put on one's best trousers to go out to battle for freedom and truth.

– Henryk Ibsen

Nor frost, nor snow, nor wind I trow, Can hurt me if it would, I am so wrapped within and lapped With jolly good ale and old.

– Anon

The hardest part of my famous Twickenham try was not resisting the English pack, but dragging the entire Irish pack over with me.

– Ginger McLoughlin

If you want your children to listen, try talking softly – to someone else.

– Ann Landers

Attending his first church service, my son turned to me and said ,Daddy, when's the interval?

– Edward Price

Any request to have the canned music turned down in a restaurant leads to it being turned up.

– Ken Lake

He has spectacularly lost his looks. He's turned into Princess Anne.

– Germaine Greer on Prince William

Moses Kiptanui – the nineteen-year-old Kenyan, who turned twenty a few weeks ago.

– David Coleman

I have dieted continuously for the last two decades and lost a total of seven hundred and fifty-eight pounds. By all calculations, I should be hanging from a charm bracelet.

– Erma Bombec

Cooking a crocodile is easy. You need two pots of boiling water, one for the crocodile and one for a rock. By the time the rock is tender, the crocodile will be cooked.

– Paul Hogan

I got my dad one of those typical Father's Day cards, with a picture of a hunting coat hanging on a peg, a decoy duck and some golf clubs leaning in the corner. It's the perfect card for him, because there's nothing Dad loves more than going out in the woods on a frosty morning and beating ducks to death with a four-iron.

– Danny Liebert

I just can't understand people who have ugly people working for them.

– Jade Jagger

To the Irishman there are only two ultimate realities: Hell and the United States.

– Evelyn Waugh

A group of closely related persons living under one roof; it is a convenience, often a necessity, sometimes a pleasure, sometimes the reverse; but who first exalted it as admirable, an almost religious ideal?

– Rose Macaulay

Conor Cruise O'Brien has done more to unify public opinion than any other person in Irish history. Thousands of people who disagree on absolutely everything else are united in their hatred of the Cruiser.

– Fergus Lawlor

All men are children, and if you understand that, a woman understands everything.

– Coco Chanel

If he tells you he likes black underwear, stop washing his pants.

– **Jasmine Birtles**

Whenever I'm confused, I just check my underwear. It holds the answer to all the important questions.

– **Grampa Simpson, The Simpsons**

The finding of a gibbet in an unexplored part of Africa gave me infinite pleasure as it proved that I was in a civilized society.

– **Mungo Park**

There are so many sons-of-bitches in the United States that they are entitled to some representation in Congress.

– **Calvin Coolidge**

And when God, who created the entire universe with all its glories, decides to deliver a message to humanity, He will not use as His personal messenger a person on cable TV with a bad haircut.

– **Jerry Seinfeld**

How come the winner of the Miss Universe contest is always from Earth? I think it is rigged.

– **Rick Hall**

All the world loves a lover – unless he's in a telephone booth.

– **Dave Tomick**

Ostrich tastes like the progeny of an unnatural and uncomfortable liaison between a duck and a sheep.

– **A.A. Gill**

I was a buffoon and an idiot until the age of forty.

– **Madonna**

I didn't even know my bra size until I made a movie.

– **Angelina Jolie**

I didn't know the facts of life until I was 17. My father never talked about his work.

– Martin Freud, son of Sigmund

I don't intend to write a book until Northern Ireland settles down a bit.

– Albert Reynolds

There's so much crap talked about bringing up a child. A fucking moron could do it. Morons do bring up their children. It's just endless love, endless patience, that's it.

– Bob Geldof

No man has ever stuck his hand up your dress looking for a library card.

– Joan Rivers

No mention of God. They keep him up their sleeve for as long as they can, vicars do. They know it puts people off.

– Alan Bennett

Don't try to make your children grow up to be like you or they may do it.

– Russell Baker

Up in the morning's no for me, Up in the morning early! When a' the hills are cover'd wi' snaw, I'm sure it's winter fairly!

– Robert Burns

My New Year's Resolution is to give up drinking out of damp glasses.

– Brendan Grace

The O.J. Simpson jury they ended up choosing had to swear they'd never heard about a case that had been in the papers every day for a year and a half. And then they ask them to rule on DNA.
These idiots didn't even get that far in the alphabet. They wondered why the N came before the A.

– Jackie Mason

In my day, we never got woken up by a teasmade. We were knocked up every morning by a man with a 6-foot pole... And we weren't having hysterectomies every 2 minutes either, like the girls these days. If something went wrong down below, you kept your gob shut and turned up the wireless.

– **Victoria Wood**

All I heard when I was growing up was, 'Why can't you be more like your cousin Sheila? Why can't you be more like your cousin Sheila?' Sheila died at birth.

– **Joan Rivers**

There is nothing worse than being stuck up in the Andes Mountains in a plane crash with your anorexic friend Freddy.

– **Denis Leary**

The more flesh you show, the higher up the ladder you go.

– **Kim Basinger**

When I was in school they showed us a sex education film about a boy calling up a girl on the phone and asking her out on a date. Nowadays I'm sure they show Nine and a Half Weeks or something starring Sharon Stone.

– **Ellen DeGeneres**

And when they were up they were up, And when they were down they were down, And when they were only halfway up, I was arrested.

– **Spike Milligan**

The only possible way there'd be an uprising in this country would be if they banned car boot sales and caravanning.

– **Victoria Wood**

My parents never wanted me to get upset about anything. They couldn't tell me when a pet had died. One day I woke up and my goldfish had gone. I said, 'Where's Fluffy?' They said, 'He ran away.'

– **Rita Rudner**

Beethoven always sounds to me like the upsetting of a bag of nails, with here and there also a dropped hammer.

– **John Ruskin**

Vince Lombardi is completely fair. He treats us all the same – like dogs.

– **Henry Jordan**

Why do airline pilots have to tell us everything they are doing? "I'm taking it up, I'm bringing it down." Do I knock on the cockpit door – I'm having peanuts now, I just thought you'd like to know?

– **Jerry Seinfeld**

God has Alzheimer's and has forgotten about us.

– **Jane Wagner**

March is a month that helps to use up some of the bad weather that February just couldn't fit in.

– **Doug Larson**

When I was a baby, my father used to throw me up in the air and then go and answer the phone.

– **Rita Rudner**

My teeth stuck out so far, I used to eat her kids' candy bars by accident.

– **Rita Rudner**

I remember when the wireless was something useful. In my day you could warm your hands on the wireless and listen to Terry Wogan. Nowadays all you can do is listen to Wogan.

– **Paula Brett**

The charms of a passing woman are usually in direct proportion to the speed of her passing.

– Marcel Proust

A man's desire for a son is usually nothing but the wish to duplicate himself in order that such a remarkable pattern may not be lost to the world.

– Helen Rowland

Progress in the Foreign Service is either vaginal or rectal – You either marry the boss's daughter or you crawl up his bottom.

– Nicholas Monsarrat

My dear Anne, it would be in vain for me to try to send you any news. I can only send you my love, and that is anything but news. It is as old as you are.

– Henry Wadsworth Longfellow

My parents were very old world. Their values in life are God and carpeting.

– Woody Allen

In my singles match I saw Hope vanishing over the horizon with her arse on fire.

– David Feherty

If I have a choice between the very horrible joke and the not so horrible, I'll always go for the very horrible one just because I enjoy that really. I like swearing as well.

– Jo Brand

Serve coffee early in the meal and very hot. If the guest burns his tongue he won't be able to taste anything.

– Phyllis Diller

If people looked like their passport photographs, very few countries would let them in.

– Doug Larson

Don't save things 'for best'. Drink that vintage bottle of wine – from your best crystal glasses. Wear your best designer jacket to go down to the post office to collect your pension. And, every morning, spritz yourself with that perfume you save for parties.

– Geraldine Mayer

Pinter's The Birthday Party was like a vintage Hitchcock thriller which has been edited by a cross-eyed studio janitor with a lawnmower.

– Orson Welles

Christmas is the time of year when virtually anything can be fobbed off as a fancy gift, provided that it's nestling in a basket on a bed of straw and packed in cellophane. Whether containing small phials of body lotion (each containing enough to cover approximately half a thigh), miniature jars of tartan-lidded service station marmalade or cute toy kittens with bows on, the straw to gift ratio is generally 90:1.

– Catherine Barnes

I don't think I've ever had one visit to the park with my kids that didn't end up with somebody needing stitches in casualty.

– Dave Lacey

In the old days it was called voodoo and you used to stick needles into a doll. Now it is called acupuncture and you just stick them straight into the person.

– Cathy Hopkins

For a working man or woman to vote Republican this year is the same as a chicken voting for Colonel Sanders.

– Walter Mondale

Never vote for the best candidate – vote for the one who will do the least harm.

– Frank Dane

My father hated radio and could not wait for television to be invented so that he could hate that too.

– Peter de Vries

We learn from experience. A man never wakes up his second baby just to see it smile.

– Grace Williams

I worshipped the ground my wife Audrey walked upon. If only she lived in a better neighbourhood.

– Billy Wilder

When friends pressed her to carry a walking stick, Princess Alice reluctantly agreed, but she had it disguised as an umbrella.

– R.W. Apple

My mother is a Muslim – she walks five steps behind my father. She doesn't have to. He just looks better from behind.

– Shazia Mirza

Johnny, keep it out of focus. I want to win the foreign picture award.

– Billy Wilder

If you live to be 100, I want to live to be 100 minus one day, so I never have to live without you.

– Winnie the Pooh

He who buys what he does not want, will soon want what he cannot buy.

– Anne Mathews

When I was a little boy I wanted to be a baseball player and join the circus. With the Yankees I've accomplished both.

– Craig Nettles

My dad was a cop, so dating was a total nightmare. The police escort I could handle, but the loudhailer from the helicopter was a bit much... 'Keep both hands on the steering wheel where we can see them.'

– Sandi Selvi

Everybody wants to save the earth. Nobody wants to help Mom do the dishes.

– P.J. O'Rourke

It is unclear from historical documentation which war the Salvation Army fought, but it is apparent from their spoils that they won.

– Dan Levin

Men are brave enough to go to war, but they are not brave enough to get a bikini wax.

– Rita Rudner

The first victory is the avoidance of war.

– Indira Gandhi

I have never understood this liking for war. It panders to instincts already well catered for in any respectable domestic establishment.

– Alan Bennett

Colin Montgomerie has the temper of a warthog recently stung by a wasp and a face like a bull-dog licking piss off a nettle.

– David Feherty

My mom was a ventriloquist and she was always throwing her voice. For ten years I thought the dog was telling me to kill my father.

– Wendy Liebman

As part of a beauty regime it was probably fabulous. As food it was like eating soggy knicker and vinegar crisps.

– A.A. Gill

I had my first son when I was 18. I was young and stupid and I grew up with the children. Having a son at 60, when I'm older and established, means that I can wallow in the parenthood thing.

– Paul Hogan

I never saw a banana till I was 14. I was immediately sick after eating it and haven't touched one since.

 – **Enid Bray**

God knew from all eternity that I was going to be Pope. You think he would have made me more photogenic.

 – **Pope John XXIII**

If I had been around when Rubens was painting, I would have been revered as a fabulous model. Kate Moss? Well, she would have been the paintbrush.

 – **Dawn French**

If murder had been allowed when dad was in his prime, our home would have been like the last act of Othello almost daily.

 – **Nancy Mitford**

I have only been to one. It was four years ago, where I had to dress up as a man because Mary was there.

 – **Sally Farmiloe**

You could not have said that I was 'as cute as a speckled pup' without expecting the speckled pup to piss on your leg out of resentment.

 – **Dolly Parton, on her childhood freckles**

Handing over the Hoover to my mother was like distributing highly sophisticated nuclear weapons to an underdeveloped African nation.

 – **Alan Bennett**

I moved to Los Angeles when I was twenty-one. I felt like a kid in a candy shop. I'd be driving down the road and – Mmmm! There was a guy and Mmmm! There was a guy! .

 – **Tori Amos, singer**

'Never trust a man who doesn't drink,' was one of my father's favourite expressions, and he died plenty trustworthy.

 – **Les Patterson**

I know where my new television set was manufactured. A label on the box said: 'Built-in Antennae.'

— **Steven Wright**

Two years ago, my Father's Day present was a hose reel. Last year it was a set of nozzles. See a pattern here? I guess it's – hard to know what to get the man who provided everything.

— **Michael Feldman**

The only law of hospitality she understood was that of speeding the parting guest.

— **E. F. Benson**

There is not one female comic who was a beautiful little girl.

— **Joan Rivers**

From where she parked the car it was just a short walk to the footpath.

— **Woody Allen**

Joan Crawford had perfect posture, but it was rather intimidating. She looked as if she had swallowed a yardstick.

— **Glenn Ford**

Dukakis never became President because his name was too much of a mouthful.

— **Bill Clinton**

When golf first started, one under par was a birdie, two under par was an eagle and three under par was a partridge. They had to change that because you couldn't get a partridge on a par three.

— **John MacKay**

I was surprised to see that Amazon.com was taking orders for a novel I hadn't even begun.

— **Lawrence Norfolk**

I don't want to say my girlfriend was loose. I think the term now is 'user-friendly'.

   – Emo Philips

I was brought up a communist. It was Lenin who came down our chimney at Christmas.

   – Alexei Sayle

The only reason we had a son was to get someone to work the video. For ten years we used it as a night light.

   – Adrian Walsh

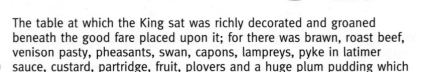

The table at which the King sat was richly decorated and groaned beneath the good fare placed upon it; for there was brawn, roast beef, venison pasty, pheasants, swan, capons, lampreys, pyke in latimer sauce, custard, partridge, fruit, plovers and a huge plum pudding which required the efforts of two men to carry.

   – Anonymous account of Henry VIII's Christmas feast at Greenwich, 1486

Oh how I wish that Charles Dickens was alive to attack such idiots [as Lambeth Council] with the eloquent mocking of his most satirical prose. Perhaps he would send his spirits to cure the misguided councillors of their tiptoeing fear of making any reference to the joy and good fellowship we find in Christmas. In any event, 'A Christmas Carol' should be made compulsory for them all so that they may know what Christmas is and Christmas can be and why it must be celebrated always.

   – John Mortimer

When I worked with Bette Davis I was never so scared in my life. And I was in the war.

   – John Mills

I am married to Beatrice Salkeld, painter. We have no children, except me.

   – Brendan Behan

When I was young, I thought money was the most important thing in life. Now that I'm old, I know it is.

   – Oscar Wilde

When the cold came before the snow, we went skating on Williams Lake across the Arm. My mother put baked potatoes in the boots of our skates. After the rowboat ferry ride, one oar almost touching the edge of the ice line on the half-frozen Arm, and the walk up to the lake, the skates were warm to put on and the potatoes cool enough to eat.

 – **Robert MacNeil**

After you've had children sex slows down. We have sex every three months now. Every time I have sex, the next day, I pay my quarterly taxes. Unless it's oral sex, then I renew my driver's licence.

 – **Ray Romano**

Life was a lot simpler when what we honoured was father and mother rather than all major credit cards.

 – **Robert Orben**

Maybe people are not as miserable as we thought.

 – **Bill Ward, hotelier, reporting no bookings so far for his Scrooge holidays for people who want a Christmas-free break**

Being married or single is a choice we all have to make, but it's not a great choice. It's sort of like when the doctor goes, 'Ointment or suppositories.'

 – **Richard Jeni**

If by the time we are 60 we haven't learned what a knot of paradox and contradiction life is, and how exquisitely the good and bad are mingled in every action we take, we haven't grown old to much purpose.

 – **John Cowper Powys**

The Gulf War was like teenage sex. We got in too soon and we got out too soon.

 – **Thomas Harkin**

Advice is what we ask for when we already know the answer but wish we didn't.

 – **Erica Jong, novelist**

As I'm sitting there playing with Barbie, washing her hair, I suddenly think, man, I gotta get a Scotch and get the hell outta all this... Look at me, I'm bathing dolls! .

    – Tim Allen

The curtain rises on a vast primitive wasteland, not unlike certain parts of New Jersey.

    – Woody Allen

My dear delightful company, I have just watched your performance of The Importance of Being Earnest. It reminds me of a play I once wrote.

    – Oscar Wilde

Watching the Aussies at cricket is like watching a porn movie. You always know what's going to happen in the end.

    – Mick Jagger

The difference between a sand bunker and water is the difference between a car crash and an airplane crash. You have a chance of recovering from a car crash.

    – Bobby Jones

In an underdeveloped country, don't drink the water; in a developed country, don't breathe the air.

    – Jonathan Raban

I

Walking past a building site on my way to the shops, I was wolf-whistled by a hunky construction worker on some scaffolding. I'm 63. It made my day.

    – Janet Lynn

Little kids in supermarkets buy cereal the way men buy lingerie. They get stuff they have no interest in just to get the prize inside.

    – Jeff Foxworthy